BLESSED
ARE YOU

BLESSED ARE YOU

A Comprehensive Guide to Jewish Prayer

Jeffrey M. Cohen

JASON ARONSON INC.
Northvale, New Jersey
London

First Jason Aronson Inc. softcover edition—1997

Book Design: Pamela Roth

This book was set in 10 pt. Palacio by Lind Graphics of Upper Saddle River, New Jersey.

Library of Congress Cataloging-in-Publication Data

Cohen, Jeffrey M.
    Blessed Are You : a comprehensive guide to
Jewish prayer / Jeffrey M. Cohen.
        p. cm.
    Includes bibliographical references and index.
    ISBN 0-87668-465-7 (hardcover)
    ISBN 0-7657-5974-8 (softcover)
    1. Judaism—Liturgy—History. 2. Prayer—Judaism. 3. Judaism—
Customs and practices. 4. Synagogues. I. Title.
    BM660.C6 1993
    296.7'2—dc20

                                                                    92-21456

Manufactured in the United States of America. Jason Aronson Inc. offers books and cassettes. For information and catalog write to Jason Aronson Inc., 230 Livingston Street, Northvale, New Jersey 07647.

To Gloria

גְּמָלַתְהוּ טוֹב וְלֹא-רָע כֹּל יְמֵי חַיֶּיהָ

And to our children—
Harvey and Lorraine
Suzanne and Keith
Judith and Lewis—
and our first grandchild, Joel

Contents

PART II   THE THEOLOGY

Foreword

The oral tradition of Judaism, codified as law by Maimonides, regards daily prayer as the fulfillment of the biblical precept to "serve the Lord with all your heart." This presupposes that prayer, even more than any other Divine commandment, being a "heart operation," requires emotional and intellectual understanding.

The Jewish prayer book is an anthology, composed over three thousand years, of individual and national creativity in word, thought and emotion. It serves the dual function of expressing and impressing truly Jewish feelings. Like an electrocardiograph, it faithfully records the impulses of the Jewish heart, and at the same time like a pacemaker it regulates these impulses when they are deficient or abnormal.

But, in contrast to machines, the agency of prayer can work only through a profound appreciation of its meaning, its words and, even more important, the wealth of thought beneath the text. *Blessed Are You* will indeed provide the searching worshiper with new vistas of understanding. Rabbi Dr. Jeffrey Cohen, with considerable experience in writing on the Jewish liturgy already to his credit, is distinguished by a felicitous combination of sound scholarship with skills in articulating it in an intelligent and edifying manner.

While the bulk of the material is drawn from classic sources, some interpretations are quite original. But these sometimes conjectural elements do not deprive the work of its impressive erudition or its significant value in guiding the reader to an appreciation of our liturgical treasures.

May this volume so flex the muscles of the Jewish heart as to keep it pulsating with spiritual vigour to evoke a ready response from Him "Who hearkens to prayer in mercy."

Lord Immanuel Jakobovits,
Former Chief Rabbi, Great Britain

Preface

Dealing analytically with prayer inevitably takes one into diverse areas of scholarship, such as biblical and talmudic history, medieval Hebrew poetry, archaeology of ancient synagogues, Jewish art, philosophy, mysticism, *halakhah*, and modern responsa. It is inevitable, therefore, that experts in any of these individual fields will be critical of the sketchiness of many of the expositions in this book, and at the same time raise their eyebrows at a number of departures from generally accepted theories. I apologize at the outset for choosing the vehicle of what is intended as an essentially popular presentation for postulating some theories that ought first to have been tested more fully on the anvil of scholarship in the pages of learned journals. My excuse for not having done so is that most of these ideas only surfaced while researching this book. Articles submitted to journals currently take over two years to appear, and a further two years for critical reaction to be published. There was therefore no alternative other than to use this work as a sounding board for a number of new theories and ideas.

Scope to innovate in the sphere of liturgy was first courageously granted by Rabba and Rav Yoseph (3rd-century Babylonian talmudists), who interpreted the mishnaic exhortation not to make one's prayer into *a fixed form* (*Berakhot* 4:4) as a challenge to the worshiper to try to introduce a new theme or thought into each and every prayer (*Berakhot* 29b). This book owes its existence to the author's belief that prayer, not only when reciting it but equally when exploring its meaning and development, is so absorbing and dynamic that the innovative spark simply cannot, and should not, be quenched. If, in consequence, some of the hypotheses appear unconvincing, then it is to be hoped that the brickbats will be aimed exclusively at the author and not at the publishers who graciously gave him an unrestricted forum for his views.

The bulk of the material contained in this volume originally appeared in a work entitled *Horizons of Jewish Prayer*, published in 1986 by the United Synagogue of London. The present volume is a revised and enlarged version of that work. I thank Mr. Arthur Kurzweil, of Jason Aronson, Publishers, for the compliment of having chosen to produce this American version, thus ensuring for it the widest dissemination.

I also thank Lord Jakobovits, former Chief Rabbi of Great Britain, for his constant encouragement and for contributing the foreword to the original edition of this book.

I acknowledge the permission granted to me by the London *Jewish Chronicle* to include many of the articles that I originally contributed to that newspaper's "Pearls of Prayer" column during the years 1982–1985.

I recall with affection the great giant of liturgical studies at Jews' College, London, in my student days, Professor Naphtali Wieder, who first implanted within me the love and appreciation of this subject. I am also mindful of the stimulation provided by my colleagues on the academic staff of the College, as well as successive generations of my students in the liturgy class.

Joy is an essential ingredient for prayer, as first enunciated in the Psalmist's plea, "Serve God with joy." Special thanks and appreciation must be given therefore to my wife, Gloria, and my children, Harvey and Lorraine, Suzanne and Keith, Judith and Lewis, for having provided that ingredient of joy in such full measure.

Note on Transliteration

The following system of transliteration from the Hebrew has been employed:

Consonants

א	–
בּ	– b
ב	– v
ג	– g
ד	– d
ה	– h
ו	– v
ז	– z
ח	– ch
ט	– t
י	– y
כּ	– k
כ ך	– kh
ל	– l
מ ם	– m
נ ן	– n
ס	– s
ע	–
פּ	– p
פ ף	– f
צ ץ	– tz
ק	– k
ר	– r
שׁ	– sh
שׂ	– s
תּ	– t
ת	– t

Vowels

short

ֲ	– a
ָ	– a
ָ	– o
ֱ	– e
ִ	– i
יִ	– iy
ֵ	– ei
יֵ	– ey
יֶ	– ay
וּ	– u
וֹ	– o
ְ	– e

Part I

The History

1

Early Forms of Prayer

The Patriarchal Period

The urge to express in words such deep emotions as fear, gratitude, confidence, happiness, pain, sorrow, and love is an instinctive one. Words have the power to release pent-up emotions, as well as to define them in rational and meaningful terms.

Where there exists a measure of conviction that our situation— happy or sad—is of concern to God, and that He can be moved to pity by human suffering, to anger by human ingratitude, and to rejoicing by human appreciation, there also exists the urge to pray. Prayer is, therefore, not merely an aspect of religious ritual, but the expression of a basic religious impulse. The neglect of prayer is inevitably the farewell salute to religion.

The talmudic sages, by attributing to Abraham, Isaac, and Jacob the introduction of daily prayer,[1] expressed, in their own way, this basic conception of prayer as the natural libretto to the melody of faith. When we speak, therefore, of the origins of Judaism, we are referring at the same time to the dialogue between the Jew and his Maker through the medium of prayer.

Even before the time of Abraham individuals certainly prayed,

3

though generally they were only motivated to do so when they were at extremes of emotion, when experiencing either agony or ecstasy. The attribution of daily prayer to the three patriarchs does not mean that from their day onward *statutory prayers* were instituted. The more spiritually sensitive among their descendants may well have prayed each day, though there is no biblical evidence to suggest this, or that any particular form or formula of prayer was employed. Prayer was entirely personal and spontaneous.

According to the great biblical commentator, Moses Nachmanides, the first recorded prayer in the Torah took the form of a confession *(Vidduy)*, when Cain, on hearing his punishment for the murder of his brother, cries out, "My sin is too heinous to be pardoned" (Genesis 4:13). This nuance is not shared by Rashi, however, who understands Cain's cry rather as a rhetorical expression of defiance: "*Is* my sin so heinous that it cannot be pardoned?"

A most important source for attempting to pinpoint the extent of the practice of private worship in the prepatriarchal period is Genesis 4:26. Referring to that same generation of Seth, Cain, and Abel, the Torah states *az huchal likro be-sheim ha-shem*. Most translations render this phrase by "At that time men *began* to invoke the Lord by name." However, the strange passive form of the verb *chalal*, "to begin" (*huchal*, instead of the expected active form *heicheilu*), convinced our talmudic sages[2] that we do not in fact have represented here the verb *chalal* in its meaning of "to begin," but rather that this verbal root is being employed in its secondary sense of "to defile." Hence *Targum Yonatan* renders this biblical phrase, "In that generation . . . people invoked their *objects of defilement* (idols) as God." *Huchal* is now related to *chulin*, the antithesis of holiness.

If this interpretation of *huchal* is correct, then this verse, rather than indicating the origin of the man-God dialogue through prayer, actually suggests the very opposite: the beginning of the spread of idolatry! No wonder then that our rabbis largely ignored the few manifestations of spirituality in the prepatriarchal period, and even managed to disparage Noah, notwithstanding his designation as "a righteous man, perfect in his generation."[3]

The extent to which prayer permeated Abraham's home, and influenced not only his family but even his servants and entire entourage, may be gauged from the account of the mission of his steward, Eliezer, to find a wife for Isaac. Eliezer expresses himself through two of the main categories of prayer: entreaty *(bakkashah)* and thanksgiving *(hodayah)*. At the outset of his mission he entreats God: "Lord of my master Abraham, send me, I pray thee, good speed this day, and show kindness unto my master, Abraham."[4] When Rebekah appears and demonstrates her kindly qualities, Eliezer offers up thanksgiving: "And the man bowed his head and prostrated himself before the Lord, and he said: 'Blessed be the God of my master, Abraham, who hath not withheld his mercy and his truth from my master. . . .'"[5] Once again, when Rebekah's family finally agree to let her go back with Eliezer, "he bowed himself down to the earth unto the Lord,"[6] in a prayer of thanksgiving.

Throughout the patriarchal period worship was primarily expressed by the offering of sacrifices, though a number of spontaneous prayers are also recorded. These were inspired by a deep yearning or urgent personal need. Isaac prays on behalf of his wife for a child[7]; his blessing of his son, Jacob, is likewise couched in the form of a prayer.[8] The exiled Jacob utters a spontaneous prayer when, on waking from his dream, he realizes that he is on the site of "the Lord's house and opposite the gate of heaven."[9] Jacob's profound sense of awe impels him to pray, though it expresses itself in purely personal terms as a plea for divine protection, accompanied by a vow of allegiance should his prayer be fulfilled.

The intolerable conditions of the Egyptian bondage would certainly have made private prayer, for relief and deliverance, a psychological necessity: "And their cry came up unto God by reason of their bondage. And God heard their groaning, and remembered his covenant with Abraham, with Isaac, and with Jacob."[10] If until this time private prayer had been the emotional pressure valve of exclusively spiritually sensitive individuals, it now became the instinctive response of the entire nation, and at the same time an indication of their growing self-awareness as God's Chosen People.

The transition from personal to communal prayer came after the Exodus from Egypt when the Israelites' social consciousness developed to the extent that they could appreciate that the happiness of the individual was largely dependent upon that of the nation as a whole. The Song of the Red Sea,[11] in which every Israelite rejoiced both in his own individual deliverance and in that of the nation also, thus represented an important stage along the path of spiritual maturity.

Psalms and the Temple Worship

It was with the composition of the psalms that the needs and aspirations of the individual and the nation merged within the context of praise and petition. King David, to whom authorship of most of the psalms is attributed, is the first to use the noun *tefillah*, "prayer" (II Samuel 7:27); and it was his devotional output, of unsurpassed beauty, that formed the foundation of Israel's worship.

As shepherd and monarch, hero and outlaw, sinner and anointed of God, warrior and decrepit old man, his experiences of life, as reflected in the psalms, were sufficiently comprehensive for any individual or community to find a parallel to their own situation, in order to draw strength from King David's conviction and hope from his ultimate triumph.

David's psalms also made a unique and pioneering contribution toward establishing the particular character and spirit of Temple worship. Poetry, song, dance, and instrumental music were henceforth the spiritual order of the day:

> Sing unto the Lord a new song,
> And his praise in the assembly of saints.
> Let Israel rejoice in his Maker. . . .
> Let them praise His name in the dance;
> Let them sing praises with the timbrel and harp.
>
> (Psalm 149:1–3)

With the building of the first Temple (970 B.C.E.) by Solomon, son of David, a more regularized form of worship was introduced. The Torah had already referred to a morning and evening sacrifice (Numbers 28:4), and this formed the basis of daily services. On New Moons, Sabbaths, and festivals special services were held and additional sacrifices offered. While the sacrifices were burning, a choir of Levites would sing selections from the psalms to the accompaniment of the musical instruments. After the sacrifice the priests would bless the assembly using the prescribed biblical formula:

> May the Lord bless thee and keep thee.
> The Lord cause His face to shine upon thee and be gracious unto thee.
> The Lord turn His countenance toward thee, and grant thee peace.
>
> (Numbers 6:24–27)

The levitical orchestra would position itself on the fifteen steps leading from the main spectator area to the women's enclosure. There was also a stage *(dukhan)* from which part of the levitical choir sang, and immediately below them the young Levites, with their high unbroken voices, provided the pleasant harmony.

It would appear that there was no congregational singing or participation in prayer on the part of the visitors and lay worshipers at the first Temple. They were there as silent witnesses to the experience, to be elevated and moved by the *numinous,* or mystic spirit, generated by the officiants; but they themselves were to observe "sacramental silence." The congregation's participation was limited to making prostrations during certain key parts of the proceedings.[12] Since private worship was not practiced by the masses with any degree of regularity, they would have been quite content to allow their priestly and levitical representatives to perform the act of worship on their behalf.

We referred above to the daily blessing of the people by the priests. According to talmudic tradition,[13] a very special form of the divine name was employed in that blessing during the first Temple period. This name, which has since been lost,[14] consisted of twelve letters, and was among the most personal names of God, more sacred than the one which superseded it: the Tetragrammaton, or four-letter name, regularly employed in the Torah.

So sacred and potent was the twelve-letter name that unscrupulous people began to invoke it for their own purposes, with some disastrous consequences. Secular use of this name was henceforth declared anathema, and it was gradually forgotten by the masses. Knowledge of it became the secret preserve of a particular pietistic fraternity within the priesthood. They would utter it during the Priestly Blessing, though indistinctly and in an undertone, ensuring thereby that its sound was drowned by the rest of the priests reciting the Tetragrammaton in loud choral unison.

According to talmudic tradition an almost identical fate seems to have befallen the Tetragrammaton during the Second Temple period. During the exile, the Priestly Blessing, together with the rest of the Temple ritual, was suspended. When the Second Temple was built, and the ritual restored, all priests used only the Tetragrammaton for blessing the people. It is conceivable that none of the priestly pietists, who originally had the privilege of employing the twelve-letter name, actually returned from Babylon to reintroduce it. Alternately, they, the grandchildren and great-grandchildren of the last priests to use the twelve-letter name in the first Temple, may not even have had the name disclosed to them. To express it on one's lips, in a heathen country and with no immediate purpose, would have been regarded as a breach of trust and holy secrecy, if not as an infringement of the second commandment.

So, for the first hundred years of the restored Temple—during the Persian period—the priests used the Tetragrammaton for the priestly blessing. The authentic vowels of that four-letter name were no secret even to the masses. According to talmudic tradition people in Jericho could even hear the sound of the priestly blessing in the Temple.[15]

It was on the death of Shimon the Righteous (circa 200 B.C.E.) that the priests stopped employing the *Shem Ha-Meforash* (Tetragrammaton) in their blessing, "so that those without status or worthiness should not learn it."[16] It is the present writer's view that to explain this rather vague tradition we have to take account of the religious and political upheavals that followed on immediately after the death of Shimon the Righteous.

The Talmud tells us of a bitter dispute among his sons over the question of the succession to the High Priesthood.[17] Onias, Shimon's younger son, who failed in his bid to succeed his father, though Shimon had favored his accession, fled to Egypt and established a rival Temple at Leontopolis. Josephus[18] tells us that the priests of Jerusalem regarded the sacrificial acts of Onias's priests as invalid and that they refused to recognize the status of those priests and disqualified them from serving in the Temple at Jerusalem.

It would seem, therefore, that "those without status or worthiness" refers to the rival priesthood of Onias. The priests of Jerusalem did not want the latter to employ the sacred name, for obvious reasons. Since Onias patterned his ritual closely upon that of Jerusalem, the only way to prevent the priests of Leontopolis from using the Tetragrammaton was for it to be withdrawn entirely from the ritual. From that time onward the ordinary priests expressed the Tetragrammaton merely as *Adonai* ("Lord"), the form later taken over into synagogue worship.

The authentic method of pronouncing the Tetragrammaton—that is, the correct vowels that should accompany its four consonants—was gradually forgotten by the masses, though it was still kept as a very closely guarded secret among the High Priestly circle in Jerusalem. According to the Talmud it was revealed by a (priestly) scholar to his disciple only once in seven years (others say twice in seven years[19]), probably for fear that the priests of Onias might become aware of it and that it might be misapplied.

It was employed, together with its authentic vowels, but once a year by the High Priest, on the Day of Atonement; though he uttered it so inaudibly that no one could have distinguished it. Rabbi Tarphon, a priest, in whose youth the Temple was destroyed, later related that while giving the Priestly Blessing—presumably on the Day of Atonement—he inclined his ear to try and catch the pronunciation of the Tetragrammaton on the lips of the High Priest behind him, but to no avail.[20]

Temple and Synagogue

In the next chapter, where we will discuss the origin of the institution of the synagogue, we will declare as most plausible the theory that views the synagogue as having arisen out of the prayer meetings of the lay fraternities *(Maamadot)*, which were established during the Second Commonwealth, as counterparts of the priestly Temple rotas. This is in keeping with the traditional concept of the relationship between synagogue and Temple.

The synagogue was both the symbol and the democratic counterpart of the elitist Temple. As long as the Second Temple was in existence—and, to some extent, even afterward—the synagogue never attempted to cast itself in an independent spiritual, or even liturgical, mold. This is what the Talmud wished to convey in its oft-quoted comment on Deuteronomy 11:13, "To love the Lord thy God and *to serve him (le-ovdo)* with all *thy heart (be-khol levavekhem)*: What is service of the heart?—that is prayer?" In other words, prayer and Temple service serve identical ends: prayer not only simulates emotionally that same sense of awe and self-renewal that the Temple sacrificial service sought to generate, but, even more, prayer actually fulfills the obligation of sacrifice where the latter cannot be performed.

The synagogue accordingly patterned itself closely upon the characteristics of Temple worship. They shared a reverence for the Book of Psalms; and both exploited to the full its unique capacity to put the worshiper into whatever mood was appropriate to the occasion. In this context, it is most significant that those responsible for the leadership of the synagogue and the development of its liturgy made no attempt, as long as the Temple was standing, to emulate sectarian factions, such as the Essenes of Qumran, in creating their own psalms, prayers, and hymns *(Hodayot)* on the model of the Davidic psalms. The synagogue did not wish to be too innovative in this direction for fear of creating a rift with Temple tradition, and impairing thereby the unity of the nation. After all, its avowed aim was to be representative, not exclusive.

There may also have been a nationalistic element in the synagogue's self-restriction to the Davidic psalms. David was the symbol of the ideal and rightful monarchy. The monarchy of the Second Commonwealth, at the time of the emergence of the synagogue, was, however, priestly-Maccabean. The synagogue was therefore determined to cling tenaciously and exclusively to the psalms, as well as expressing, in a number of blessings and prayers, its hope for a restored Davidic monarchy.

That apart, the otherwise close relationship between synagogue and Temple was underlined by the fact that the synagogue ensured that its times of services always corresponded with those of the Temple. Thus, the morning service *(Shacharit)* was recited at the very hour that the morning *Tamid* ("Continual Offering") was brought in the Temple; and the afternoon service *(Minchah),* likewise, was recited at the time when the *Tamid Shel Bein Ha-Arbayim* ("Afternoon Continual Offering") was brought.

Another way in which the synagogue affirmed its dependence upon the Temple was through the essential nature of its services, which, like those of the Temple, were primarily communal. There are hardly any prayers in the statutory services wherein the worshiper, emphasizing his individuality, addresses God in the first person. Prayer—like the Temple worship—is a communal exercise; hence it requires a *minyan,* a quorum of ten worshipers. The individual is not lost amid the ranks of his coreligionists. On the contrary, surrounded and supported by them, encouraged and aroused to a greater degree of vibrant spirituality by their proximity, he is, in fact, enabled, with greater facility, to tap his own latent sources of religious energy and sensitivity.

When praying alone, without the stimulus of the *minyan,* the identical formulae of communal prayer are employed. Its essential character cannot be set aside. The individual has to "home in" to the prayers of the community and identify with them. He even has to recite his own prayers at the very same time that the communal worship is taking place in synagogue. The individual, in this situation, is merely precluded from reciting those "Sanctifications" *(Kaddish, Kedushah,* and *Borakhu),* which involve a reader's summons to the congregation to participate, and a response by the latter.

The relationship of synagogue to Temple is also to be seen in the special privileges reserved for the priests within the synagogue system. The *Kohein* ascends the steps to bless the congregation before the Ark, just as he did in the Temple, and a ritual of formal washing of his hands by the Levites is performed before the blessing, to recall the *Kiddush Yadayim,* sacred washing, in Temple times prior to performing the sacrificial act. At a later period the *Kohein* was given the prerogative of being "called up" first to the Reading of the Law, and, according to the Talmud, the biblical prescription "And you shall sanctify him" (Leviticus 21:8) requires that, in general, he is to be regarded as having a higher status—and honored accordingly—within the synagogue and community.[21]

The fact that synagogues face toward the Temple at Jerusalem, and that worshipers must themselves face in that direction when reciting the central prayer, the *Amidah*, also acknowledges the link between the two institutions. Some also see this reflected in the relationship between reader and congregation, which evokes that of priest and petitioner in the Temple setup.

The Palestinian Talmud (*Berakhot* 1:1) actually casts the worshiper, rather than the *chazan*, in the role of priest. It establishes the law that while saying the *Amidah* the worshiper must keep his legs close together in order to emulate the priests who, when ascending the altar, had to shuffle along so slowly that, when one foot was placed in front of the other, their legs were hardly separated.

The emergence of synagogue prayers from the matrix of Temple sacrifice was also responsible for a number of other halakhic regulations governing prayer that were also clearly influenced by sacrificial law. Hence, just as any extraneous or inappropriate thought while offering the sacrifice—such as an intention to eat of its meat later than the prescribed time limit or outside the prescribed sacred precinct—rendered the animal *piggul*, rejected, so is a proper *kavvanah* (intention) necessary for prayer. Similarly, the reason why the central prayer, the *Amidah*, must be recited standing is that that was the Temple regulation governing sacrifice.

The law that a person should endeavor to have a permanent seat (*makom kavua*) in his synagogue, so that his prayers are always uttered from the same place, is likewise rooted in the closely regulated Temple system whereby each category of sacrifice had its particular location (for most sacrifices this was the north) in relation to the altar, from which it had to be slaughtered, as well as a fixed place where the blood had to be sprinkled.

The recommendation that one should be dressed in dignified attire when attending synagogue is also inspired by the fact that the priests wore special robes when performing the Temple service.

Examples of the dependence of synagogue upon Temple have recently been augmented in an illuminating article by Theodore Friedman,[22] who has demonstrated that even in the realm of architecture the synagogue was influenced by, if not modeled directly upon, the layout of the Temple.

Before the 3rd century C.E., the Torah scrolls were housed in an anteroom of the synagogue, and brought in as required.[23] It was comparatively late, therefore, that an Ark, in the form of a niche in the eastern wall of the synagogue chamber, was introduced. The original arrangement was preferred to the more respectful one of having the Torah in the actual synagogue chamber, in order to be reminiscent of the Solomonic Temple layout, wherein the Torah scrolls were housed in the

Heikhal, the chamber leading into the Holy of Holies where the Ark was accommodated. Hence, in early talmudic times, the synagogue also placed the scrolls in an adjacent chamber.

The basilica style of architecture, where two rows of parallel columns effectively divide the prayer hall longitudinally into three areas, was adopted for all ancient synagogues. Friedman sees this as another clear attempt to provide a physical reminder of the Temple layout, wherein the most impressive "Chamber of Hewn Stones" *(Lishkat Ha-Gazit)* was designed in basilica style.

The intriguing fact that, in all excavated synagogues, stone benches are always located against the side walls, and never in the central nave, is similarly explained as an attempt to follow Temple precedent. No one, other than kings of Davidic descent, was permitted to sit down in the central area *(azarah)* of the Temple. With the development of a longer synagogue service, many people could not remain standing. They introduced benches, therefore; but, again following the Temple regulation, they prohibited people from sitting in the central area.

There was a widespread feature of having steps leading to, and connecting, various sections of the ancient excavated synagogues. Steps led up to the synagogue building itself, and, in some synagogues where the Ark was housed within the prayer hall, a few steps always led up to the Ark. Friedman regards this feature as quite obviously patterned upon the Temple, wherein there was a multiplicity of steps. As one entered the Temple one proceeded from one level to the next by means of various flights of steps. There were twelve steps as one made one's way from the outermost enclosure, called *Soreg,* into the Women's Court by way of the Eastern Gate. There were fifteen steps leading from the Women's Court to the Court of the Israelites, and so on. The greater the sanctity of the particular area, the higher up was its location, with the Holy of Holies being at the very highest elevation.

Friedman explains in the same way the enigmatic statement of Rav Chisda that, "one should always enter into a synagogue by means of two doors,"[24] which was responsible for the universal practice of having a vestibule leading into the prayer chamber itself. This is also shown to be based upon the Temple arrangement wherein the area for prayer, the "Hall of Hewn Stone," was reached by passing also through Nicanor's Gate.

At precisely what period during the history of the Second Commonwealth the Temple succeeded in developing an authorized liturgy, we cannot be sure. Neither can we determine whether the Temple borrowed its prayers from the early Synagogue or vice versa. All we have is the later mishnaic tradition that the Temple liturgy included the daily recitation of the *Shema* and its blessings, the Ten Commandments, selected psalms for the levitical choir, a series of blessings which might have been the ones later augmented to make up our *Amidah*,[25] a period of silent meditation and private prayer uttered by the worshiper in a fully prostrated pose,[26] and the Priestly Blessing of the people.

It would appear from our sources that there was, however, a developed Temple liturgy of *Selichot* (penitential prayers) to be recited on the fast days instituted during the incidence of drought,[27] as well as prayers to accompany the blowing of the *Shofar* on Rosh Hashanah, the formal confessions uttered by the High Priest on Yom Kippur, and the "short prayer" he uttered after emerging on that day from the Holy of Holies.[28] Most of these, however, were prayers that only the officiating Priest, Levites, or members of the *Maamadot* recited, and that could not easily be incorporated into a daily liturgy for recitation in the prayer houses.

After each blessing the congregation responded with the formula, *Barukh shem kevod malkhuto le-olam va-ed* (Blessed be His name, whose glorious Kingdom is for ever and ever). This was subsequently replaced by the simple *Amen*. There was no universally accepted text. There was agreement, however, regarding the themes for a particular prayer or service, but much local variety existed from the point of view of form and style. Only in talmudic times was some attempt made toward standardization.

2

Synagogue Prayer

The Origin of the Synagogue

The origin of the synagogue as the central institution in Jewish life is shrouded in mystery. Scholars are widely divided on this subject. One view, vigorously, if unconvincingly, expressed by Louis Finkelstein,[1] suggests that the synagogue was already a developed institution during the period of the classical prophets of the first Commonwealth (9th–6th centuries B.C.E.). Its prayer meetings were held on Sabbaths and New Moons at the homes of the prophets. Hence, when the Shunamite woman, whose child, unknown to her husband, was in a coma, tells the latter that she is going to the prophet's house, he replies, rather perplexed, "But today is neither New Moon nor Sabbath!" (II Kings 4:23).

Evidence such as this is not convincing, however, since, while the prophet may well have "held court," and exhorted the people spiritually at his home, there is absolutely no evidence that *regular* worship took place there on such occasions. The prophet was, however, available to pray on behalf of individuals for their personal needs; and it was for this purpose that the Shunamite woman went to enlist his services (II Kings 4:33). Furthermore, even if the prophet Elisha did conduct prayer

15

meetings at his home on Mount Carmel (II Kings 4:25), the fact that this lady had to make the arduous journey from Shunem to Elisha's residence, both on this occasion and, presumably, periodically on a "Sabbath or New Moon," suggests that local meetinghouses for prayer did not exist. Indeed, when she tells her husband that she is rushing "to the man of God" (II Kings 4:22), he doesn't ask her which particular man of God. The implication is clearly that Elisha was the only recognized spiritual authority. The idea of a network of "prayer houses," presided over by competent leaders—"men of God"—is therefore absolutely untenable.

While Finkelstein's theory, that such a developed institution of the synagogue was carried to Babylon with the exiles (586 B.C.E.), is implausible, the alternate view—that it emerged out of the needs of the exiles living in Babylon during the next half century—is shared by an impressive array of scholars.[2]

The essence of their view is that during the exile, when the sacrificial cult was interrupted, prayer came to be regarded as a more effective vehicle of religious expression. Whereas the Temple had emphasized class distinction and the priestly monopoly in religious administration, the exile leveled social barriers by reducing the whole community to the status of plebeians. It was through the medium of prayer that specific expression could be given to this new spirit of equality. No priests were needed as intermediaries for prayer, as they had been for sacrifices; no expense of travel to, and accommodation in, Jerusalem was required for prayer; and no distinctions of wealth or status could color—or discolor—the simple act of worship, whereas they had been so evident in the flamboyancy of the sacrificial cult.

Proponents of this theory of the exilic origin of the synagogue maintain that the exiles, seeking a measure of security and identification with their kin in a foreign and heathen environment, would inevitably have gathered together spontaneously, particularly on Sabbaths, feast, and fast days, to reaffirm their loyalty to their ancestral faith and to keep alive their hopes for restoration. They would have faced toward the homeland and offered up prayers, including confession of the sins which had brought such harsh judgment upon their nation. They would have chanted poetic laments similar to those found in the Book of Lamentations and in the psalms.

There is one particular rabbinic interpretation that is generally adduced to support the idea of such prayer meetings during the exilic period. It is applied to one significant reference in Ezekiel, prophet of the exile: "Although I have scattered them among the countries, yet have I been to them *as a little sanctuary (mikdash me'at)* in the countries where they are come" (Ezekiel 11:16). Rabbi Isaac[3] explains the "little sanctuary" as a reference to the synagogues and schools of learning in Babylon, where God's spirit resided after it was banished from the ruined Temple.

Scholars who employ this interpretation, to support the idea of synagogues during the Exile, conveniently ignore the fact that this interpretation of the Ezekiel verse is immediately contested in the Talmud by another authority who believes that the "little sanctuary" refers to one specific Babylonian spiritual center, the *Bet Rabbeinu Shebebavel*, which was not founded until 700 years after the exile, in the period of Rav, disciple of Judah the Prince (2nd–3rd centuries c.e.).

The author of this interpretation in the Talmud, R. Eleazar, is not troubled by the problem of making the prophet Ezekiel refer to one particular academy of learning some 700 years later. His main objective seems to be simply that of refuting R. Isaac's view that there actually was a network of "synagogues and schools of learning" so early in Jewish history.

While meetings for prayer and study may, indeed, have taken place from time to time in Babylon, the notion that a new dynamic institution, engendering the sort of religious spirit we associate with the exercise of regular worship, grew out of those meetings, just does not seem to be borne out by what we know of the history of that period. The Isaiah of the Babylonian captivity is still preoccupied with preaching against idolatry,[4] and even the cream of the exiles, those imbued with idealism and yearning for Zion, who returned to Palestine when Cyrus the Persian gave permission (538 b.c.e.), do not seem to have been exposed to, let alone imbued with, anything approximating the intense religious spirit that the institution of the synagogue would have injected into their lives. Their widespread intermarriage, desecration of the Sabbath, and ignorance of Torah—from which even the priests and Levites were not immune—is unequivocally chronicled in the Books of Ezra[5] and Nehemiah.[6] Furthermore, even a cursory reading of these books creates the clear impression that the priestly and cultic influence had remained predominant in Jewish life. It is the priests and Levites who preside over the reorganization of national life, centered upon the Temple, immediately after the return from Babylon. Amid all the references to the preparations for the rebuilding of the Temple, the donations, requisitioning of materials, appointed officials and their vestments, etc., there is not one allusion to a prayer hall, a prayer leader, or even to the future use of the Temple for such a purpose. Had the prophets of the Exile been prayer leaders, or had they succeeded in establishing the concept of the synagogue and regular worship among the masses, it is inconceivable that facilities for prayer would not have been incorporated into the design and curriculum of the new spiritual center.

The popular term — *Bet Kneset* — that was coined for this institution also provides some indication of its period of origin. It seems to have largely escaped the attention of scholars that the root of this word — *Kanas* — hardly appears in the earlier books of the Bible, and is restricted to very rare usage in the late books of Ecclesiastes, Esther, Chronicles, and in but two of the psalms.

It seems highly unlikely that they would have employed an, as yet, archaic or obscure verb to create from it a name for a new, vibrant institution which they were hoping to popularize! Nothing would be more likely to distance the masses from it than to give the synagogue an unfamiliar title.

The inference is clearly that it was only when the root *Kanas* gradually became popularized, in the subsequent, late Persian, period, that it would have been regarded as a suitably well-known appellation (perhaps even a new "in" word) for the rapidly evolving network of prayer houses.

We are thus inevitably drawn to the late Persian and early Greek period, during which to postulate the rise of the institution of the synagogue, though the influences that shaped its rise may well be discernible some centuries earlier. We will, consequently, have to go back a little in time to note some of these influences.

From Private to Public Worship

Although, as we have already noted, spontaneous private prayer became *de rigueur* through the bitter experiences of the Egyptian bondage, yet, with national independence and growing prosperity, the need and stimulus for prayer at the individual level lapsed. The common folk rarely offered up their own prayers — hence Eli, High Priest of the sanctuary at Shilo, mistakes Hannah for a drunkard when he sees "her lips moving, but no sound emerging" (I Samuel 1:13). It was assumed at that time that one really required a prophet or priest to act as intermediary for private petitions (see I Samuel 12:19, 23).

It was possibly not just the rarity of an individual offering up a private prayer, but also its protracted nature (I Samuel 12:12) that aroused his suspicion. If so, this might give us some important insight into the form of personal prayer at that time (12th–11th centuries B.C.E.). Moses' brief prayer on behalf of his sister, Miriam, when she contracted leprosy, "Lord, please heal her" (Numbers 12:113), may therefore be considered the paradigm for what was considered an appropriate private petition at that period. Although Moses' plea was of a personal nature, the Torah states, "And Moses *cried out (va-yitzak Mosheh)* to the Lord, saying. . . ." It would seem then, that even private prayers were generally declaimed, perhaps loud enough for the heavens to hear![7] This would provide a further explanation for Eli having regarded the silently praying Hannah as a drunkard.[8]

But Hannah had clearly been taught to believe that the longer the prayer, the more the likelihood of it being answered. Lengthy private prayers were therefore new to Eli on both counts. He preferred formal sacrifice – yet another reason for his harsh treatment of Hannah.

Hannah's view of the efficacy of lengthier prayer ultimately gained in popularity. Some four hundred years later the great prophet Isaiah, castigating a sinful Israel, attempts to disabuse them of the idea that "countless prayers," even of a communal nature, would appeal to God:

> When you lift your hands outspread in prayer,
> I will hide my eyes from you.
> Though you offer *countless prayers,*
> I will not listen.
>
> (Isaiah 1:15)

It would seem then that the ordinary folk did not pray on a regular basis,[9] believing that direct communication with the deity was something only a man of God could achieve on one's behalf. Communal prayer was undertaken exclusively at times of great national concern – such as in the face of drought or war – or when public thanksgiving for deliverance had to be expressed. This remained essentially the situation throughout the first commonwealth and the period of the Exile, with the exception that private petition eventually became the prerogative of every individual, without the need of an intermediary. However, it was only at times of great personal crisis or celebration that the individual would be moved to offer such a prayer.

Regular worship, *as a purely spiritual exercise,* was not the norm. Thus, when the prophet Jeremiah sends a letter to the refugees in Babylon, he exhorts them to "seek the welfare of any city to which I have carried you off, and pray to the Lord *for it:* on its welfare your welfare will depend" (Jeremiah 29:7). Prayer is still motivated by self-interest. It is still petitionary. He does not expect them to pray daily for the welfare of their own souls. He does not envisage that they will build houses for prayer: "Build houses and *live in them*" (Jeremiah 29:5), he advises.

And even in his vision of the restoration of the nation to its land Jeremiah does not foresee the existence of houses of worship in each city. Even personal celebrations, such as weddings, will take place in the precincts of the one focus of spirituality, the Temple:

> Yet in this place shall be heard once again the sounds of joy and gladness, the voice of the bridegroom and the bride; here too shall be heard voices shouting "Praise the Lord of Hosts for He is good, for His love endures for ever," as they offer praises and thanksgiving *in the house of the Lord*.

Religious Rallies

It was the second commonwealth movement of *Soferim* ("Scribes"), founded by Ezra (440 B.C.E.), and setting as its objective a spiritual revival rooted in the diffusion of Torah knowledge among the masses, that may be said to have provided the greatest impetus for the rise of the popular institution of the synagogue. They broke down the priestly monopoly of spirituality and enabled the ordinary Jew to undertake his ritual practices with confidence and enthusiasm (see Nehemiah 8:13–18).

Ezra and Nehemiah convened religious rallies whose program provided the blueprint for some of the central elements of synagogue worship. They instituted the public reading and exposition of the Torah (Ezra 7:10; Nehemiah 8:1; 9:3; 13:1) from a raised wooden platform—the forerunner of our *Bimah* (Nehemiah 8:4). They introduced blessings to be recited over the reading of the Law, and encouraged the people to bow and recite *Amen, Amen* after them (Nehemiah 8:6). They accompanied the reading of the Torah with a full explanation of the meaning of the verses, and they interpreted the laws clearly and fully (Nehemiah 8:8). This was to develop into a great and inspirational exegetical tradition of Aramaic *Targum* and midrashic exposition in the generations ahead, which in turn gave birth to the synagogue sermon and *shiur*.

At one of these rallies, instead of the Torah reading and exposition occupying most of the time, equal time—about three hours—was devoted to "worship and confession" (Nehemiah 9:3). It was at this service that we meet for the first time what was later to become another notable characteristic of synagogue liturgy: the reader's invitation, or instruction, to the congregation to "bless the Lord"—*Borakhu et ha-shem* (Nehemiah 9:5). A section of the lengthy prayer that was uttered on that historic occasion is actually incorporated into our daily morning services (Nehemiah 9:6–11).

Ezra and Nehemiah were themselves staunch upholders of Temple Judaism, and in the signed covenant whereby they bound the people to uphold the laws of the Torah (Nehemiah 10:1) they lay great emphasis on the cult and on ensuring adequate financial support for the priestly and levitical Temple administrators (Nehemiah 10:32–40). Nevertheless, the public rallies and prayer meetings they had introduced must have caught the imagination of the nation. Without doubt, on their return to their villages and communities, religious meetings would have been organized every Sabbath—and in some even more frequently, on Mondays and Thursdays—to read the Torah, discuss its meaning, and offer up prayers, petitions, and thanksgiving.

Men of the Great Assembly

We know little about the nature of Jewish religious life during the next few centuries, other than a few talmudic traditions regarding the "Men of the Great Synagogue" (or "Assembly")—the *Anshei Kneset Ha-Gedolah*—who were the successors of Ezra and the *Soferim*. Significantly, however, all these traditions point in one direction: toward the intensification of prayer and the evolution of a synagogue liturgy.

They are credited with having introduced the *Shemoneh Esrey* ("Eighteen Blessings" of the weekday *Amidah*),[10] various other blessings, *Kiddush* and *Havdalah*,[11] as well as having made strenuous efforts to ensure that Torah scrolls and *tefillin* were available for all.[12] All these innovations and provisions presuppose regular worship, and we may assume that, at least by the close of their period, prayer had begun to make its influence felt as an intrinsic part of the religious life of the nation.

In *Pirkei Avot* (1:2), Shimon the Righteous is described as "one of the last survivors of the *Kneset Ha-Gedolah*." Unfortunately we cannot determine precisely the chronology of *Pirkei Avot's* "Chain of Tradition," as it contains many omissions. It is impossible to date this Shimon as having lived at the end of the Persian period—wherein the Men of the Great Synagogue are generally placed—and modern scholars generally identify him with Shimon II (219–199 B.C.E.). If this identification is correct, the activities of the *Kneset Ha-Gedolah* would have spilled over into the Greek period by more than a century. This seems far more plausible than the traditional view that telescopes the activities of this movement into a few decades of the Persian period. However, this is rather frustrating for our immediate purpose in attempting to determine precisely when a formal synagogue service made its first appearance, for it means that it could have been any time between the period of Ezra (440) and Shimon (200).

The Greek period is, indeed, a plausible setting for the evolution of the synagogue. Greek ideas, of democracy and democratic institutions, which infiltrated Judaea around 330 B.C.E., may well have given a vital boost to the efforts of the *Kneset Ha-Gedolah* who were committed to making the democratic institution of the synagogue a worthy competitor—and ultimate successor—of the priestly autocracy that governed the Temple.

Placing the development of synagogue prayer between 330 and 200 B.C.E. is totally in line with the scholarly view regarding the final compilation of the psalms. Sigmund Mowinckel[13] argues convincingly that they were collected together to achieve their final form "sometime before the year 300 B.C.E., maybe even fifty years earlier."[14]

He also asserts that "the Psalter cannot under any circumstances be later than about 200 B.C.E."[15] It would hardly be stretching the imagination to suggest that the upsurge in the popularity, and the expansion, of the synagogue during this period prompted the collection and editing of the psalms in order to provide a hymnal for local synagogal usage.

Mishmarot and *Maamadot*

The latter theory, to account for, and date, the rise of the synagogue, synthesizes well with that of Solomon Zeitlin,[16] who views it as an offshoot of the network of twenty-four *Maamadot*—lay fraternities—which was organized throughout Judaea, corresponding to the twenty-four *Mishmarot*—duty-rotas of priests—who officiated at the Second Temple altar for a full week, twice a year. When the turn of a particular priestly *Mishmar* came around, the corresponding fraternity of laymen (*Maamad*) would accompany the priests and Levites at the altar, and bring the sacrificial act to a close by reciting prayers and biblical selections relating to the sacrifices.

Those laymen who lived far from Jerusalem, and could not make the journey, would assemble together in their own localities and hold prayer meetings. It was from these prayer meetings that the institution of the synagogue probably developed.

Zeitlin attributes this organization of *Maamadot* to the Pharisees, that is to the later Second Temple period, which we have already established, for other reasons, as the most plausible time. He believes that the daily offering *(Korban Tamid)* was originally a private sacrifice, and therefore a privilege only the wealthy classes could afford. The Pharisees, on the other hand, who represented the interests of the lower classes, set as their goal the democratization of the Temple institutions. They therefore not only made the daily sacrifice a public offering, paid for out of communal funds, but also gave equal participation in the sacrificial ritual to the laymen of Judaea by establishing these twenty-four rotas of *Maamadot*. The synagogue thus began as a movement for social and religious equality; and, in its administration and the many opportunities it offers for the active participation of laymen in the conduct of its services, it has retained that essential character until the present day.

We mentioned above that throughout most of the biblical period the popular belief was that a holy intermediary was required in order to present petitionary prayer to the Almighty.

During the later period of the Second Commonwealth the role of "holy intermediary" for petitionary prayer was taken over by those who served as members of the *Maamadot*, the lay prayer-rotas. In addition to their prescribed prayers and Torah readings, they also observed fasts and offered up prayers on behalf of their brethren in danger. Specific days during the week of their rota were allocated to prayer for specific dangers.

> On Monday they prayed for those on the high seas; on Tuesday for those traveling across deserts; on Wednesday for children afflicted with croup, and for those in danger of contracting it; on Thursday they prayed that the pregnant women should not miscarry and that the nursing mothers should have no difficulty feeding their young.[17]

It is obvious that specific petitioners in any of these categories would approach their representatives and request them to have their particular predicament in the forefront of their minds, and even to mention them by name in a specific petition, when uttering prayers for that special condition.

The Temple–Synagogue Rapprochement

The famous story of *Choni Ha-Me'agel* (Honi the Circle Drawer)[18]–who lived during the first century B.C.E.–not only betrays the period into which the idea still survived that a holy man was required as intermediary for petitionary prayer, but, more significantly, it also gives us an indication of precisely when the rapprochement between Temple and synagogue really began to gain momentum.

There had been a three-year drought in Palestine, and a message was dispatched to Choni that he should pray for rain. When his initial petition was not answered, he drew a circle and called out to God, "Your children look toward me as one who has Your ear. I swear by Your great name that I will not move from out of this circle until You have mercy on Your children." Raindrops began to fall, whereupon Choni cried out, "I asked for more than this!" It then came down with such vehemence — each drop being the size of the mouth of a barrel — that people feared for their lives. Choni thereupon demanded that this be replaced with a more acceptable rainfall.

The reaction of the religious authorities to Choni's miraculous abilities is interesting. Shimon ben Shatach, leader of the pharisaic party, chided him for his insolence in making such precise demands of God; though Shimon recognized that God did indeed indulge Choni's every wish, "like a spoiled child." He told him that "if it was not that you were Choni, I would have put you under a ban of excommunication for your conduct!" The Sanhedrin, on the other hand, sent a congratulatory message to him: "A generation impoverished through sin, you have delivered through your prayers."

Bearing in mind that the Sanhedrin held their sessions in the Chamber of Hewn Stone in the Temple, and were consequently under the influence of Temple Judaism (this may still even have been the Sadducean, priestly Sanhedrin, which Shimon ben Shatach managed ultimately to replace with Pharisees), their acknowledgment of the superior efficacy of prayer over Temple sacrifice marks a significant turning point in the struggle of the synagogue for official recognition by the Temple leadership.

Synagogue Buildings

The question of whether or not at such an early period there were buildings exclusively designated as synagogues is also problematic. A popular reference, to support the theory that a network of "synagogues" existed for several centuries before the destruction of the Temple, is Psalm 74:8, which might well emanate from the Maccabean period (165

B.C.E.): "They have burned all the meeting places of God *(mo'adei El)* in the land." This is conceivably a reference to synagogues that existed before Antiochus invaded and devastated Judaea.

Scholars are skeptical about this, on the grounds that there is not a single reference to a synagogue in the chronicle of destruction, persecutions, and atrocities described in the first Book of Maccabees (1:21–62). This is easily explained, however, since the obvious preoccupation of the priestly Maccabees was with the restoration of the Temple. They might well have regarded the destruction of synagogues as unfortunate, but not as tragic. The Temple in their eyes made synagogues unnecessary.

While Philo, Josephus, and the New Testament do attest to the existence of synagogues, in both Palestine and the Diaspora, in the 1st century, and while this is corroborated by early inscriptions (at Delos[19]) and by Bible scroll discoveries (at Masada), yet it must be admitted that no archaeological excavation has yet uncovered a building in Judaea from before the 2nd century C.E. that can indisputably be identified *exclusively* as a synagogue, rather than as a multipurpose assembly hall. This includes the so-called synagogues at Masada[20] and Herodium! The earliest dated synagogue is that of Dura-Europos (circa 240 C.E.). The popularly held view that there was a synagogue in the Temple itself is grounded neither in clear textual evidence nor archaeological verification.

So, until the 1st century C.E., most people simply prayed in the city squares of their own localities. Synagogue architecture—if one can use the term—was domestic architecture. At first the private homes of prophets, and, at a later period, of sages, served as meeting places for prayer. With the establishment of academies of learning *(Battei Midrash)*, these took over this function on a daily basis. The need for separate synagogue buildings probably arose as a result of conflicts of interests and requirements, and differences over such things as times of services and use of building, between the lay worshiping fraternity and the scholars and students whose building they shared.

The multipurpose nature of these earliest "synagogues" explains why not one of those discovered at Gamla, Masada, Herodium, or Delos was endowed with a specially designated area to serve as the *Aron Kodesh*, and house the sacred Torah scrolls.

The explanation is quite simply that the regular multipurpose usage of the chamber required that it be kept neutral, and that the scrolls be housed in a separate anteroom, used exclusively as a sacred store. Only several centuries later was the need felt to designate permanent and exclusive halls as "synagogues," and to endow them with a permanent Ark section. It has been suggested that "this was apparently related to the popular need for a clearer religious self-definition. The wider display and use, in the later period, of such Judaic symbols as the *Menorah*, Ark, *Lulav*, and *Shofar*, which were not employed during the period of the second Temple, is also evidence of that need, which was possibly necessitated by the rise of Christianity."[21]

After the Bar Kochba rebellion (135 C.E.) the Jews were expelled from Jerusalem. This led to the establishment of new settlements in Galilee and the Golan heights, many of which grew into vibrant centers of religious life and talmudic study. The ruins of over one hundred synagogues from that period have been discovered in that area.

3

Prayer in Talmudic Times

Studying and Praying

One of the pentateuchal sections dealing with the Sabbath laws is introduced by the verse *Vayyakhel Mosheh,* "And Moses *assembled* all the Israelites" (Exodus 35:1). The noun *kehillah* ("a congregation") derives from that verb; and this association prompted an interesting midrashic observation:

> God said to Moses: Divide the Israelites into large *congregations* and expound publicly to them the laws of the Sabbath. In this way future generations will learn from you to establish congregations every Sabbath in their academies of learning *(Bet Ha-Midrash),* for the purpose of Torah study and halakhic instruction. Thus will my great name be praised among my children.[1]

Significantly, there is no reference here to *prayer* on the Sabbath. The main purpose of assembling the people is to study Torah! This Midrash clearly sets out to promote the institution of the *Bet Ha-Midrash* ("House of Study"), which, in talmudic times, served the dual purpose of study and prayer—academy and synagogue. Primacy is here ac-

27

corded, however, to its role as academy. And it is on *Shabbat*—when people are not preoccupied with work—that they are expected to "assemble" in large numbers, primarily for study of Torah, but also for prayer.

It would seem then, that in the talmudic era—as now—the vast majority of Jews were once-a-week attenders. According to Moses Nachmanides, this *Shabbat*-only spiritual convocation, summoned for, and united in, communal prayer, is even implied in the biblical reference to the Sabbath as *mikra'ei kodesh*, "a holy summons" (Leviticus 23:2). This term suggests that this is the day—if on no other—when Israel should assemble in the House of God, for prayer and praise, in response to the "holy summons" to sanctify this day.

There is more than a tinge of resignation underlying the talmudic statement: "The Sabbaths and festivals were only instituted in order that we might occupy ourselves with Torah on these occasions."[2] This falls considerably short of the biblical ideal of daily study—"meditating therein by day and by night" (Joshua 1:8). The talmudic sentiment was therefore explained later to apply only to "workers who are fully occupied with their work the rest of the week, and only on *Shabbat* are they able to come and immerse themselves in Torah."[3] Since "Six days shalt thou labor and do all thy work" is also a divine prescription, there is, therefore, a tacit justification here for noncompliance with Joshua's ideal of full-time study.

On *Shabbat*, however, there was no dispensation, and everyone was expected to repair to the "academy-cum-synagogue" to study and to pray.

Study and prayer were not regarded as separate spiritual exercises. The *Shabbat* morning program wedded them together in such an interactive manner that it became natural to regard the public reading from the Torah, as well as the *derashah*, or exposition, that accompanied it, as devotional acts of worship. Thus was forged the unique character of Jewish prayer.

Henceforth it was a matter of course that the synagogue service should be interspersed with readings and study passages, not only from the Bible, but also from various collections of rabbinic literature: *Mishnah* (passages from the first codification of rabbinic law, by Judah Ha-Nasi, late 2nd century C.E.), *Beraita* (supplementary rabbinic law), and *Aggadah* (midrashic exposition). The twinning of the synagogue and the *Bet Ha-Midrash* meant that the Jew prayed while he studied, and studied while he prayed. There could be no greater "praise" of God than to read and study His Law. There could be no greater devotional act than to discover, and rediscover, the subtle shades of meaning underlying His word and His will. It is facetious to think that man can talk to his Maker for hours, and still command God's interest and attention. Far more appropriate it is that we should allocate time for God to talk to us— through the medium of His revealed word: the Written and the Oral traditions.

The *Amidah*

The central composition of every Service is the *Amidah* ("Standing Prayer"), and a measure of its importance lies in the fact that in talmudic literature the generic term *tefillah* ("prayer") referred specifically and exclusively to the *Amidah*, unless otherwise qualified. In talmudic times it was also the only prayer that had to be recited aloud by the prayer-leader (*chazan* or *sheliach tzibbur*) from a position of prominence before the Ark. The synagogue *gabbai*, when inviting someone to lead that composition, would simply say: *Avor lifenei ha-tevah*, "pass before the Ark," or *bo ukerav*, "Come and approach (the Ark)."

It was also, at first, the only prayer that, as its name implies, required the worshiper to be in a standing position for its recitation, as an indicator of its special importance. This may seem surprising when we consider that we are not required to stand for the twice-daily recitation of the other main prayer, the *Shema*, even though it enjoys a higher status as a biblically mandated composition ("these words . . . you shall recite . . . when you lie down and when you rise up"— Deuteronomy 6:7)!

We may conjecture that while the biblical status of the *Shema* clearly did not require enhancing, the *Amidah*, on the other hand, by reason of its being only a rabbinic composition, required all the weight and authority the rabbis could muster in order to establish its obligatory recitation. Insisting that it be recited while standing would clearly serve to emphasize the importance with which it was invested.

The *Amidah* comprises three main sections: the first three blessings are designated as *shevach*, praise of God; the intermediate thirteen blessings constitute *bakkashah*, pleas for personal and national needs; and the last three blessings are *hodayah*, thanksgiving for divine bounty. On Sabbaths and festivals, however, when it was not regarded as appropriate to adopt the stance of a humble and needy petitioner, but rather to hail, joyfully and confidently, the sanctity of those special holy days, the thirteen intermediate blessings are accordingly replaced by one lengthy blessing, called *Kedushat Ha-Yom* ("sanctity of the day").

While there is a popular tendency to attribute the composition of the *Amidah* to a single age, and to assume that it was introduced and made statutory by some early rabbinic synod, this is not in fact how it came about. The first point to note is that our *Amidah* does not represent the original version that evolved in Palestine, but is rather a Babylonian revision of it, produced quite a few centuries afterward. Since Babylon overtook Palestine as the main center of Jewish learning and religious life, from the 4th century C.E. onward (see chap. 4), it was able to frame its version of the prayers in accordance with its own particular rules and principles, as discussed and clarified in the Babylonian Talmud and the later works of the *Geonim*, the heads of the great Babylonian academies.

It is clear that the rabbis of the Talmud had no single authoritative view regarding the origin of the *Amidah*, and hence we find a number of mutually contradictory "suggestions" as to its authorship and period of origin:

The Patriarchs instituted the [*Amidah*] prayers (*Berakhot* 26b).

Moses instituted the formulae of the [*Amidah*] prayers (Jerusalem Talmud, *Berakhot*, chap. 7).

120 Elders, among whom were several Prophets, instituted the *Shmoneh Esrey* ["Eighteen Blessings"] according to the accepted order (*Megillah* 18a).

The Men of the Great Synagogue [4th–3rd centuries B.C.E.] instituted for Israel the blessings, the [*Amidah*] prayers, the Sanctifications and the *Havdalah* rituals (*Berakhot* 33a).

It was the early sages who prescribed the recitation of the *Shmoneh Esrey* for Israel (*Sifre Devarim*, sec. 343).

While it is the first quotation above that is popularly taught in our Hebrew schools, to the extent that it has become almost an axiom of faith to throw back the origin of that main statutory prayer to the very beginnings of Jewish history, it will now be appreciated that that is but one of several suggestions that, taken together, span a period of some 1,700 years, from the Patriarchal period (1900 B.C.E.) until the "early sages," who are probably to be identified with the early Pharisaic teachers of the 3rd–2nd centuries B.C.E., referred to in the first chapter of the *Ethics of the Fathers*.

The fact that there is such a wide difference of opinion in the talmudic literature indicates clearly that the *Amidah* was acknowledged by all the early sages as an ancient composition whose origin is shrouded in mystery, and about which one can but speculate.

Indeed, this remains the consensus view of scholars regarding its origin, namely, that the individual blessings evolved independently over several centuries, having been created, in the main, to meet specific national needs and various social and religious situations. As prayer and prayer-houses became popularized, through the efforts of the Pharisees, a need was felt for some consistency of practice; hence the introduction of a central prayer, the *Amidah*, comprising the eighteen blessings (*Shmoneh Esrey*), whose popularity gradually won for them general acceptance.

This evolution into a statutory *Amidah* was a slow and painful process, with many of the greatest talmudists of the 1st century only grudgingly accepting this trend toward standardization, and remaining apprehensive that it would destroy the element of spontaneity that had characterized prayer from biblical times until then, and spell a take-over of the expression of religious fervor and sentiment by specialist composers and theologians. The following passage reflects those differences of opinion on the question of the status of the *Amidah*, as well as the variant methods of reciting it in the academies of the scholars referred to:

> Rabban Gamliel said: A man must recite each day the Eighteen Bless-ings. Rabbi Joshua said: [it is sufficient if he recites] the essence of the Eighteen. Rabbi Akivah said: If he is able to recite the full Eighteen fluently, he should do so; if not, he may recite merely the essence of them. Rabbi Eleazar said: Whoever puts his [*Amidah*] prayer into a fixed mold, deprives it of its petitionary quality.[4]

It is clear that we have reflected here the stages of the evolution of the *Amidah*, from a series of generally accepted blessing formulations, which were at first recited aloud by any knowledgeable reader, in no particular order of blessings and conforming to no fixed or authorized text. As long as the reader reflected the overall sentiments of the accepted *themes*—the "essence"—he had fulfilled the expectations of the members of the prayer quorum.

There is an interesting midrashic story regarding Rabbi Eleazar Chisma (1st century) that reflects the anarchic state of prayer in the synagogues of Judea at that period, before the view of Gamliel won sway, and a standardized order of service and a fixed *Amidah* became statutory:

> Rabbi Eleazar came to a place, and he was invited to lead the *Shema*. "I'm not knowledgeable (of your custom)," he replied. "Then stand before the

Ark [and lead us in the *Amidah*]," they said. "I do not know it [in its full form]," he replied. Thereupon the townsfolk turned to those accompanying the visitor, and said, mockingly, "Is this really Rabbi Eleazar? Is this the same whose scholarship you have been boasting about? He truly does not deserve the title *Rabbi!*" Eleazar's face grew pale, and he promptly went off to Rabbi Akivah, and prevailed upon him to teach him the full version of the *Amidah*. After some time, Eleazar returned to that particular place. This time he readily accepted the invitation to lead the service, after which the people called out: *Itchasem Rabbi Eleazar* ("Eleazar has become un-muzzled!"). And from that time onward he was nicknamed *Eleazar Chisma*.[5]

The ignorance of that sage is easily explained, however, when we note that he was a disciple of Rabbi Joshua, cited above. In opposition to Rabban Gamliel, who wanted to impose the full version of the Eighteen Blessings, Rabbi Joshua believed that to recite the essence of those blessings was sufficient. There is no doubt, therefore, that that was precisely his own tradition and that of his academy. Thus, it is quite reasonable to assume that his disciple, Rabbi Eleazar, brought up in that tradition, never had cause to recite the full version, and was therefore unable to accept the honor of those townsmen. The latter, simple folk, uninformed about the variant liturgical practices of the synagogues around the country, would naturally have assumed that their practice of reciting the full version was standard!

Clearly, among those congregations and places that were accustomed to recite merely the essence of the Eighteen, there was considerable variety of custom, particularly as regards the length of their extempore blessings. This is reflected in the following charming passage:

A disciple once stood [as reader of the *Amidah*] before the Ark in the academy of Rabbi Eliezer, and he drew out his prayers inordinately. "What a long-winded chap is this one!" said his colleagues to their teacher. Rabbi Eliezer replied: "Did he prolong any more than Moses, our teacher, of whom it is said, 'And I petitioned before the Lord for forty days and forty nights' (Deuteronomy 9:18)?" On another occasion, a disciple acted as reader before Rabbi Eliezer, and he was unusually brief. "What an abbreviator is this chap!" complained the disciples. Rabbi Eliezer replied: "Is he any briefer than Moses our teacher, whose prayer [for his sister, Miriam] was, simply, 'Please, God, heal her, please' (Numbers 12:13)!"[6]

The Earliest *Amidah*-type Blessings

While there are no formulae or lists of blessings prescribed in the Torah for regular or even periodic recitation in the context of prayer, scholars believe that some of those earliest blessings that we have alluded to, as precursors of the later *Amidah*-type blessings, are already foreshadowed in one of the postbiblical books of the Apocrypha, the Book of Ben-Sira (Ecclesiasticus), written around 170 B.C.E.

While the formula *Barukh attah* had clearly not yet become normative, this work employs the vocative *Hodu le* . . . ("Give thanks to . . ."), with the response, *Ki le-olam chasdo* ("For His loving-kindness endures forever"), borrowed from Psalm 136:1–3, 26. Ben-Sira 51:12 preserves a contemporary prayer with a list of thirteen of these *Hodu*-type blessings, most of which contain formulae of blessing conclusions *(chatimot)* that found their way subsequently into the statutory prayers with which we are familiar from our prayer book, or which at least echo key phrases from it:

Hodu le-El ha-tishbachot (Thanks to the God of praises)

Hodu le-shomer yisrael (Thanks to the Guardian of Israel)

Hodu le-yotzer ha-kol (Thanks to the Creator of all things)

Hodu le-go'el yisrael (Thanks to the Redeemer of Israel)

Hodu li-mekabbetz nidchei yisrael (Thanks to Him that gathers in the dispersed of Israel)

Hodu le-boneh iyro u-mikdasho (Thanks to the Builder of His city and His sanctuary)

Hodu le-matzmiyach keren le-vet David (Thanks to Him who makes the house of David to flourish)

Hodu le-vocher bi-vnei Tzadok le-khahen (Thanks to the One who chose the sons of Tzadok as his priests)

Hodu le-magen Avraham (Thanks to the Shield of Abraham)

Hodu le-tzur Yitzchak (Thanks to the Rock of Isaac)

Hodu la-avir Ya'akov (Thanks to the Mighty One of Jacob)

Hodu le-vocher be-tziyyon (Thanks to the One who chooses Zion)

Given the freedom to innovate in that early, pre-Gamliel period, it is not surprising to find references in the talmudic literature to several clusters of blessings, including alternative *Amidah* collections, all comprising different numbers of blessings, different themes and formulae, and different systems of ordering the blessings.

The morning prayers of the priests in the Temple constitute one such collection:

The Supervisor would say to them: "Recite one of the [pre-*Shema*] blessings." And they would do so. They then read the Ten Command-

ments and the three paragraphs of the *Shema,* after which they recited three
blessings in unison with the people: *Emet ve-yatziv,* the *Avodah* blessing, and
the priestly blessing. On Sabbaths they would recite an additional blessing
for the priestly duty-rota who had just completed their week of service.[7]

Thus we see from here that the morning service of the priests in the
Temple did not contain anything like eighteen blessings. We also notice
that the *Emet ve-yatziv,* which in our prayer scheme is the concluding
blessing of the *Shema,* leading into, but quite separate from, the *Amidah,*
was regarded at that time as intrinsic to the "three blessings" that clearly
represented an early type of self-contained *Amidah.* This may be another
reason why the later talmudic tradition insisted that there be no
interruption—even for the recitation of *Amen*—between the *Geulah* (i.e.,
Emet ve-yatziv) blessing and the beginning of the *Amidah.* This preserves
an echo of the time when the former was an intrinsic part of the *Amidah*
genre.

Other examples of *Amidah*-type collections are the prayers of the
high priest on Yom Kippur. This group, comprising eight blessings,
centered around the reading of the Law for that day, though only the
first of the blessings was a Torah blessing, the rest representing an
independent liturgy, indeed, an alternative *Amidah:*

> And he recites after it [the Torah reading] eight blessings: (i) the Torah
> blessing, (ii) the *Avodah* (i.e., *Retzei*), (iii) the thanksgiving *(Modim),* (iv) the
> prayer for forgiveness of sin *(Selach lanu),* (v) a special blessing for the
> Temple, (vi) for the divine presence to rest on Israel, (vii) for God to accept
> the sacrifices of the priests, and (viii) a petition for God to accept all the
> prayers of His people.[8]

On fast days there was another specially prescribed liturgy, comprising six special blessings added by way of a supplement to the regular
prayers. The significance of this collection is that four of the six blessings
(the other two being the *Zikhronot* and *Shofarot* verses recited on Rosh
Hashanah) comprise the recitation of an entire psalm (Psalms 120, 121,
130, and 102), after each of which a special concluding *berakhah* is recited
(see *Mishnah Taanit* 2:3). This might well reveal the earliest stage in the
evolution of blessings: a psalm, rounded off with a concluding blessing.

Moves toward Standardization

As we have observed, it was the Patriarch, Rabban Gamliel II of Yavneh
(80–110 C.E.), who was insistent that, from among all the extant variant

liturgies, one fixed and standardized version be authorized and made incumbent for daily recitation.

He entrusted to his pupil, Shimon Ha-pakuli, the task of editing the blessings and putting them into the most appropriate order (*Berakhot* 28b). The actual choice of blessings was probably already made for him, on the basis of the themes that were in general vogue in most of the rabbinic prayer-houses and academies. The discovery, in the Cairo *Genizah*, of many variant formulae of the ancient blessings suggests that his main task was to collate all the formulae of blessings brought to his notice, and to decide which version had the greatest merit. No doubt he selected individual blessings, phrases, and even single words from all the different versions, and blended them together into a universally acceptable *Amidah*.

He did not concern himself with the particular situation that first inspired each of those eighteen blessings, with the result that no specific historical information has been preserved regarding most of them. It has thus been left to modern scholars to make conjectures.

It has been assumed that a blessing like *Re'ey ve'anyeinu* ("Look upon our affliction") was composed during a period of oppression and national trauma. Its origin might well have been during the Babylonian exile—hence the phrase "and redeem us speedily for Thy name's sake." Again, it has been conjectured that the blessing *Barekh aleinu et ha-shanah ha-zot* ("Bless for us this year") was originally created as a blessing for the new year.

The blessing *Hashivah shofteinu* ("Restore our judges") probably originated in the period 30–70 C.E. The Talmud states that "forty years before the destruction of the Temple, the Romans removed from the Jews the authority to judge capital crimes, and drastically curtailed the power of the Sanhedrin" (J.T. *Sanhedrin* 1:1). This blessing is clearly a plea for judicial independence.

The blessing *Al ha-tzaddikim ve-al ha-chasidim* ("Toward the righteous and the pious extend Your mercies") was conceivably introduced during the period of the Maccabean struggle (167–165 B.C.E.). "The righteous" are those who stood loyally by their faith and took up arms against the forces of Antiochus. The *chasidim* figure prominently in the account of the struggle. Many of those pietists were slaughtered by the Syrians when at first they refused to take up arms on the Sabbath and defend themselves.

Rabban Gamliel probably had three main reasons for his determination to standardize the prayers. First, he realized that, with the Temple in ruins, a new spiritual impetus was required, one which the synagogue and daily worship could best provide. Second, his period witnessed an upsurge of Christian missionary activity, coinciding with the composition of the Gospels and their dissemination among Jewish communities. It was also a period of rapid expansion for the new religion as it captured the teeming masses of Graeco-Roman pagans, disenchanted with the naive system they had inherited, and searching for meaning for their lives in the context of a monotheistic religion with a message of divine care and concern. There is evidence that most turned first to Judaism, but found its prerequisite of circumcision, as well as its exacting Sabbath laws, too much to take on.

Gamliel was constantly pestered by _minim_, members of the new faith who delighted in engaging him in disputation; and he was especially alarmed at the infiltration of new Christians, indistinguishable at that time from their fellow Judean Jews, pressing their prayers and literature onto an unsuspecting Jewry. The simple, uneducated folk could not be expected to distinguish whether a religious text left in a synagogue was Orthodox or sectarian. Neither, given the flexibility and spontaneity allowed in the framing of prayers, could they know whether one called upon to act as reader was a secret adherent of the new faith and was uttering acceptable or unacceptable religious sentiment. Hence Gamliel's decision to establish, once and for all, a fixed and authorized order of daily prayer. It was for the same reason that he chaired a synod that decided which sacred works were to be regarded as "biblical" and holy, and which as "external" and profane.

Gamliel's third reason may have been his wish to stem the disturbing fashion of charismatic or ecstatic prayer that was becoming fashionable among those early Christians and was appealing even to some of his own colleagues and disciples. In the absence of a fixed and regulated liturgy, they were emboldened to give expression to their own, often wild, outpouring of exaggerated body language and meaningless phraseology, claiming that it was the Spirit that was working on them.[9]

Ironically, the most distinguished of Rabban Gamliel's colleagues, Rabbi Akivah, seems to have been a devotee of this type of rapturous praying, for, "when he prayed by himself, a man would leave him in one corner and find him later in another, on account of his many genuflections and prostrations."[10] Akivah was, of course, an unrivaled master of mysticism,[11] and it would be natural to suppose that he would have approached the exercise of prayer from that perspective. We may speculate that pupils and admirers of Akivah might have felt tempted to emulate his mode of worship, but without the requisite spiritual receptivity. In the light of this potentially dangerous trend—especially given the corresponding spread of mystical and ecstatic prayer in Christian circles—Gamliel may have felt further impelled to introduce the discipline and rational spirit of an officially sanctioned and statutory order of service.

As we have observed, Gamliel created his authorized central prayer out of a number of extant blessings, clusters of blessings, and theologically significant formulae, which, though the products of specific situations, yet were sufficiently comprehensive to be able to be applied to the needs and aspirations of every age.

Eighteen or Nineteen Blessings?

While the *Amidah* is popularly referred to as the *Shmoneh Esrey* (*eighteen* blessings), the number of blessings it actually contains is nineteen! This suggests that it began as a unit of eighteen, to which a further blessing was added. The generally quoted explanation is that the added blessing was the twelfth, *Ve-la-malshinim*, the condemnation of the heretics.

Our Babylonian version of this blessing is quite tame:

Let there be no hope for slanderers; and let all wickedness perish in an instant. May all Your enemies be speedily cut down. May you speedily uproot and crush, cast down and humble the dominion of arrogance, speedily in our days . . .

The original version, as recited in ancient Palestine, and as discovered this century in the Cairo *Genizah*, represents a far more passionate condemnatory targeting of various groups who were a thorn in the flesh of the 1st century Jewish community of the holy land:

La-meshummadim al tehi tikvah *u-malkhut zadon meherah te'aker* *be-yamenu*	Let there be no hope for apostates; and may the haughty kingdom (Rome) be speedily overthrown in our days.
ve-ha-notzrim ve-ha-minim ka-rega *yoveidu*	And may the Christians and other heretics perish in an instant.
yimmachu mi-sefer ha-chayyim	May they be erased from the Book of Life, never to be inscribed to-
ve-im tzaddikim al yikatevu	gether with the righteous.

Our tame Babylonian version is to be explained quite simply by the fact that Babylonian Jewry was never troubled by any of the schismatics referred to in the Palestinian version. There were no Christians in Babylonia, where Jews lived an independent, autonomous existence under the largely tolerant and benign rule of successive Parthian and Persian dynasties, committed to the dominant religion of Zoroastrianism. As a cohesive, self-regulating community, Jewry there was also untroubled by any problem of heretics or apostates. Thus, the anachronistic and totally unsuitable Palestinian version of that blessing was replaced by one containing softer and more general condemnation of those kingdoms and individuals who reject the yoke of heaven.

The impression that this was the blessing that was added at a later time, to make up the total of nineteen, was derived in fact from a superficial reading of the main talmudic passage dealing with the editing of the *Amidah*, a passage that is vague and sketchy in the extreme:

> Why does the *Mishnah* refer to *eighteen* blessings? Surely there are *nineteen!* Rabbi Levi explained: that is because the blessing against heretics was introduced later, at Yavneh.[12]

This neat explanation is rendered problematic, however, a few lines further on, when the Talmud describes the creation of that "blessing against heretics" in the Yavneh academy:

> Rabban Gamliel said to the sages: "Is there anyone competent enough to frame a blessing against heretics?" Samuel Ha-katan stood up, and created one. The following year, though he tried for two or three hours to recall it, he still forgot it.

We see from here that, although Samuel was able to frame a suitable imprecation against Christians and other enemies, yet, for all that, it did not win popular acceptance, to the extent that none of his colleagues committed it to memory or asked him subsequently to repeat it for them to introduce into their synagogues. The result was that by the following year even Samuel himself had forgotten his own blessing, notwithstanding a valiant attempt lasting for "two or three hours!"

One reason why Samuel made no attempt, at that second synod, to frame an entirely new blessing against heretics, to replace the one he had forgotten, is that there was already a preexistent blessing that could be adapted in the absence of anything more suitable. This was the *Birkat Ha-Perushim*, the "Blessing against Separatists," referred to in the *Tosefta*, an early source contemporaneous with the *Mishnah*. In the long history of the Pharisaic struggle against various internal and external religious and national threats, there would have been a natural instinct in most periods to invoke divine aid against them through the creation of various prayers, polemical compositions, and blessings for their downfall. Since those existing versions of that blessing predated the Christian era and the beginning of the period of Roman oppression in Judea, and were therefore in need of drastic revision to accommodate references to those particular problematic situations, Gamliel probably felt that a *de novo* composition was preferable.

It is more likely, however, that Samuel Ha-katan's "inability" to recall his previous year's imprecation against the heretics – as well as the synod members' refusal to memorize it and to introduce it into their synagogues and academies – may well have been fear of Roman recriminations against anyone publicly uttering seditious sentiments or any statement critical of the Roman administration. Judea was littered with the corpses of those who threatened the occupying power politically or even merely theologically.

There is the famous story in the Talmud[13] of three leading sages and an associate, Judah ben Gerim, who was a secret informer to the Romans. They were discussing the situation under Rome. One sage praised the roads, marketplaces, bridges, and bathhouses that Rome had introduced, whereupon Rabbi Shimon bar Yochai observed that everything they did was for their own advantage: roads and marketplaces to put harlots thereon, bridges to levy tolls, and bathhouses to glorify and delight their bodies. Judah ben Gerim reported Shimon's criticism widely, with the result that the governor issued a proclamation that he be apprehended and executed. Samuel Ha-katan and his colleagues, fellow members of Gamliel's synod, were thus well aware of the dangers involved in following that Patriarch's instruction to introduce either a modified version of the old *Birkat Ha-Perushim* or an entirely new invective against Rome and the lesser threat of Christianity.

It seems obvious therefore that Samuel Ha-katan, famous in his generation for his humility and peace-loving nature,[14] would have been the least likely person to have volunteered to compose such a denunciation, unless forced to do so by his lord and master, Gamliel, whose authoritarianism is referred to in so many talmudic passages.[15]

Let us return to the first of the two explanations (though they are, in fact, interrelated) that we have offered for Samuel's reticence to frame a new condemnatory blessing, namely, because there was already one in existence. This is confirmed by the passage in the *Tosefta* referred to above:

> The Eighteen Blessings instituted by the sages correspond to the eighteen divine names in Psalm 29 *(Havu La-shem)*. One should insert any reference

to *minim* (Christians) into the *Blessing against Separatists* . . . and any reference to David into the Blessing for Jerusalem.[16]

This passage discloses to us what, in fact, the *Genizah* fragments have confirmed, namely that the *Amidah* that Gamliel was promoting consisted of only eighteen blessings, which included an old blessing against separatists/heretics, and also a single blessing for Jerusalem, city of David, which, according to the *Tosefta* could be expanded to include a reference to King David and/or his messianic identity. We know this single, composite blessing from the *Genizah* documents:

Rachem Ha-shem Eloheinu	Have mercy, Lord God,
al yisrael amekha	upon Israel, Your people,
ve-al yerushalayim	and upon Jerusalem
iyrekha ve-al tziyyon	Your city, and upon Zion
mishkan kevodkha	Your glorious habitation,
ve-al heikhalekha	and upon Your Temple,
ve-al me'onkha	and upon Your dwelling-place,
ve-al malkhut	and upon the kingdom of
Bet David	the house of David
meshiyach tzidkekha.	Your righteous Messiah.
Barukh attah Ha-shem	Blessed art Thou, O Lord,
elohei David boneh	God of David, builder of
yerushalayim	Jerusalem.[17]

We are now in a position to understand how the *nineteen* blessings came about. It was, in fact, a Babylonian creation. The authorities of 3rd-century Babylon took that original Palestinian *Amidah* of eighteen blessings and made out of it an extra blessing. This was done by subdividing the above composite blessing for Jerusalem and David, and allocating a separate blessing to both. The newly added, nineteenth blessing is our *Et tzemach David*, which refers exclusively to David, rather than, as in the Palestinian version, his having to share honors with Jerusalem.

Thus, instead of the Palestinian synthesized conclusion: *Elohei David boneh yerushalayim* ("God of David, builder of Jerusalem"), Babylon was able to provide two blessings, with two separate conclusions: *Et tzemach David*, with its Davidic conclusion, *Matzmiyach keren yeshu'ah* ("Who causes *messianic-Davidic* salvation to spring forth"), and *Ve-li-yerushalayim iyrkha*, with its conclusion, *Boneh yerushalayim* ("Builder of Jerusalem"). We can now see that the popular view that the additional blessing was the one against heretics: *Ve-la-malshinim*, or its Palestinian precursor, *La-meshumadim*, is quite erroneous!

The Development of Services
and Prayers

In the face of considerable opposition Gamliel declared an evening service to be obligatory.[18] Although Daniel[19] and the psalms[20] make reference to a three-times daily act of worship, this was clearly the practice of pious individuals, but had no obligatory force. His opponents objected to Gamliel's proposed innovation on the obvious grounds that there had been no evening sacrifice in the Temple. Such an innovation would appear, therefore, to be creating a precedent for breaking the bond that had hitherto existed between Temple and synagogue. Gamliel justified his decision, however, by pointing out that the entrails of the late afternoon sacrifice continued to smoulder on the altar at nightfall, and therefore this was also a "period of goodwill" during which to petition the Almighty. One wonders whether or not Gamliel also wanted to ensure that no opportunity was left for heretics or the followers of the ecstatic tradition to introduce their own form of evening service in the absence of an officially prescribed version!

A *Musaf* ("Additional") service was now introduced on Sabbaths and festivals, to correspond with the additional sacrifice that had been offered on those days. An essential part of all these services was a prayer for the restoration of the Temple and a plea for divine pardon for sins.

The renascence of Jewish learning after the destruction gave impetus to the concept of study as a mode of worship. The idea gained currency that study of the laws of the sacrifices was especially significant in that it effected a vicarious atonement.[21] Hence it was that *Korbanot*, mishnaic portions dealing with categories of sacrifices and details of the cult, entered the liturgy.

Many prayers, now incorporated into our congregational liturgy, originated as the private devotions of individual talmudists. These were perpetuated by their pupils and ultimately won general popularity. An example of this is the *Yehiy Ratzon* recited as a prelude to the announcement of the new moon. According to the Talmud,[22] this was a private prayer recited by Rav[23] after he had finished his daily prayers. Similarly, the private prayer of Mar, son of Ravina, *Elohay Netzor leshoniy mera*, became so popular that it was introduced into the official liturgy as the concluding prayer of every *Amidah*.

The talmudic sages attempted to steer a middle path between standardization of the liturgy and greater spontaneity. Thus they established a fixed formula for the *berakhah*, so that the opening and closing phrases of a prayer were regulated,[24] to embody agreed ideas or motifs, but left to individual or communal choice the wording of the body of the prayer.

Bet Ha-Midrash Prayer

Although the Temple and the synagogue were the main fountainheads of liturgical composition, the *Bet Ha-Midrash*, the academy of talmudic learning, also originated its own distinctive models of prayer. These were inspired by the *derashah*, the public exposition of the weekly scriptural portion, and were especially composed as an introduction or conclusion to the discourse. Their theme is, naturally, the Torah; and they take the form of praise to the Giver of the Torah, tribute to its wisdom and perfection, or a plea for a true understanding of its message and strength of purpose to fulfill its demands. At the conclusion of the discourse the thoughts of the preacher inevitably turned to the messianic era. By contrasting the contemporary conditions of hardship and oppression with the delights to be enjoyed *le-atid lavo*—in the time to come—the homilist would be moved to offer a prayer for the redemption of Israel and the inauguration of the Kingdom of heaven.

Our *Siddur* is replete with such *Bet Ha-Midrash* compositions, and in a number of instances the subject matter leaves us in no doubt as to their origin and purpose:

> *Yehiy ratzon le-fanekha . . . she-yibaneh beit ha-mikdash bi-mheirah ve-yameinu ve-tein chelkeinu be-toratekha* (May it be Thy will . . . that the Temple be speedily rebuilt in our day and grant our portion in thy Law).

> *Yehiy ratzon . . . le-khonein et beit chayyeinu u-le-hashiv et shekhinato be-tokheinu* (May it be the will . . . to establish the Temple and restore His divine presence in our midst).

The above prayers clearly served as conclusion to a *derashah*, exposition or study session, dealing with laws relating to sacrifices or Temple ritual.

> *Yehiy ratzon . . . le-kayyem banu chakhmei yisraeil, heim u-nesheihem u-veneihem u-venoteihem, ve-talmideihem be-khol mekomot moshvoteihem* (May it be the will . . . to preserve among us the wise men of Israel; them, their

wives, their sons and daughters, their disciples in all the places of their habitation . . .).

Such a prayer, or, more accurately, a tribute to scholars and their families, might well have been recited originally at the opening ceremony of a newly established academy of learning, or at the ordination ceremony of a new rabbi.

Another prayer that originated in the talmudic *Bet Ha-Midrash* is the *Kaddish Derabbanan*, with its prayer for "peace, grace, loving-kindness, mercy, long life, etc." to be granted "to Israel, her rabbis and their disciples, and the disciples of their disciples, and to all who engage in the study of the Law." Sometimes a specific reference to a distinguished scholar and leader was inserted into this *Kaddish*. At the induction ceremony of the *Resh Galuta*, the leader of Babylonian Jewry, his name was inserted near the beginning: "May He establish His Kingdom during your lifetime *and during the lifetime of our leader, the Exilarch."* During the period of Maimonides, Egyptian and Yemenite communities would include, in every *Kaddish*, the phrase "and in the lifetime of our master and teacher, Moses ben Maimon."

The *Kaddish* recited at the cemetery by children, after the interment of parents, is the same *Kaddish* recited at a *Siyyum*, the ceremony of concluding a talmudic tractate. Its origin was clearly in the *Bet Ha-Midrash*, and the reference to "the world that is to be created anew, wherein He will revive the dead and raise them up into life eternal" was included merely as a reminder and assurance that the reward of life eternal awaits those who frequent the *Bet Ha-Midrash* and spend their lives in Torah study. It was only later that these references to afterlife made this *Kaddish* an obvious choice for recital at the burial service.

The *Uva le-tziyyon go'eil* also originated in the *Bet Ha-Midrash* context. After the morning service, groups of scholars would stay on for a study circle that would traditionally close with the recitation of verses of consolation from the prophets that foretold the messianic redemption, as well as verses of praise of the Torah. The *U-va le-tziyyon* verse ("And a redeemer shall come unto Zion"—Isaiah 59:20) was a particularly popular choice, since they applied the continuation ("And my words that I have put in thy mouth") to the Torah they had just studied, the merit of which, they believed, would hasten the redemption. When, as a result of persecution or economic necessity, it was no longer possible to remain behind in synagogue for a study circle, the practice of reciting such verses was not allowed to lapse, and they were incorporated into the statutory morning service itself.

The early association of this prayer with study circles may also be detected in the second half of the passage, in the section commencing

Barukh eloheinu she-braanu likhvodo, which is simply a benediction over Torah study. A further echo of the original function of this whole composition is still heard in the practice of some old-style *maggidim* (preachers or talmudists) to conclude a discourse with the petition *U-va le-tziyyon go'eil ve-nomar amen.*

Obligatory Prayers

Rabbi Gamliel's efforts to establish a standardized and regular liturgy received great support from one of the most outstanding scholars and leaders of the following generation, Rabbi Meir (circa 150 C.E.). The latter went even beyond the demands of Gamliel, and insisted that "a man is duty-bound to utter one hundred blessings each day."[25]

R. Meir supported his statement with a proof text from Deuteronomy (10:12): "And as for thee, O Israel, *what (mah)* doth the Lord thy God require of thee. . . ?" R. Meir offered this verse as a mnemonic, since the word *mah* is close in pronunciation to the word *me'ah,* "a hundred."

Whether or not R. Meir intended to impose a specific obligation of one hundred blessings, or meant it merely as a round number, we cannot tell. The very loose inference from Deuteronomy is hardly impressive as an authoritative halakhic rationale. Apart from this, we have no reason why one hundred should have been a particularly significant number in the liturgical context. Yet we do know that later generations did assume that R. Meir was promoting that specific number, and strenuous efforts were made to recite one hundred blessings each day.

On weekdays, where three *Amidot,* each of eighteen (or nineteen) blessings, were recited, there was no problem in reaching that target. On Sabbaths and festivals, however, with an *Amidah* of only seven blessings, it was difficult to achieve. This did not deter a later scholar, R. Chiyya son of Rav, who reached the target of one hundred blessings by smelling various spices and eating sundry delicacies on those occasions.

The *Siddur* of One Hundred Blessings

The very first written compilation of prayers—as it occupies a mere four pages of print it can hardly claim the accolade of being the first *siddur—*

was conceived under the influence of R. Meir's dictum. It was the Gaon of Sura, Natronai (9th century), who, on being asked by the community of Lucena in Spain to spell out which particular "hundred blessings" R. Meir had had in mind, wrote his responsum, enumerating all those blessings.

Natronai offers us, for the first time, a tradition to account for R. Meir's requirement of just one hundred blessings. It seems that R. Meir was inspired by an episode toward the end of King David's reign, when some mysterious epidemic caused the death of one hundred men every day. The King discovered by mystic meditation that by uttering precisely one hundred blessings each day the epidemic could be halted! Natronai's obscure tradition goes on to find a proof text which is supposed to allude to this, otherwise unknown, episode: "The sayings of David, son of Jesse, and the sayings of the man *raised on high*" (II Samuel 23:1). The latter phrase in Hebrew is *hukam ol*, the numerical value of *ol* being one hundred. According to the author of this tradition, *hukam ol* is to be understood as, "one hundred men *(ol) were saved*" (*hukam*, literally, "were raised up," i.e., from the grave).

The *Arukh Ha-Shulchan* (I, 46:2) describes how our halakhic authorities labored to try and reconstruct the precise one hundred blessings to be recited each day:

> Some counted one hundred and five (i.e., Karo's *Bet Yoseph* commentary); others did succeed in reaching one hundred, though only for fast days (i.e., *Magen Avraham*). According to my humble opinion, however, there are, indeed, exactly one hundred to be recited, on the assumption that it is the custom to eat one proper repast each day (i.e., a formal meal with bread, Grace, etc.).

Arukh Ha-Shulchan proceeds to enumerate the 100 blessings, as follows: The early morning blessings (excluding *mekaddesh et shimkha barabim*, which is posttalmudic, and consequently not included in Rabbi Meir's reckoning) together with the blessings over *tzitzit* and *tallit*, as well as the two blessings over the *tefillin*, total twenty-six. The two blessings of *Barukh she'amar* and *Yishtabach*, the two blessings before and the one after the *Shema*, and the nineteen of the *Amidah*, bring the total to fifty. Add to this the thirty-eight of the two *Amidot* of *Minchah* and *Maariv*, plus the two blessings before and the three after the *Shema* in the latter service, as well as the blessing *Ha-Mappil* before retiring to sleep at night, make a total of ninety-four blessings. The last six blessings are recited over the formal meal of the day, namely for washing the hands, eating bread, and the four blessings of the Grace After Meals.

Prayer as a Vehicle of Polemic

Prayer is not only a vehicle of devotion but also a profession of belief. As such it was inevitable that polemical material should have entered the liturgy as the adherents of the normative majority strove not only to vindicate their own beliefs but, at the same time, to counter dissidents and sectarian minorities. Yet, however strong the feeling against such dissidents, the sanctity of prayer was never compromised by incrimination or abuse. The argument was invariably kept at the theological level, with the object of attack rarely being explicitly named. Instead, the folly of the particular doctrine was hinted at by the insertion of a conspicuous textual emendation or by emphasizing the importance of the particular doctrine whose validity was being impugned. Examples of such polemic are the following:

(a) The *Yigdal* composition, recited at the beginning of the daily morning service and at the end of the Sabbath and festival evening services. This is not only a most rhythmic and succinct catechism of basic Jewish beliefs, based upon Maimonides' famous Thirteen Principles of Faith, but is also a refutation of the views of both the sectarian opponents of Orthodoxy as well as of Judaism's "daughter religions." A few examples from *Yigdal* will demonstrate this underlying purpose.

"He is One, and there is no oneness like His" (*Echad ve-ein yachid ke-yichudo*). This is clearly aimed at Christianity, with its doctrine of a trinitarian aspect of God, and is reinforced in the next line: "He has no bodily form or physicality" (*Ein lo demut ha-guf ve-eino guf*).

Another line states: "He granted His rich gift of prophecy (*Shefa nevuato*) to the men of His choice, in whom He gloried." This is an affirmation that it is the classical, biblical prophets of Israel who have an exclusive claim to prophetic inspiration, as opposed to such false claims made, for example, by, and on behalf of, Mohammed.

"God will never alter or change His law for any other" (*Lo yachalif*) is quite clearly aimed at the New Testament and the Koran, both of which claimed to have superseded Israel's Torah.

The last two lines, which affirm the future coming of the Messiah and the Resurrection of the Dead, are also aimed at those who rejected those cardinal doctrines. The Sadducees and the early Christians both denied belief in a future Messiah; the former because the doctrine is not enunciated in the Pentateuch, the latter because of their claim that the messianic era had already dawned with the arrival of Jesus. (Because, as time moved on, it became clear to the early Christians that the messianic conditions associated with his "coming" had clearly not materialized, they were forced to make room in their theological speculation for the convenient doctrine of a "Second Coming"!)

The final and climactic line of *Yigdal*, which affirms the Resurrection of the Dead, is also aimed at Sadducees and Karaites who rejected the idea for the identical reason that they rejected any other doctrine not clearly expressed in the biblical text.

Another prayer recited at the beginning of the morning service is *Elohai Neshamah*, which affirms that the God-given soul is pure. . . . "You created it, You formed it, You breathed it into me and You preserve it within me." This overemphasis on the divine origin of the soul, and the fact that God directly breathes it into each individual body, just as He did to Adam, is an implied refutation of the Christian doctrine of original sin. The implication is that the soul cannot possibly be tainted when it is breathed into man by God Almighty!

(b) The second blessing of the *Amidah* with its sixfold reiteration of the doctrine of resurrection. This was probably composed with the Samaritans and Sadducees in mind, both of whom denied the existence of life after death.

(c) The verse "Who forms light and creates darkness, makes peace and creates evil" occurs in Isaiah 45:7. When this verse was inserted into the liturgy, the phrase "and creates evil" was replaced by "who creates all things." The excision of a biblical phrase could only have been justifiable on serious polemical grounds; and it is suggested that the retention of the authentic biblical version might have provided fuel for the adherents of the dualist Persian (Zoroastrian) religion. The latter believed that the world was created and preserved by two opposing forces, light and darkness, which manifest their existence in good and evil respectively. The reference to God as the creator of evil was accordingly altered in order not to lend support to such a view.

(d) An inverted form of polemic may be detected in the removal of the Ten Commandments from its place of honor in the daily liturgy.[26] This was done in the face of the "insinuations of the heretics," namely, the Pauline Christians who rejected the validity of the other laws of the Torah while upholding the Ten Commandments. By demoting the latter, the rabbis underlined the equally binding nature of all the laws of the Torah.

(e) One of the most distinguished of the 12th-century circle of German pietists *(Chakhmei Ashkenaz)*, Rabbi Ephraim bar Yaakov of Bonn, states that it was for polemical reasons that a special blessing *(al sefirat ha-omer)* was prescribed over the counting of the *Omer*. Whereas there are other examples of biblically prescribed counting of days, such as for those afflicted with a contaminating bodily flux *(zav)*, or a leper, who must count seven clean days (Leviticus 13:4–5; 15:13), or a woman after childbirth (Leviticus 12:1-5), yet no blessing was prescribed for those situations!

R. Ephraim declares that the blessing was introduced by the Pharisees in the context of their famous, and bitter, dispute with the Sadducees over the meaning of the verse, "And you shall count for yourselves *from the morrow of the Sabbath* seven full weeks" (Leviticus 23:15). The Sadducees took the phrase literally, and began counting on the first *Sunday* (literally "morrow of the Sabbath") after Pesach. The Pharisees, on the other hand, maintained that "Sabbath" in this context, means, more broadly, "day of rest," and refers to the first *Yom Tov* of Pesach. We consequently begin to count "on the morrow" (i.e., from the eve of the second diaspora day) of Pesach.

In order to demonstrate their supreme confidence in the veracity of their interpretation, against that of the Sadducees *(le-hotzi mil-libban shel tzedukkim)*—states R. Ephraim—the rabbis introduced the special *berakhah* over the *Omer*. The blessing boldly asserts that *"God* commanded us to count the *'Omer'*—from the day when Pharisaic (rabbinic) Judaism does so!"

(f) A much later form of polemic was directed against the 8th-century sect of Karaites. They denied rabbinic interpretation of Scripture and accepted what, in their view, was the literal meaning of the text. They came to the conclusion that the biblical law prohibiting the kindling of a fire on the Sabbath was meant to apply even if such lights and fires were lit before the Sabbath commenced. They consequently extinguished all lights before the Sabbath and spent the day without heating or light.

To stress the error of this doctrine the rabbis introduced into the Friday night service the recitation of *Bameh Madlikin.*[27] This Mishnah discusses the type of wick and oil that should be used to light the home on the Sabbath, and it was read during the service as a mark of confidence in the rabbinic tradition. The introduction of a special benediction over Sabbath lights also owes its origin to this conflict. This practice, introduced by some of the Geonim—religious leaders of Babylonian Jewry—was meant to affirm that not only was it *permitted* to have lights burning, but that it was a positive *command* to do so.

4

Babylon and Palestine

The two main centers of world Jewry in talmudic times (1st–6th centuries) were Palestine and Babylon. Religious as well as political and social conditions in these countries differed considerably as a result of pressures brought to bear by the ruling powers. In Palestine the Jews were subjected to continual oppression and religious restrictions by the Romans. This became intensified in the 4th century when Christianity became the official religion of the Roman Empire. The inevitable result of this was that anti-Roman and anti-Christian polemic became a prominent feature of the Palestinian religious literary tradition.

In Babylon, on the other hand, the rule of the Parthian dynasty was generally friendly toward the Jews. This enabled Babylonian Jewry to organize itself into an autonomous community, enjoying almost complete independence under the authority of the *Resh Galuta*–Prince of the Exile, or Exilarch–descendant of the royal house of David and honored by the Parthian kings with the rank of Prince. Even under Persian domination, when conditions were not so happy, the essential cohesion of the community was not impaired.

It is not surprising, therefore, that there were considerable differences between the liturgies that evolved in those two countries. This applied not only to the subject matter of the prayers but also to the regulations governing the conduct of the service and the customs associated with prayer.

49

With the decline of Palestine, from the 4th century, Babylonian Jewry, guided by its famous academies of learning—especially Sura and Pumbedita—began to gain general acceptance for its own traditions. The original liturgy of Palestine was not preserved intact, though a considerable amount of it was absorbed into that of Babylon. Of the two great academies of Babylon, both of whom adopted independent approaches toward liturgical principles, it was the academy of Sura that was more amenable toward preserving the Palestinian heritage.

It is clear from certain responsa from geonic times[1] that for a lengthy period there was no clear-cut geographic demarcation line between communities that adopted the disciplined approach of Babylonian liturgical reform and those who tenaciously held on to the original, and more expansive, Palestinian traditions. One responsum refers to a single community in Africa that was split down the middle over which version to employ. This was probably the community of Kairwan in North Africa where this battle for liturgical domination raged fiercely until, finally, the Babylonian influence proved dominant.

The *Piyyutim* of Palestine

The original Palestinian liturgy had contained a large number of *piyyutim*, poetic supplements to the standard prayers. Palestine, as the home of mysticism, midrashic lore, and sacred poetry, was more sensitive to aesthetic literary artistry, as an authentic form of spiritual expression, than was Babylon, which viewed its primary role as that of custodian of halakhic and ritualistic tradition. With the decline of such authority in Palestine, the Babylonian Geonim felt that a fairly strict control had to be exercised by them, particularly in such a sensitive area as prayer. They wished to ensure that what was being recited remained not only in consonance with the halakhic principles that were being applied in other areas of Jewish life, but that the prayers being sanctioned were also comprehensible, clear in the sentiments they were expressing, and relevant to the feelings of ordinary Jews. They adhered closely, therefore, to the principle that it is forbidden to depart from the pristine form in which the talmudic sages had originally couched their prayers.[2] It is also probable that the generally negative Babylonian attitude toward the Palestinian *piyyut* was occasioned by their fear that such poetry might become a vehicle for disseminating Palestinian traditions, and enhancing the prestige of the Palestinian Talmud, at the expense of their own Babylonian Talmud, which had already become authoritative for all Jewish communities in Western countries.

Such an attitude may also have arisen as a reaction to what Babylon may have regarded as Palestine's exaggerated emphasis on poetry to an extent where the urgency and force of the actual statutory prayer becomes totally dissipated by this enormous volume of poetic supplement. That this was the reality of the situation, not just a baseless fear, becomes clear from the Cairo *Genizah*, where we discovered that Palestine had special *piyyutim* not merely for each of the festivals or fast days, but also for inclusion on ordinary weekdays. M. Zulay published special *Yotzrot*[3] (poetic pieces for inclusion in the *yotzer ha-meorot* blessing before the *Shema*) prescribed for recitation on Sundays, Wednesdays, Thursdays, and Fridays of each week. Each composition referred to the significance of that particular day in the order of Creation and the special acts of Creation that took place on that day.

It is clear from the examples published that Palestinian congregations did not make random selections of just one or two of these *piyyutim* for inclusion in their statutory service, but that they had to recite the entire collection. This was because all the poems were created as an integrated liturgical presentation which threaded its way through the entire service. Thus, the *piyyutim* for Sundays, for example, employ succeeding words of the Psalm for the first day of the week (*Lashem ha-aretz umelo'ah*) as the opening words of each line of poetry in the blessing both before and after the *Shema*. The second words of each succeeding line of *piyyut* form a name acrostic. To omit or be selective from any of this would be to impair the essential unity and conception. In the *piyyutim* for several days of the week, each stanza commences with a reference to that particular day: *barvi'iy* ("On the fourth day"), *bachamishiy* ("On the fifth day"), etc.

The Babylonian authorities were probably also sensitive to the fact that people who had to get to their places of work at an early hour would simply not tolerate a protracted service of this kind!

Opponents of *Piyyut*

The famous Saadia Gaon (9th–10th centuries) was particularly zealous in this direction, and he applied his blue pencil to a large number of liturgical compositions and blessings, eliminating expressions that, in his view, departed from or impaired the original structure, injected ideas that were not directly related to the basic theme of the passage, or constituted departures from tradition.

A well-known example of such censorship is Saadia's objection to the line *Or chadash al tziyyon ta'iyr* ("O cause a new light to shine on Zion") at the end of the first of the blessings before the morning *Shema*. According to Saadia this sentiment, which petitions for the messianic "light" to shine on Israel, had no place in a blessing whose theme is thanksgiving for the *natural* light of the sun that "renews the act of Creation each day." In this particular instance, however, Saadia's opinion did not carry the day, as it was felt that such an urgent messianic sentiment required to be expressed, and that the metaphorical association with the subject of "light" was natural enough for such a contextual association to be made.

Saadia also refused to authorize any blessing that was not directly referred to in the Talmud. The Cairo *Genizah* has provided us with many texts of Palestinian prayers, poetic compositions, blessings, and formulae, containing the type of supplementary ideas and sentiments to which Babylonian authorities like Saadia took exception. The principles that were applied to our *Siddur*, and the form it subsequently assumed, are the creation of the Babylonian Geonim.

Traces of Early *Piyyut*

While the Geonim excluded a large amount of Palestinian *piyyut* from the version of the liturgy that they authorized, yet it is still possible to detect, in our own prayer book, vestigial lines from those early poetic compositions. One example of this is in the *Geulah (gaal yisrael)* blessing that leads into the morning *Amidah*:

Tzur yisrael	O, Rock of Israel,
Kumah be-ezrat yisrael	Rise up to the help of Israel.
Ufdei khinumekha	And deliver, as you have
yehudah ve-yisrael	promised, Judah and Israel.
Go'aleinu ha-shem	Our Redeemer, the Lord
tzevaot shemo kedosh	of hosts is His name, the
yisrael	Holy One of Israel.

Another example of a poetic remnant of this kind is found in the *Tachanun* prayer:

Shomer yisrael	O Guardian of Israel,
Shemor she'eirit	Guard the remnant of
yisrael	Israel.
Ve-al yovad yisrael	And suffer not Israel to perish;
Ha-omrim shema	Those who utter "Hear
yisrael	O Israel."

From the High Holyday liturgy we are also familiar with the following example:

Zokhreinu la-chayyim	Remember us unto life,
Melekh chafeitz ba-chayyim	O King, who delightest in life,
Ve-khotveinu be-sefer	And inscribe us in the
ha-chayyim	book of life,
Le-maankha elohim	For thine own sake, O
chayyim	divine source of life.

These few examples[4] exemplify the basic characteristics of this earliest stage of liturgical poetic expression. They employ the same basic structure of the quatrain (the four-lined stanza), and there are, generally, only two or three words in each line. They date from a period before proper rhyming of end syllables had been developed, and the poetic element is achieved merely by repeating the same word at the end of each line and by maintaining—more or less—a uniform number of stresses in each line.

They will also be seen to conform to a unified system in their method of expression. The opening line (in *Zokhreinu la-chayyim,* it is the second line) addresses God directly, by referring to one of His attributes. The second line introduces the plea or petition, which is generally expanded upon, or made more specific, in the following line. The final line either refers to one of God's well-known attributes, which convinces the poet that God will truly fulfill the petition (as in above examples one and three), or it refers to a particular merit, possessed by Israel, which should secure the fulfillment of the petition (example two).

This earliest attempt at garnishing the basic prayers with poetic supplementation may well date from the very beginning of the talmudic period, if not earlier.

In the light of our foregoing remarks it will come as no surprise that the *piyyutim* did not attain to the honored place they now occupy in our liturgical tradition until after they had struggled for their very existence against some formidable opposition.

Attitude of Maimonides

Moses Maimonides is uncompromising in his condemnation of the license with which *chazanim* were giving free rein to their poetic emotion:

> We cannot approve of what those foolish persons do who are extravagant in praise, fluent, and long-winded in the prayers and hymns they compose in the desire to approach the Creator. They describe God in attributes which would be an offense if applied to a human being.
>
> If they find some phrase suited to their objectives in the words of the prophets, they employ them in their literal sense, to derive new expressions from them and to form from them numerous variations. Such authors write things which partly are pure heresy and partly contain such folly and absurdity that they cause those who hear them to laugh.
>
> If slander and libel are a great sin, how much greater is the sin of those who speak with looseness of tongue, describing God by attributes that are far beneath Him.
>
> (*Guide for the Perplexed,* chap. 59)

Maimonides' fear of describing God in exaggerated terms must be viewed in the light of his concept that we may only employ "negative attributes" in relation to God, declaring what He is *not*, not what He *is*. Our naive attribution of power, wisdom, or kindness to God is false, in that our very understanding of these concepts is derived only from an analogy with their manifestation in human beings.

This flood of sacred poetry, which was rapidly altering the whole character and spirit of the synagogue service in Maimonides' day, displeased him for philosophical reasons. There were other authorities who were opposed to it for the practical and political reasons we have referred to above, namely the fear that Palestinian *piyyut*, reflecting the halakhic and midrashic traditions of the Palestinian Talmud, would undermine the authority of the Babylonian Talmud, which was now binding upon most of Jewry.

Another obstacle that the *piyyutim* had to overcome is that one requires to be a competent rabbinic scholar to identify and unravel the numerous midrashic allusions with which *piyyut* abounds. These are frequently merely hinted at by the employment of a single link word. One also requires to have a mastery of the Hebrew Bible in order to understand the meaning of the rich imagery which is frequently culled from rarely studied chapters of Job, Ezekiel, and Isaiah.

Many suggestions have been offered to account for the mystical spell cast by the High Holydays. One thing it will not be attributed to is our comprehension of the liturgical texts we read.

And yet, in some mysterious way, those unintelligible Hebrew words—and the soulful melodies that infuse them with emotion—do seem to be able to speak directly to the heart of every Jew.

Pioneers of *Piyyut*

In the last few centuries of the talmudic period (4th–6th centuries C.E.) the *piyyut* was brought to a developed stage through the pioneering genius of a school of Palestinian poets. The initiator seems to have been one Yosi ben Yosi, and his method was perfected some time later by two of the most famous names in liturgical poetry, Yannai and Eleazar Kallir.

It was the revival of interest in the Hebrew language on the part of the Aramaic- and Greek-speaking community that provided the impetus for the development of new and more complex poetry, from the point of view of both content and form. Yosi supplied this need by being the first to weave ideas and quotations from mishnaic, talmudic, and midrashic literature into a poetic framework. He also experimented with artistic devices, such as alphabetical acrostics, alliteration, and occasional rhyme.

Yosi Ben Yosi

For all that, hardly anything is known of Yosi's life and activities, just as little is also known of the state of liturgical Hebrew poetry in the period leading up to his own day. This is because there are so few examples of poetry from the talmudic period. The most notable examples are *Aleinu, Al kein nekaveh, Attah zokher maasei olam,* and *Attah nigleita baanan kevodekha,* all of which were composed for the *Musaf* of Rosh Hashanah.

Yosi wrote a great deal of his poetry as a supplement to the *Avodah* (description of the Temple Service) on Yom Kippur. Perhaps it was because of this that the tradition became current that Yosi had been, in fact, a High Priest—a view quoted as fact by Joseph Karo in his *Bet Yoseph* commentary to the *Tur*.[5] This view would obviously place Yosi in the period before the destruction of the Temple (70 C.E.), a view with which no modern scholar would concur.

There is, indeed, much scholarly speculation and dispute on the question of precisely when and where Yosi lived. Rappoport placed him among the 10th-century Spanish poets, on the grounds that only the Sephardim recite his *Avodah* poetry. S. D. Luzzatto also thought that Yosi lived in the geonic period, though Zunz and Graetz preferred the 7th–8th centuries. H. Brody identifies Yosi and Yannai with two rabbis of the same names mentioned in the Palestinian Talmud.[6] If this identification is correct, it would mean that they lived around the 4th–5th centuries. As we know that Yosi lived about a century before Yannai, it seems clear then that we must place Yosi at the end of the 3rd and beginning of the 4th century, a view that is now generally accepted.

Where he wrote his poetry is equally baffling. Rappoport's view, that he was a Spaniard, is rejected by Graetz on the grounds that such a profound mastery of rabbinic literature as Yosi betrays in his poems could never have been found in a Spanish scholar at such an early period, nor was the Hebrew language as yet so well known in that country.

The fact that the Babylonian Geonim mention Yosi, and accepted his poetry into their prayers, suggests that he was either Babylonian or Palestinian. Some scholars believe that he did, indeed, hail from Babylon since he signs his name with the designation *Ha-yatom*, and there was actually a Babylonian place name *Hayetom*. The generally accepted view, however, is that Yosi was Palestinian, and that *Ha-yatom* means "the orphan," which would explain why he was named after his father, Yosi ben Yosi. This is not conclusive evidence on its own, however, since people were named after living relatives in antiquity, as they are in most Sephardic communities to this day. The likelihood of his being Palestinian is increased, however, by the fact that the name Yosi was very popular in ancient Palestine.

Yannai and Kallir

Yannai introduced into Hebrew poetry the name acrostic, and he was the first Hebrew poet to weave his name into poetry in this form. According to Professor J. Schirman,[7] it was the early Jewish poets who were responsible for the introduction of rhyme into Western poetry. The use of such devices as an aid to memory was specially vital in the light of the rabbinic refusal to sanction the writing down of prayers.

During the next few centuries Yannai's poetry became so popular that its influence on subsequent Hebrew poetry was enormous. His style was imitated so faithfully that it is often difficult to separate the work of the master from that of his emulators. Yannai composed many *Kerovot*, poetic insertions into the blessings of the *Amidah*.

Kallir, traditionally the pupil of Yannai, was the most prolific synagogue poet of the Ashkenazi rite, though almost nothing is known of his life and activity. He devoted special attention to *Yotzrot*, poetic insertions into the blessings before and after the *Shema*. Some scholars are of the opinion that these were originally written as substitutes for the recitation of the *Shema* at a time when the Persians, who occupied Palestine between 614–628 C.E., banned its recitation. The threefold daily affirmation of the unity of God would have offended against the dualistic beliefs of the Persians. Hidden amid a profusion of poetry, however, it would be difficult to detect or anticipate its recitation.

While this theory is interesting, it is, nevertheless, untenable for the reason we have already indicated, namely that it seems clear that these pioneers of our synagogue poetry lived, and were creating their *Yotzrot*, at a period much earlier than the 7th-century Persian occupation of Palestine.

Yannai and Kallir, through their poetry, made significant contributions toward Hebrew philology and the development of the Hebrew language. Where a Hebrew word was not available in the classical literature to express a particular idea, they coined a new word or word-formation. The output of these early poets adorns the Ashkenazi festival and High Holyday liturgies. The Sephardi communities, on the other hand, preferred to adopt the *piyyut* of their own Spanish poets, such as Ibn Gabirol, Judah Halevi, Abraham and Moses Ibn Ezra.

The effects of persecution—particularly the Crusades—on the Franco-German (Ashkenazi) communities made them desire some literary outlet to express and chronicle their emotions. The result of this was the rise of a great school of Ashkenazi *paytanim*, headed by the Kalonymos family and Simeon ben Isaac.

5

Medieval **Siddurim** *and* *Prayer Rites*

Early Liturgical Compilations

An official objection to committing prayers to writing continued until well after the close of the talmudic era. Two factors were probably responsible: first, since prayer also embodied polemic, there was the danger of cruel repercussions should the enemy read the invective Israel had called down upon their heads; second, written texts could easily be altered to conform with sectarian views and heresies.

Nevertheless, in the 8th century, Yehudai Gaon already refers to the existence of unofficial prayer books. He does not authorize their general introduction, but he does permit the reader to use a written text on occasions such as the Day of Atonement when the service is prolonged by unfamiliar compositions.

During the succeeding century written texts must have been smuggled into the synagogues, subsequently becoming an indispensable aid to prayer. It was popular pressure for a standard prayer book that had prompted the community of Lucena to write to Natronai Gaon (c. 850) about the talmudic reference to *me'ah berakhot*,[1] the obligation to recite one hundred blessings each day. His response, listing the blessings in full constituted the nucleus of the first prayer book.

Natronai's successor as Gaon was Amram bar Sheshna (858–870). His *Seder Rav Amram* constitutes the first attempt to produce a systematic text of the prayers, rather than a mere list of blessings. This *Siddur* was quoted extensively by Rashi, Tosafot, and Karo, though it was only as recently as 1865 that a complete manuscript of the work was discovered and published. Amram had included in his *Seder* a halakhic section dealing with explanations of the liturgy and regulations governing prayer, which greatly added to the esteem in which the work was held throughout France and Spain. Curiously, its influence in Eastern communities was minimal.

By far the greatest liturgical work of the Middle Ages was the *Siddur* of Saadia Gaon (892–942), one of the most illustrious of Jewish scholars. Accompanying the Hebrew text of his *Siddur* are regulations regarding prayer and synagogal customs. The latter are written in Arabic and embody Saadia's criticisms of a number of existing prayers and compositions that either "have no root in tradition" or "spoil the intention of the prayer they come to supplement." Saadia traveled extensively, and his decision to compile an authorized prayer book was clearly prompted by "the neglect, addition, and omission" he witnessed in the synagogues at home and abroad. His solution was to provide a prayer book that he hoped would further his ambition of unifying the Jewish world.

The great philosopher and halakhist, Moses Maimonides (1135–1204), also compiled a prayer book, entitled *Seder Tefillot Kol Ha-shanah*, which is incorporated into his code of law, the *Mishneh Torah*. Maimonides strongly opposed any interruptions in the standard service, even for the sake of reciting a private petition. This was another reason for his implacable opposition to the recitation of *piyyutim*.

Maimonides' version became authoritative for the communities of the Muslim world, particularly Egypt and Palestine. In Yemen the influence of Maimonides resulted in a fusion of his version and the existing tradition based on *Siddur Saadia*. This synthesis, called *Takhalil*, held at bay any outside influences until the 20th century.

Standardization of the liturgy was not confined to the Orient, and a considerable contribution was made by the School of Rashi in Troyes, Northern France. One of Rashi's close disciples, Simchah b. Samuel (d. 1105), from the town of Vitri, compiled a prayer book—the *Machzor Vitri*—reflecting the existing rite. This was much the same rite as followed by the preexpulsion Jews of England, as well as the Ashkenazi communities of southwest Germany. After the expulsion of the Jews from France in 1322, this French rite was preserved by three Italian communities, Asti, Fossano, and Moncalvo, and is popularly referred to as *Minhag Afam*.

Ashkenazi and Sephardi Rites

The liturgies of the Ashkenazi and Sephardi communities have always been characterized by differences.[2] Why these differences existed was never satisfactorily explained until Leopold Zunz, who laid the groundwork for the study of the liturgy during the last century, propounded the theory that they are not merely due to the varying traditions of medieval Germany and Spain, but have their origin in the more ancient distinction between the liturgies of Palestine and Babylon.

The influence of the Babylonian rite dominated the Arab countries, especially Spain, which frequently sought the guidance of the Babylonian Geonim. The Palestinian ritual did not, as might be supposed, die out as Jewish life waned in that country, but was transplanted to Christian Europe to become the basis of the Ashkenazi tradition. Southern Italy, during the 8th and 9th centuries, strove to become the cultural heir of the Palestinian tradition, and the early *paytanim* who hailed from that area based their compositions on Palestinian models. Having preserved the liturgy of Palestine, Italian Jewry constituted the vehicle whereby it was transferred to Franco-Germany.[3]

From the 11th century the two liturgies diverged further as German rabbis tried their hand—with varying success—at liturgical and poetic expression. The most notable contribution to the Ashkenazi ritual during this period was by the Kalonymos family—Kalonymos ben Meshullam, Moses Kalonymos, and his sons, Kalonymos and Yekutiel.

The Crusades left an indelible mark on the liturgy as memorial dirges and *Kinot* ("laments") were composed to describe and bemoan the tragedies. The *Aleinu* prayer, especially dear to the martyrs, many of whom recited it as they breathed their last, was moved from its position in the Rosh Hashanah liturgy to a place of honor at the conclusion of every service throughout the year.

The countries east of the Danube developed, in the course of time, their own variations of the Ashkenazi ritual. Differing traditions with regard to the order of the prayers and the inclusion or exclusion of certain compositions and phrases were responsible for the variations found in the prayer rites of Poland, even in the individual towns and provinces of these countries.

It was the Polish rite that became dominant in England, a fact to which the title page of *Singer's Prayer Book* still testifies.

Among preexpulsion Spanish Jewry three distinct rituals existed: those of Castille, Aragon, and Catalonia. Even after the expulsion their adherents retained their own usage in the synagogues they established in their host countries. Thus, around 1540, the fourteen congregations in Salonika each followed a different rite. Only at the beginning of the 17th century was some sort of uniformity introduced into the eastern Sephardi ritual.

The original Castillian ritual was first printed in Venice in 1522, and it is upon this rite that the English Sephardi ("Spanish and Portuguese") prayer book was based.

Another rite worthy of mention was that followed by Jews living in the Balkan countries. Their prayer book, the *Machzor Romania*, was first printed in Constantinople in 1510.

The *Machzor Roma*, representing the old Italian rite, had the distinction of being the first prayer book to be printed (Soncino, 1486). The Italian tradition represented a synthesis of the ancient Palestinian as well as the Babylonian rites.

The Influence of Mysticism on the Liturgy

The influence of Jewish mysticism on the liturgy is seen in two ways: first, the vast number of prayers whose authors were mystics and whose compositions were suffused with mystical doctrine, and, second, the application of mystical interpretation to the existing traditional liturgy.

With regard to the former, symbolism naturally played a dominant role in the style of the compositions as the mystics strove to discover the key to hidden worlds and to the First Cause of existence. Such a key, it was believed, lay embedded in the fabric of the sacred word, and only by means of the correct mystical introspection, or *kavvanah*, would the kernel of reality, nestling under the surface of the sacred words of the prayers, be revealed.

The history of Jewish mysticism goes as far back as the Pharisaic circles of the Second Temple (2nd century B.C.E.) who made the first chapter of Genesis *(Maaseh Bereishit)* and the first chapter of Ezekiel, with its vision of the divine Throne Chariot *(Maaseh Merkavah)*, the subjects of secret discussion and interpretation. The influence of "Merkavah Mysticism," which attempts to reproduce in words the *mysterium tremendum*—the awesome mystery that surrounds God's majesty—continued down the centuries, to influence the earliest Palestinian *paytanim* of the school of Kallir.

The second approach to mysticism through prayer was developed particularly by pietist circles in medieval Germany. These *Chasidim* not only composed mystical hymns, such as the *Shir Ha-Kavod*—Hymn of Glory—and the *Shir Ha-Yichud*—Unity Hymn—but also indulged in speculation regarding what underlay the text of the liturgy.

They sought to apply special devices and techniques that would lead them to the substratum of true meaning and mystical significance. The most frequently employed devices were *Gematria* (calculating the numerical value of the Hebrew words in order to link them to other words and phrases of equal value), *Notarikon* (considering the individual letters of words as abbreviations for whole phrases or sentences), and *Temurah* (interchanging of letters to make other words). "The Chasidim thus discovered a multitude of esoteric meanings in a strictly limited number of fixed expressions."[4]

Safed and Chasidic Prayer Rites

Isaac Luria was the founder of a famous school of mystics in Safed in the 16th century. The mystical conception of prayer was a dominant theme in their system, and their influence on the liturgy was enormous.

They introduced a new service—*Kabbalat Shabbat*—which precedes the evening service on Friday night. This service of welcome to the Sabbath concludes with the poem *Lekhah Dodi*—"Come, My Beloved"—which has been described as "perhaps one of the finest pieces of religious poetry in existence."[5] The mystics of Safed also composed Sabbath table hymns, as well as mystical formulae to serve as aids to concentration before the performance of religious duties and the recitation of important prayers. They also introduced colorful customs, such as the staying awake during the entire nights of Shavuot and Hoshana Rabba to recite a *Tikkun*, a specially compiled, mystically significant, order of service.

Liturgy has always been the most convenient vehicle by means of which sectarian religious groups have sought to give expression to their unique complexion, as well as to their independence of mainstream authority. It is not surprising, therefore, that Chasidism should have had early recourse to liturgical reform.

Immersed, as Chasidism was, in the spirit and doctrine of the kabbalistic literature, and especially in the teaching derived from it by Luria's mystical school at Safed, it is readily understood why, some two centuries later, the chasidic authorities should have decided to adopt the prayer rite of that school as the basis of their own liturgical reform. The Safed school had been founded by descendants of refugees from Spain; hence the (inaccurate) application of the term *Nusach Sefarad* (Sephardi rite) to describe the chasidic rite inspired by that school. Chasidism, in fact, chose for itself the specific rite initiated by Rabbi Isaac Luria (1534–72), the most distinguished of the Safed mystics.

Luria was born of an Ashkenazi father and Sephardi mother, a cross-fertilization that is also apparent in the prayer rite that he introduced, being an amalgam of the Polish Ashkenazi rite and various innovations and changes based upon the Sephardi rite as followed in Palestine at that period. This was characterized by a trimming of the *piyyutim,* compensated for by the addition of a number of extra psalms, as well as various blessings and compositions woven around the esoteric traditions of the Kabbalah.

The principle underlying his changes and innovations was that of providing a version that was an expression and representation of that essential mystical element without which prayer, according to the Lurianic system, could not be totally effective. This was the element of *Kavvanah,* which, for them, emphasized intention, reflection, and med-itation upon the various mystical combinations of the divine name. This, it was believed, would result in an upward release of impulses that would accrue to the cause of the creation of harmony in the realms of the *Sefirot,* the various creative emanations from the divine source. This, in turn, generates a reciprocal flow of blessing and grace to the world. In introducing his own liturgical adaptations Luria was motivated by the desire to frame prayer formulae in such combinations as would not only promote the correct *Kavvanah* but would also facilitate these mystical objectives.

Luria's rite, the *Nusach Ha-Ari* ("Rite of the divine Rabbi Isaac"), after the initials of his popular cognomen, was initially adopted by individual mystics and *chasidim.* The circle of the *Baal Shem Tov* ("Master of the Good Name"), founder of the chasidic movement, used it in their private meetings at Medziboz, though in public they did not dare to recommend or introduce any departure from the standard Polish Ashkenazi rite.

It was Dov Baer, Maggid of Meseritch (d. 1772), who gave the imprimatur to the *Nusach Ari* as the official prayer rite of the chasidic movement. The ensuing abandonment by the *chasidim* of the standard Ashkenazi rite, and the establishment of a network of *shtibls* ("prayer rooms"), played a major part in arousing a violent reaction to the movement on the part of the authoritarian communal and rabbinic leadership of Poland and Russia. However, the dissolution, in 1764, of the Council of Four Lands, the supreme synod of Polish Jewry, certainly emboldened the *chasidim* to pursue their independent policies without fear of effective and violent communal recriminations.

Dov Baer's authorization of the *Nusach Ari* was later published, together with his other literary compositions, in a work entitled *Maggid Devarav Le-Yaakov*, by his disciple, Solomon of Lutzk. This work defends the chasidic espousal of the Lurianic rite by emphasizing its unique superiority over other rites. To demonstrate this, Dov Baer drew attention to the mishnaic tradition that there were thirteen prostrations in the Temple, one for each of the thirteen gates; there being one gate for each tribe, and a thirteenth gate for those who were unaware of their tribal ancestry.[6] This is to be linked to another popular rabbinic tradition that, corresponding to the earthly Temple, there is a celestial Temple also containing gates for each tribe.[7]

Prayer constitutes the vehicle that enables each person to enter the heavenly Temple via his own tribal gate. The need for diverse liturgies arose from the fact that each gate has its own special combination. At times when everyone knew their tribal ancestry, it was naturally essential for people to follow the liturgical rite of their own tribe, which unlocked their own heavenly gate. However, once ignorance of tribal ancestry became rife, it was necessary to provide a liturgy that unlocked the thirteenth gate so that all Jews could gain entry. "Luria, through his familiarity with the paths of heaven, was enabled to create a liturgy which achieved this purpose; and it is better, therefore, to follow his rite which is suitable for everybody."[8]

Introductory formulae, recited in mystical circles before the performance of a *mitzvah*, were transmitted to Chasidism via the Lurianic system. These generally commence with the words *Le-sheim yichud kudsha berikh hu u-shekhinteyh* ("In order to achieve the unification of the Holy One, blessed be He, and His *Shekhinah*") or *Hareini (Hinneni) mukhan u-mezuman* ("Behold I am ready and spiritually prepared"). To understand the notion of "unifying the Holy One with His *Shekhinah*," and precisely how prayer can help to achieve such a union, requires a deep study of chasidic lore. Oversimplified, it is the ultimate objective of the complex doctrine of *tikkun*, which means the necessity, and ability, of the *chasid* to repair and perfect the world.

In the mystical tradition as popularized by Isaac Luria (as opposed to the esoteric principles of the earlier Zoharic writings) the doctrine of *tikkun* becomes a cornerstone of the entire interactive mystical mosaic. Its scope actually extends beyond the objective of merely perfecting the world, and embraces not only the idea of restoring the primeval harmony of the entire cosmos, but even the very daring notion of perfecting the harmony and unity of the divine being.

The Kabbalists believed that, at the very dawn of the creative process, the *Sefirot* (creative emanations, or self-extensions, from the essence of God) were too potent to be contained within their vessels, which were similarly made of spiritual light. What ensued was a cataclysmic *shevirat ha-keilim*, "breaking of the vessels," which caused a spillage of primary divine substance to become diffused and strewn all over the cosmos.

This fissure in the divine composition—referred to as the separation of The Holy One and His *Shekhinah*—can only be repaired, and God made "whole," by the process of *tikkun*. This is achieved by man performing to the full his sacred task of redeeming all the evil in the world, through Torah, *mitzvot*, and prayer. Every manifestation of good and every act of vanquishing evil sends back to the heavenly source some of those rays of spiritual light that were lost to God's being at the dawn of creativity. When the entire process of *tikkun* will have been completed, in the messianic era, then, as the *Aleinu* prayer asserts, "God will be One and His name one."

The effectiveness of those mystical meditations, as aids to concentration, was recognized outside of mystical and chasidic circles, and a number of them infiltrated into the Ashkenazi prayer book. Examples of the latter are the meditations before putting on the *tallit* and *tefillin*, shaking the *Lulav* and counting the *Omer*.

Hayyim Joseph David Azulay (1724–1806), in his *Machazik Berakhah* (489:3), inveighs against the recitation of these kabbalistic meditations—which include references to holy names and celestial beings—by those who do not fully understand their profound significance. He also draws attention to the numerous errors that have crept into the formulae through the carelessness of copyists and printers. These are readily apparent, Azulay asserts, when comparing them with the authentic version as transcribed by Chaim Vital and his son, Samuel. Azulay therefore urges that no one should recite a meditation until he has personally cross-checked the authenticity of his own version against the master copy of Vital that is kept in Egypt. The uninitiated, warns Azulay, are forbidden to recite the meditations even from a correct version.

Azulay's strictures were widely noted, and many modern-day authorized editions incorporate a much abbreviated version of the meditations, omitting the recondite mystical references.

Shneur Zalman of Lyady (1745–1813), founder of the *Chabad* tradition, concerned at the proliferation of rituals and compositions within the loose orbit of the Lurianic tradition, analyzed over sixty versions of the ritual. His edited rite, garnished by many of his own meditations and supplied with a kabbalistic commentary, was published in 1800. This prayer book, known as *Dem Rebbin's Siddur*, is authoritative for *Chabad chasidim* down to the present day.

The Spirit of Chasidic Prayer

For the *chasid*, prayer is not just something that one *recites*. It is rather an exercise that one performs, or an experience that one *enters into*. The *chasid* must liberate himself from his surroundings, and, more important, from self-awareness, if he is to attain to the appropriate communion with God. The ideal is *bittul ha-yesh* ("annihilation of the self"); and *shokling*, rhythmic movements of the body that are now a characteristic of praying throughout the Orthodox community—was highly regarded as a stimulus to that objective. Some *chasidim* would shout out aloud while praying, or flail their hands heavenward. Shneur Zalman of Lyady would repeatedly smite the wall with his hand, in order to reinforce his pleas to God on behalf of his petitioners, to the extent that blood would flow. Some chasidic theoreticians even conceived of prayer as an act of mystic union akin to copulation—with the *Shekhinah*. Accordingly, *shokling* was a physical manifestation of that spiritual coupling!

There is no room for inhibition within the chasidic system. The true *chasid* must truly abandon himself to his Maker, and singing and dancing are the essential means by which he strives to generate the ecstasy that will enable him to express his *deveikut*, his emotional "cleaving" to God.

The term most frequently employed in chasidic writing on prayer is *hitlahavut*, "burning ardor (for God)," from the Hebrew word *lehavah*, "a flame." But that desire for God has to be so overwhelming that any other *machshavot zarot* ("extraneous thoughts") are totally excluded. If those thoughts are present, and are focused upon one's own qualities and achievements, that is truly unacceptable. If those distractions are erotic in nature—and Chasidism faced up to the predominance of the sexual urge at both conscious and subconscious levels, and its capacity to intrude even during prayer, long before Freud alerted us to the extent to which we are affected and conditioned by our sexuality—then we have to take measures to banish those thoughts.

Chasidism dealt with this by introducing the doctrine of the "elevation of strange thoughts." This was a technique not of sublimation, but of thought conversion, whereby the beauty or desirability of the woman is latched upon and used not as a sexual but rather as a mental and spiritual stimulus. The *chasid* is taught to "elevate" those thoughts by substituting the beauty of God for the physical beauty that is currently bewitching him. He is taught how to immediately contrast the pale reflection of beauty that humans are endowed with, on the one hand, and the supreme divine source of authentic and enduring beauty, on the other.

Similarly, if it is pride and self-importance that distracts him, he is taught how to convert those into consideration of the authentic and justifiable pride that the Almighty and Omniscient God alone can feel, in comparison with which his own achievements are totally vain and unworthy of any such superior feelings.

An essential concept in Chasidism is the capacity of the *Tzaddik*, the holy leader and mentor, to storm the gates of heaven through his prayers, and even to reverse an adverse heavenly decree. This is based on a talmudic maxim: "The Holy One, blessed be He, decrees, and the righteous may annul that decree." The *Tzaddik* has the miraculous capacity either to direct heavenly grace in the direction of a particular petitioner—securing for him "children, life, or sustenance"—or, if he deems it necessary, to arrest the flow of that grace. Inevitably it gave the *Tzaddik*, in the eyes of his followers, a divinelike capacity, a power over life or death. Not surprisingly, therefore, *chasidim* will intercede with their *rebbe* and seek his guidance, help, and inspiration on personal, family, religious, and business matters, great and small.

An entire literature exists on the subject of the origin of this supernatural power possessed by the *Tzaddik*. The most well known explanation is the parable offered by the Maggid of Meseritch:

> When a king is based in his royal palace, he will only leave it in order to stay for a short time at an equally magnificent palace where he will receive the same regal consideration. However, when the king has to undertake a journey abroad, along foreign highways and byways, then he is quite prepared to stay even in the most humble of dwellings where hospitality is offered, as long as the place is spotless.

> For our many sins, the divine King, the *Shekhinah*, is nowadays in exile, remote from His palace. He is prepared, therefore, to dwell in any spotlessly pure soul. He is content to enter the "humble dwelling," which is the soul of the *Tzaddik*, and allow him to determine the direction of divine grace.

When the *Tzaddik* stands at the head of his followers, leading them in prayer, he is not, therefore, merely a prayer leader, or even a *shliach tzibbur*, a "representative of the congregation," as described by the Talmud. He is nothing less than the personal transporter of their petitions. He can soar heavenward, bearing those petitions to other worlds, the worlds of the primeval emanations of the divine *Sefirot*, where unity, harmony, and grace prevail undiluted, and where mercy and loving-kindness flow unimpeded. And even if a severe decree has been made from on high, the soul of the *Tzaddik* is quite able to attach the petitions of the doomed person to other worlds where no such decree was ever uttered, and to carry from there a sufficiency of grace to neutralize the original decree.

Prayer in Chasidism is a totally absorbing activity. For the *Tzaddik* it is a feverish activity involving the traversing of time and space. "Serve God with joy" is a key concept in this system. That spiritual joy is generated most readily when one is convinced that "salvation is close at hand." The proximity of one's *rebbe* is, for the *chasid*, the most effective instrument of securing that salvation.

6

The Modern Period

Printing, Textual Studies, and Scientific Works

Printed prayer books began to appear toward the end of the 15th century. Printing inevitably resulted in greater uniformity, and many local variations of standard rites soon passed out of existence.

Another effect of printing was to render the office of *chazan*— prayer leader—less important. Until the advent of printing, the *chazan* would recite the prayers alone for the sake of those worshipers who did not know them by heart. Few worshipers could have afforded a handwritten manuscript of the prayers. The congregation would silently repeat the words after the *chazan*. Now that a *Siddur* was available to all, the need for the *chazan* was considerably reduced.

A uniform text does not necessarily mean an accurate text, and most editions abounded in printer's errors, omissions, arbitrary additions, grammatical mistakes, and misleading rubrics. Throughout the 18th century attempts were made to remedy this situation with the regular publication of corrected editions. This, in turn, stimulated scientific investigation into the origin of the prayers, which began in earnest at the beginning of the 19th century.

A major contribution to the study of liturgy was made by Wolf Heidenheim (1752-1832). In order to establish an authoritative and correct text he compared scores of ancient manuscripts. He set up a printing press at Rödelheim in 1799, where he produced an edition of the festival *machzorim* with a Hebrew commentary and German translation (1800). In 1823 he published his *Siddur Safah Berurah*, a text of the daily prayers with a German translation.

Scientific investigation into the origin of the prayers now commenced in earnest, with the publication in 1832 of the first of Leopold Zunz's classical works on the subject *(Vorträge des Jüdischen Gottesdienstes)*. A contemporary of Zunz, Leser Landshuth, made a notable contribution to liturgical studies with the publication in 1845 of an appendix to the *Siddur* of Hirsch Edelman *(Siddur Hegyon Lev)*, in which he traced the origin of Hebrew prayers. In 1855 he produced a study on the Passover *Haggadah*, followed, two years later, by his chief work, *Ammudei Ha-Avodah*, on liturgical poetry. In the same year, Zunz's second work *(Synagogale poesie des Mittelalters)* appeared, followed, in 1858, by his *Ritus*, in which he traced the emergence of the various liturgical rites. He crowned his life's work in 1865 – one year before his death – with the publication of his *Literaturgeschichte der Synagogalen Poesie*, which, while giving an account of the history of Hebrew poetry, also depicted the intellectual and social life of the Jews of Germany, Italy, and Spain.

In 1868 Heidenheim's *Siddur* was superseded by what has been described as the "*Siddur* par excellence," the *Avodat Yisrael* of Seligman Baer. Baer had access to Heidenheim's manuscripts and unpublished notes, and, having made the study of the *Masorah* – the traditional text of the Hebrew Bible – his main occupation, and having produced critical editions of most of the biblical books, he applied the same methods to the *Siddur*. His text of the prayers was accompanied by a commentary, *Yakhin Lashon* ("Preparatory Study of the Language"), wherein he gives variant readings, sources, and an explanation of the text.

The Cairo *Genizah*

There is hardly a single area of Medieval Jewish history and literature that has not been illumined by the early material discovered in the Cairo *Genizah* by Solomon Schechter in 1898. Schechter's trip to Fostat in Old Cairo was on behalf of Cambridge University, where he held the post of reader in rabbinics; and the 140,000 pages and fragments he discovered there, in an inaccessible attic of the ancient Ezra Synagogue, he brought back to Cambridge and deposited in the University library. It has been estimated that an equal number of manuscripts and fragments were also discovered by a variety of other scholars, researchers, and bibliophiles. Most of their discoveries were ultimately deposited in national libraries throughout the world.

The original synagogue dated back to 882, and for centuries it remained an important place of worship and seat of learning. Among the great luminaries who frequented it and who taught there were Moses Maimonides and his son, Abraham. Scores of letters bearing Maimonides' signature were discovered there. Its store of worn-out texts, used both for synagogue worship as well as study, contained a vast amount of material that was hitherto totally unknown, and spanned nearly a thousand years of literary activity in a variety of lands, notably Egypt, Palestine, Babylonia, and Spain. The worshipers at the Ezra Synagogue, in the early centuries of its existence, included many who still observed the customs and traditions of ancient Palestine. They still recited many of the liturgical compositions of the earliest Palestinian poets, which, with the almost total decline of Palestine as a center of Jewish religious life, were lost until they were brought to light in the Cairo *Genizah*.

The work of sifting through and classifying the fifty or so boxes, jam-packed with pages, documents, books, and fragments, was an enormous task, calling for reserves of patience in addition to great expertise in Semitic linguistics, rabbinics, biblical studies, and bibliographic knowledge. A torn fragment of a hitherto unknown Hebrew original of the postbiblical (apocryphal) book of Ben-Sira (Ecclesiasticus) might be lying on top of an Arabic commercial document. A page of rules relating to the organization of the Essene community (Damascus Covenant) of the last century B.C.E. might be stuck to a folio of *piyyut* from medieval Spain. Documents reflecting the struggle between rabbinic Judaism and the Karaite offshoot might be interleaved with pages of Yiddish letters and poems from the 15th century. It takes highly skilled and competent scholars in order to identify the nature and origin of each item, and much of the material first required to be professionally restored, utilizing the most up-to-date methods, before it could be deciphered.

This was but the first stage before the important work of cataloging every item could begin, to enable scholars to go directly to the material relating to the subject and period they are researching. Schechter could not devote himself to this task in the systematic manner it required, since, four years after his discovery of the *Genizah*, he left Cambridge to assume the post of President of the Jewish Theological Seminary of America. It is only in the past twenty-five years that the *Genizah* has received the expert attention it required, with the establishment of a special Taylor-Schechter *Genizah Research Unit* under Dr. Stefan Reif, assisted by several research assistants and workers.

The classification and publication of *Genizah* material relating to liturgy has revolutionized our understanding of the influences, trends, and movements that have shaped the development of the various prayer rites of Jewish communities in many countries. We are now frequently enabled to determine the various stages of development that specific compositions and prayers underwent, from their beginning, as a simple basic expression or formula, to a final lengthy and composite piece. In many instances we are able to appreciate that a problematic word or phrase, or an apparently awkward grammatical or syntactical form, in a particular composition, is entirely removed by our discovery of a superior reading in a *Genizah* version. We are frequently able to understand now – on the basis of *Genizah* text readings – that a particular version that has come down to us may have undergone considerable revision, for stylistic, theological, or halakhic reasons, and sometimes as a result of the intrusion of the censor, or even through Jewish internal, preventive censorship. In a number of instances not only are we enabled to plot the various changes and revisions that a composition has undergone, but we are, at the same time, given a glimpse into the attitudes, conditions, and tensions that constrained that particular community to make such changes.

Since 1976, the work of the Taylor-Shechter *Genizah Research Unit*, in the fields of conservation, microfilming, cataloging, publications, and research on the material, has become increasingly widely known and appreciated. This has been achieved by means of the unit's regular newsletter, *Genizah Fragments*, and the indefatigable efforts of its director to raise both funds and awareness, the latter by welcoming congregational groups and interested visitors.

Since research and scholarship cannot develop without its essential critical tools, of which bibliographical data is paramount, the research unit made its priority the compilation of a 600-page bibliography of all the *Genizah* fragments currently in the possession of the Cambridge University Library. This invaluable aid, *Published Material from the Cambridge Genizah Collections – A Bibliography 1896-1980* (Ed. Stefan C. Reif), appeared in 1988.

Elbogen's Liturgical History

Ismar Elbogen (1874–1943) is still regarded as having provided the classic and most authoritative presentation of the history of the liturgy in all its facets. This is contained in his pioneering work, *Der Jüdische*

Gottesdienst in Seiner Geschichtlichen Entwicklung (Frankfurt-am-Main, 1913; Hebrew edition, Tel Aviv, 1972).

This systematic and comprehensive work clarified the origin of the two main liturgical traditions of Babylon and Palestine, and the relationship between them. It also provides a most detailed treatment of the kernel of the morning service, the *Shema* and its blessings, and the *Amidah*, tracing each stage of the evolution of the phraseology of the blessings.

Elbogen analyzes the history of the Reading of the Law and the *Haftarot*. He attributes the institution of the public Reading of the Law to Ezra, though he departs from the traditional view in postulating a progressive expansion of the institution. He believes that the Torah reading was introduced originally exclusively for the three pilgrim festivals of Pesach, Shavuot, and Sukkot as a springboard and vehicle for an exposition of the laws and customs of these holy days. Another of its purposes was to provide an opportunity for the public to hear the biblical sources of the festivals explained in a manner calculated to justify and vindicate the orthodox interpretation in the face of the independent and frequently conflicting exegesis of the Samaritans. From the pilgrim festivals the custom of the public Reading of the Law developed, says Elbogen, to Rosh Hashanah and Yom Kippur, and, at a later period, to the four special Sabbaths before Pesach, from which it was extended to become a weekly, Sabbath institution.

A most important section of his work relates to the rise and development of the *piyyut*. Sacred poetry was enabled to enter the liturgy, he claims, only after the conclusion of the Amoraic period of the talmudic era (circa 5th century), by which time the principle parts of the synagogue service—upon which these poetic insertions were based—had already been standardized. Elbogen provides an excellent survey of the contribution of the leading liturgical poets in Palestine and in all the lands of the dispersion. He also explains the various genres of sacred poetry, the influence of mysticism on the liturgy, and the earliest *Siddurim* and *Machzorim* of the geonic period. Elbogen's unique critical acumen, and his encyclopedic knowledge of rabbinic sources, made his work not only a *sine qua non* for the study of liturgy, but also a model scholarly presentation that was to influence subsequent research in so many areas of Jewish culture.

Elbogen's masterpiece was still regarded as a standard work some sixty years later. The unusual step was therefore taken of publishing an updated Hebrew edition of the work in 1972. Joseph Heinemann served as editor, assisted by leading liturgical scholars. The German text was translated by one of Elbogen's former students, Yehoshua Amir, and the far simpler Hebrew title of *Ha-tefillah Be-Yisrael (Prayer in Israel)* was given to the work.

Elbogen's original is allowed to speak for itself. Wherever necessary, the editors interpose supplementary comment, in brackets and smaller print. This gives a resumé of current scholarly opinion and describes material that has come to light—particularly from the *Genizah*—since Elbogen's day, explaining how such new knowledge has altered many cherished liturgical principles and axioms of the past.

The Schocken Research Institute

As regards liturgical poetry, mention must be made of the pioneering contribution made by the scholars of the Schocken Research Institute for Medieval Hebrew Poetry in Jerusalem. The Institute was founded by a Polish philanthropist and patron of Hebrew culture, Salman Schocken (1877–1959), who invested much of his considerable fortune into collecting what soon came to be one of the largest and most important libraries of Judaica in the world. Schocken also took under his wing budding scholars and writers, and he became S. Y. Agnon's patron and publisher from the very beginning of his literary career. The family publishing house has, in fact, become synonymous with contemporary Jewish culture.

The Research Institute, with the Schocken library as its nerve center, was opened in Berlin in 1929, and was safely transferred to Jerusalem in 1934. Its first director was Haim Brody, former chief rabbi of Prague, who accompanied the Institute when it moved to Palestine. Brody had already made his name in scholarly circles through his worthy anthology of medieval Hebrew poetry, *Mivchar Ha-Shirah Ha-Ivrit*, which he edited together with M. Weiner. At the Institute, Brody edited the secular poems of Moses Ibn Ezra (1935) and produced a commentary on the poetry of Yehudah Ha-Levi, shedding considerable light on the whole school of Spanish Hebrew poets.

Most notable among the scholars who were attracted to join the staff of the Institute were Menachem Zulay, Chaim Schirmann, and Abraham Habermann.

Menachem Zulay studied the rise and development of the Babylonian liturgy, in which subject he gained his Ph.D. at the University of Bonn in 1933. In the following year he settled in Jerusalem and began work at the Institute. He played a prominent role in the Institute's efforts to collect photographs of unpublished fragments of Hebrew poetry from the *Genizah* which, as we mentioned above, had found their way into the libraries of many different countries. These poems were edited and published by the Institute as the basis of definitive works. Zulay devoted himself particularly to the poetry of Yannai, rescuing this most important father of synagogue poetry from almost total scholarly obscurity.

Zulay is best known for the work he published in 1938, *Piyyutei Yannai*. To mark the tenth anniversary of Zulay's death, in 1964, the Institute published a further work by him on the poetic traditions of the school of Saadia Gaon.

Zulay's distinguished colleagues at the Institute also illumined the field of liturgical as well as secular Hebrew poetry with their volumes of research articles, particularly the series entitled *Yediot Ha-Makhon Le-cheker Ha-Shirah Ha-Ivrit*, and in their pathfinding publications in their special fields of interest.

Chaim Schirmann made a notable contribution to our understanding of the development of liturgical poetry, by publishing a collection of hitherto unknown poems from the *Genizah*, emanating from various periods and many different centers of Jewish cultural life. Of special note are his two important anthologies, one of Italian Hebrew poems from the 9th century until the modern period, and the second covering the poetry from Spain and the Provence from the 10th to the 15th centuries.

Abraham Habermann's output was prolific and diverse, covering the fields of literary history, Hebrew printing, Franco-German liturgical poetry, and the Dead Sea Scrolls. Of particular importance is his *Toledot Ha-Piyyut Ve-ha-Shirah*, a comprehensive history covering over two thousand years of poetic tradition.   .

Two other scholars who brought German scholarship to the State of Israel, and who have made outstanding contributions to the scientific study of liturgy, are Daniel Goldschmidt and Joseph Heinemann.

Goldschmidt is best known for his critical editions of the Passover *Haggadah* and the Rosh Hashanah and Yom Kippur *Machzorim*, though students of liturgy are also greatly in his debt for a prolific output of critical editions of classic sources, particularly his *Seder Rav Amram*, the *Selichot* and *Kinnot* according to the Lithuanian and Polish rites, Maimonides' *Seder Ha-Tefillah*, the *Machzorim* of Greece, Rome, and the Balkans, as well as the *Siddurim* of the Ashkenazim and Sephardim of the contemporary State of Israel. His studies have been collected into a volume entitled *Mechkerei Tefillah Upiyyut* (*On Jewish Liturgy*, Jerusalem, 1978).

Heinemann's particular contribution was to reveal the literary forms underlying the liturgy in talmudic times. His best-known work is entitled *Ha-Tefillah Bi-Tekuphat Ha-Tanna'im Ve-ha-Amora'im (Prayer in the*

Period of the Tanna'im and the Amora'im), wherein he analyzes the earliest formulae of prayer, the structure of the basic *berakhah* terminology, the primitive *piyyut* and prayers emanating from the Temple, the evolution of unique genres of prayer originating in the *Bet Midrash* (rabbinic academy) and the synagogue, and the process of standardization of the *Siddur*, which was the preoccupation of the scholars of Babylon in the geonic period. Heinemann's major essays and studies, published in a wide variety of scholarly journals and publications, were collected and published in 1981 by his pupil, Avigdor Shinan, in a book entitled *Iyyunei Tefillah (Studies in Jewish Liturgy)*.

The discovery of the Dead Sea Scrolls, in 1947, has also provided an additional perspective from which to view the fascinating panorama of Jewish liturgy.

Prayer in the Vernacular, Editions and Translations of the Prayer Book

The use of the vernacular in prayer seems to have been especially favored by the Sephardi communities in the East, and was probably introduced soon after the exile from Spain in 1492. Especially on Rosh Hashanah and Yom Kippur it was their practice to read prayers in Spanish, a tradition preserved by the Sephardi communities of the Balkans until their destruction in the Second World War. A remnant of this is preserved to the present day by the English Sephardim who read the *Haftarah* (selection from the Prophets) on the Fast of Av in Spanish.

The Ashkenazim, on the other hand, resisted until much later such a concession to ignorance of Hebrew. Due to their emphasis on rabbinic learning, there was an informed laity who could understand the prayers, coupled with the fact that the Yiddish language, with its liberal admixture of Hebrew, also provided the average Jew with some idea of the meaning of the prayers.

Soon after the advent of printing, an Italian translation of the Roman ritual appeared (Bologna, 1538), the Italian being translated into Hebrew characters. Before the close of the century translations appeared in Spanish and Yiddish. In 1617 a translation into Portuguese was published in Amsterdam for the benefit of the Marranos.

During the 18th century translations into French, Dutch, and modern German were published. The latter was produced in 1786 by David Friedlander. Since he was a leading figure in the Mendelssohnian movement, the translation aroused opposition among the German Orthodox community who henceforth equated translation of prayers with Reform Judaism.

Orthodox opposition to translated editions hardened some thirty years later when a new *Prayer Book for Sabbath Morning and the New Year* was issued for the Berlin Reform community. Now, for the first time, German translation actually became a replacement for prayer in the original Hebrew.

The reformist trend was now gaining great momentum, and a new prayer book, bearing the significant title *Die Deutsche Synagogue*, appeared in 1817. This was characterized by many variations, omissions, and innovations: prayers in German instead of Hebrew, abridgement of core Hebrew prayers and blessings, random selection and combination of Ashkenazi and Sephardi versions, and abolition of the silent *Amidah* recited by the individual worshiper. They also replaced the *Shacharit* service *Kedushah* with that of the *Musaf Amidah*. Their reason for so doing was that they objected to the nationalistic plea for a speedy return to Zion *(mattai timlokh be-tziyyon . . .)* contained in the *Shacharit* version of the *Kedushah*. According to Jakob J. Petuchowski, the early reformers were obviously less troubled by the metaphysical description of angels conversing, as contained in the *Musaf* version, than by the totally unacceptable reference to a restoration to Zion! The latter concept was in stark conflict with their basic philosophy of integration into German society and an equal stake in German nationalism.[1]

Another—though in this instance less objectionable—objective of most of the Reform prayer books that have been issued over the past one hundred and fifty years has been to minimize the number of *piyyutim* recited, on the grounds that they are too lengthy, their allusions too complex, and their sentiments outdated. Joseph Heinemann points out the contemporary irony underlying the vigorous opposition on the part of the Orthodox community which Reform's expurgation of *piyyutim* initially engendered: "The historical irony of this is apparent to all, particularly to the inhabitants of the State of Israel today; for here a kind of silent revolution had taken place with the abolition of the majority of the *piyyutim* in nearly every synagogue—and there has not been a voice raised in objection!"[2]

The *Siddur*, which is meant to serve as a unifying spirit in Jewish religious and community life, acted, in fact, within Reform, as a divisive influence, since each community created an arbitrary liturgy for its members without conformity to any generally accepted principles or guidelines. In some prayer books any association with the traditional, historically hallowed, prayers was merely coincidental. This was the case in the Reform community of Berlin, whose prayer book was almost entirely in German, apart from some key phrases from *Shema* and *Kedushah*. In the Hamburg Temple, however, established in 1818, the prayers were based directly upon the traditional prayer book, though all references to a restoration to Zion, or to the ancient Temple ritual of sacrifices, were expunged. They also abandoned the *Haftarah, Yekum Porkan,* and *Ein Keloheinu.* The present-day tendency is to return to the spirit and form of the Orthodox *Siddur* and an almost exclusive retention of Hebrew as the language of prayer.[3] In the same year that Friedlander's German edition appeared (1786), the first translation of the Ashkenazi rite into English was made, in New York, by Isaac Pinto.

Singer's, Rinnat Yisrael, and Art Scroll

Simeon Singer's edition of the *Siddur* was produced in London in 1890, under the "sanction and authorization" of the Chief Rabbi, Dr. N. M. Adler. Its official title was the *Authorised Prayer Book of the United Hebrew Congregations of the British Empire.* Not surprisingly, and also because of the popularity of both the Reverend Simeon Singer and his edition, the latter was popularly and universally referred to as *The Singer's Prayer Book.* Quite remarkably, a century and countless editions later, this is still the case. It found its way into most synagogues of Great Britain, even those outside the orbit of the United Synagogue and the halakhic authority of the chief rabbi, and there was a steady demand for it even in the United States. Its appeal was not only due to the compact nature and beauty of the edition or the literary merit of Singer's translation, but also for the very practical reason that the public-spirited Montefiore family defrayed the entire cost of production, enabling the book to be sold for the heavily subsidized price of one shilling (7 cents)!

Its aim was "to unite accuracy and even literalness with due regard to English idiom, and to the simplicity of style and diction which befits the language of prayer."[4] Those same criteria were also borne in mind in 1990, when an entirely new edition, with a modern idiomatic translation, was commissioned, under the editorial direction of Lord Immanuel Jakobovits. This is the "Centenary Edition," issued to coincide with the 100th anniversary of the first edition of 1890.

It has to be said that there are clear signs that *Singer's* no longer enjoys quite the preeminence that it once had in Britain. *Singer's* still partakes of the spirit of the Anglo-Jewish religious establishment, which is unacceptable to the "Right Wing" communities, with their own religious mentors, and to the ever-growing segment of young people who have spent a few years in Israeli *yeshivot,* and who return with new religious allegiances in the "*yeshivah* world." Their newly acquired mastery of Hebrew means that they no longer require a translated edition, and their priority is rather for an edition that has some traditional commentaries and laws of prayer, and feels more like a *sefer* (a traditional text) than the *Book of Common Prayer,* which *Singer's* has consistently resembled.

Hence the growing popularity of the Israeli *Siddur Rinnat Yisrael* (1970) and, particularly, the exquisitely produced American *Complete Art Scroll Siddur* (1984).

The *Rinnat Yisrael* still remains, surprisingly, the only prayer book, of the three under consideration, to include an Order of Service for Yom Ha-Atzma'ut and Yom Yerushalayim. Its layout is far less congested than the other two, and its script much larger and clearer. A special *Diaspora version* was produced in 1982. Although its introduction, rubrics, instructions accompanying the various prayers, and month-by-month liturgical "Guide to the Jewish Year" are all in English, yet, quite inexplicably, the brief footnote elucidations of the meaning of difficult Hebrew expressions in the prayers have been retained in Modern Hebrew! It was not considered necessary to provide an English translation of the Hebrew prayers, perhaps on the assumption that those who required such a translation would be more likely to prefer *Singer's.* Yet an exception is made in the case of the two Aramaic prayers, *Brikh shemei* and *Yekum Porkan,* and the Aramaic *Zemirah* (Sabbath table hymn), *Yah Ribon,* which are endowed with an accompanying translation! This is presumably based on the most questionable assumption that although Diaspora Jews could not reasonably be expected to understand Aramaic, yet the Hebrew of the prayers and the Modern Hebrew of the footnotes would be quite within their ability to comprehend!

The *Complete Art Scroll Siddur,* by contrast, has English on nearly every one of its 992 pages. It is large and thick, with a commentary that is, in itself, of full book length. With consummate skill the publishers have managed to crowd upon nearly every page of both the Hebrew and English sides a multivariety of typographical styles, character sizes, and devices. These include shaded backgrounds for prayers and insertions that are added on special occasions only, bordered highlighting of more detailed halakhic instructions, asterisks indicating that that word or phrase is treated in the commentary, and numbered footnotes providing the scriptural sources of every verse that has been melded into the prayers. Most admirable is the technique of arranging the parallel Hebrew and English texts in such a way that the first and last phrases of the translation of each passage run parallel to those of the Hebrew text. Similarly, each English paragraph begins with the initial Hebrew word of the corresponding passage of the Hebrew text, in order to ease cross-checking (for some reason this was omitted on p. 77).

It is difficult to think of anything that has been overlooked in this *Siddur*; and, although a full review is outside the scope of this book, it must be said that the commentary has come in for considerable criticism on the grounds that it is simplistic, overly pietistic, and exclusive of any academic source identified with modern liturgical scholarship, and outside the established rabbinic and halakhic fraternity.

The popular Routledge edition of the festival prayers (1906) set out to provide a translation that would be stylistic and inspirational. To that end it employed the services of some distinguished literary figures in Anglo-Jewry, such as the great Israel Zangwill. Their elevated and self-conscious verse may have suited 19th-century taste, but to the modern ear it is almost as incomprehensible as the Hebrew original. The Birnbaum edition (1951) has produced a more readable and less pretentious translation, with some helpful notes; but the use of archaic vocabulary, aggravated by the "thee," "thou," and "thy" syndrome, must deprive it of its claim to modernity.

The very propriety of including free renderings of the *piyyutim* (poetic compositions) into vernacular poetry, within an edition of the *Machzor*, has been questioned by some on the grounds that, apart from diverting attention away from the Hebrew text and its required recitation, it also transforms the devotional prayer book into a mere book of poetry.

The result of this, it is alleged, is that many sacred hours of the High Holydays are spent in critical literary appraisal instead of in prayer.

It is argued that, even though the original *piyyutim* may be unintelligible, they are, at least, in the sacred language, comprising biblical and rabbinic allusions written by sages under the influence of the holy spirit, and consequently invested with the mystical power of moving human hearts to repentance and the Almighty to mercy. No poetic translation, on the other hand, however felicitous, can lay claim to that mystic or spiritual capability.

7

The Liturgy of Ethiopian Jewry

The Ingathering

In the early 1980s, the Jewish world awoke to the significance of the arrival in Israel of a large number of refugees from Ethiopia; and against a background of increased Marxist oppression and a serious famine—which galvanized welfare agencies around the world to give it priority rating—an audacious rescue operation was undertaken to airlift thousands of our starving black brethren to a new life in Israel. The remnant of the community was airlifted, in the equally dramatic "Operation Solomon," in 1991. Inevitably, a host of problems yet confront this small community as they struggle to adjust to the millennial gap that separates their primitive way of life, which has hardly changed in two thousand years, from the westernized, technological society that is Israel's ideal and reality.

In addition to social problems of education and integration, and the inevitable discrimination on the grounds of color that they encounter from some quarters, there are also religious problems. The question of their status as Jews took some time to be resolved by the leading rabbinic authorities, and there was some resentment on the part of the community that they had to undergo a token ceremony and ritual of conversion. Segments of the chasidic community totally reject their claim to Jewish status and openly cold-shoulder them.

The name *Falasha*, by which they were traditionally known, means "an exile," "a wanderer," in their Ge'ez language. It was a term of opprobrium applied to them by their Ethiopian neighbors to remind them that they were immigrants and not members of the indigenous population. This insult they were able to use to their advantage to substantiate their claim to have been, indeed, exiles from ancient Palestine where they originally formed part of the Israelite tribe of Dan. They claim to have originated specifically from notables of Jerusalem who accompanied Menelik, the child born of the union of Solomon and the Queen of Sheba, when he was returned to his maternal homeland. Those notables did not, or could not, return to Palestine, and remained in Ethiopia where they continued down the ages to practice their (biblical) religion. Because of its basically unpleasant connotation, the Ethiopian community prefers to be known as *Beta Yisrael* (House of Israel), a name that also underlies their ancestral identity. There are actually several other theories regarding the origins of the Falashas. Although Israel's chief rabbis have accepted the authenticity of the tradition that they hail from the tribe of Dan, one of the Ten Lost Tribes conquered by the Assyrians in 721 B.C.E., President Ben-Zvi, on the other hand, thought that they descended from Jewish soldiers posted in Upper Egypt by the Persian emperors. Others believe their founding fathers to have been Jerusalemite refugees from the destruction of one or other of the Temples. Ethiopian chronicles suggest that before the conversion of Ethiopia by Syrian missionaries, in the 4th century C.E., the biblical style of Judaism practiced by the Falashas was very widespread. They are, therefore, the descendants of those who stubbornly and heroically refused to convert.

Having been detached from the subsequent evolution of the Israelite religion into its "rabbinic" form, they knew nothing of talmudic and medieval halakhic traditions; and their liturgy obviously has a totally different complexion from that of mainstream Judaism. They did not read Hebrew, and therefore did not possess a "traditional" *Sefer Torah*. Their sacred literature is the Bible, which they had only in book form, in the Ge'ez language. *Keriat Ha-Torah* took the form of a "Bible reading," followed by an explanation in Amharic. *Aliyot* were, accordingly, not part of their tradition. Ritual immersion and prayer—which, on Sabbaths and festivals, took up most of the day—were of great importance, and the synagogue, or *mesgid*, was their central institution. Its courtyard generally contained a stone altar for the offering of the Paschal lamb and other festival sacrifices.

As they integrate into the State of Israel, and adopt the religious traditions of the Oriental Sephardi community, it is inevitable that they will forget their native liturgical rite. It is therefore of value to record some of its features.

A Rare Ethiopian *Siddur*

The description of the *Siddur* of Ethiopian Jewry given below is derived exclusively from a text published in Paris in 1876 by the Orientalist, Joseph Halévy, who transcribed the prayers into Hebrew from their Ge'ez original. It is a slim volume, just twenty-eight columns, the last three of which contain the prayers to accompany the sacrificial act.

In the introduction to his *Seder Tefillot Ha-Falashim*, Halévy tells us that he visited the *Falashim* in 1867 as an emissary of the Alliance Israelite Universelle (the international Jewish organization, founded in Paris in 1860), and the text upon which he bases his Hebrew version was written down for him by the scribe of their community, one Zerubbavel ben Yaakov, in the village of Kavta. Halévy also acknowledges the interest taken in this project by the London-based *Society of Hebrew Literature*, who published and distributed it.

The community had institutions akin to monasteries and nunneries, where men and women consecrated themselves to a life of abstinence and piety. The prayers that Halévy transcribed carry a devotional introduction that acclaims one Abba Saqwén, founder of such a monastic order in the 13th century, as having been their chief composer of liturgy. The present liturgy, it is stated, contains Abba Saqwén's compositions, as well as "the prayers of the angels and the saints." Indeed, apart from the final section, bearing the heading *Tefillat Ha-Korban* ("Prayer over the Sacrifice"), there is only one main heading to the compilation—"Prayer of the Angels to the One God." The content of the prayer that immediately follows makes it quite clear, however, that the *Angels' Prayer* has in fact come adrift from its superscription. What follows is very much a mortal composition, containing a litany of divine attributes and praises, introduced by the words *kiy attah* (*for thou art* . . . the grace of the righteous; *for thou art* the crown of the pure; *for thou art* the strength of the weak), *Tehillah* (*Praise to* . . . the Most High; *Praise to* the Lord . . .), *Halleluyah* and *Barukh Ha-Shem*. In one passage the attribute *Ein Sof* (Infinite), familiar from Jewish philosophical writings, is employed.

In the *Tehillah* line (p. 4) there is a quaint sentiment, in brackets, expressing thanksgiving for the gift of Abba Saqwén's prayers: "Praise to the Lord for having given me this book, the work of Abba Saqwén. May the One God support me." This was probably inserted by Halévy's scribe, Zerubbavel, who later inserts within brackets another personal gloss (p. 23), where he actually refers to himself by name, petitioning God to include him, and his father and mother, in the heavenly banquet that will be held in the hereafter in honor of the righteous. Such a mystical idea—found in the midrashic literature—is unlikely, however, to have been an early, native Ethiopian Jewish tradition. Similarly, Zerubbavel's colophon—quoted by Halévy in his final footnote—expresses the plea that God should grant him the privilege of writing down, once again, the prayers of his community "in the heavenly Jerusalem, with Abraham, Isaac, and Jacob, for all eternity, Amen."

Biblical doxologies, which will be familiar from our own prayer book, include: *Barukh ha-shem ha-mevorakh* ("Blessed be the Lord, who is to be blessed"); *Barukh ha-shem elohei yisrael* ("Blessed be the Lord, God of Israel"); *Kadosh, kadosh, kadosh ha-shem tzeva'ot* ("Holy, Holy, Holy is the Lord of Hosts"); *Barukh ha-shem elohei yisrael min ha-olam ve-ad ha-olam* ("Blessed be the Lord, God of Israel, from eternity unto eternity"); *Lekha ha-shem ha-gedulah ve-ha-gevurah ve-ha-tiferet ve-ha-netzach ve-ha-hod* ("To You, O Lord, belongs the greatness, might, glory, eternity, and splendor"), and *melekh mehulal* ("King who is praised").

A large proportion of the *Siddur* is taken up with recitations of divine attributes, mostly rooted in biblical phraseology. God is hailed as *magbiah shefalim* ("Raiser of the lowly"), *ozer gibborim* ("Who girds the mighty with strength"), *rishon beliy reshit ve-acharon beliy acharit* ("The First without beginning, and the Last without end"), and *machlish gibborim bi-gevurato* ("Who weakens the strong by His strength").

Angels, as intermediaries and as fellow worshipers of God, figure prominently in the prayers of the community. One lengthy composition enumerates all the angelic hierarchy, and depicts them at prayer, flanked by "the angels in the heavens and those within the thunder and lightning; those at the ends of the earth and those in the seas; and those who run the course together with the sun and the moon." It then proceeds to detail a timetable of services, specifying the hour of the night when each of those groups of angels is permitted to offer its particular praise of God:

> For the first two hours of the night it is the turn of the souls of the righteous forefathers ("Adam, Abel, Abraham, Isaac, Jacob, Moses, Aaron, and David the King of Israel"). The third hour of the night is given over to the judgment of Hell, when fire rages to the depths of Sheol. No

prayers are appropriate at that time. At the fourth hour of the night the *Seraphim* recite *Holy, Holy, Holy.* . . . At the fifth hour, the (angels of the) seas offer praise; at the sixth hour, the clouds; and at the seventh, the whole universe is still, and only the Spirit of God hovers over the face of the waters.

In the eighth hour of the night the gates of the earth are opened, so that the growth of vegetation can proceed; and in the ninth hour the angels bring the prayers of men before the presence of the Most High. They open the gates of heaven so that God may hear the prayers and pardon all the sins of men.

A later composition tells us the precise formulae of praise employed by each category of angel. In such a context we are not surprised to find direct petitioning of angels: "Pray for us, O angel Michael; make supplication for us, O angel Gabriel." One obscure category of angel, known only from the book of Daniel (4:10,20), has equal place in these prayers. These are the *iyrin*, "Wakeful Ones," or "watchers."

One paragraph of the *Siddur* takes the form of a confession for sin. It commences with a variation of the well-known verse from Isaiah (1:18), which it proceeds to express from the human standpoint: "If *my* sins were as numerous as the sand of the seas, or as heavy as iron, let them become like snow or water. Forgive me all my sins, pardon my iniquities." There then follows a list of otherwise unknown personal names of angels, culminating in the plea, "May the power of these names deliver me, *so-and-so* son of *so-and-so.*"

There are, indeed, quite a number of opportunities for the worshiper to insert his own name into a petition, to make the plea more personal and urgent. Similarly, the threefold *Kedushah* (Sanctification) is employed quite frequently within the context of a single service. In one passage its ending is rendered in the second person, to read "Holy holy holy. . . . The ends of the earth are filled with *Your* glory" (*melo kol katzvei eretz kevodekha*).

Such variations of biblical verses are quite common and inevitable, given their ignorance of the Hebrew original. Thus, for example, the Thirteen Divine Attributes (Exodus 34:6–7) are quoted (p. 23) in a form that suggests that they have been confused with some other source. Again, there is a lengthy, and fairly accurate, quotation from Exodus 32:13, but, following the phrase *arbeh et zarakhem ke-khokhvei ha-shamayim* ("I will multiply your seed like the stars of the heavens"), there is an unwarranted insertion: *ve-kha-chol asher al sefat ha-yam* ("And like the sand on the sea shore"), which obviously crept in by confusion with Genesis 22:17. In quoting the words uttered by God to Cain, after he had killed his brother, the verse reads *hinneh kol demei hevel alu eilay* ("Behold, the sound of the blood of Abel has risen to Me"), whereas the actual Hebrew text does not have the first word, *hinneh,* and reads, "The sound of the blood *of your brother cries out to me from the ground.*"

Employment of Biblical Verses

There are frequent examples of biblical passages whose entire context is recited in our *Siddur,* but of which this rite has extracted only the opening phrase or one sentence. Thus, only the first half of the verse *Va-yehi bi-nso'a ha-aron* (Numbers 10:35) is recited (p. 12), and only the two verses *Zeh eiliy ve-anveihu . . .* and *Ha-shem ish milchamah . . .* from the Song of the Red Sea (Exodus 15:1–19), which we read in its entirety. This is particularly so in the case of the Book of Psalms, which the Ethiopian liturgists greatly relied upon.

There is a parallel to our *chazan's* summons to the congregation to "Bless the Lord who is to be blessed" *(Borakhu et ha-shem ha-mevorakh).* This reads as follows: "And now, you people of the Lord, arise, stand, and bless the Lord our God, and all the holy beings that are with Him."

The affirmation *Amen* occurs only once, and the double affirmation, *Amen ve-amen,* but a few times, though not in the context of a response to a blessing. Indeed, there are no blessings in this liturgy in the form that we have them. A statement may open with the phrase *Barukh ha-shem* ("Blessed be God who . . ."), but there is no closing blessing or doxology.

While we generally invoke only the merit of the three forefathers in our blessings *(zekhut avot),* this is not the case in the Ethiopian rite, as the following quotation will demonstrate:

> Furthermore I say: For the Lord do I wait patiently with great desire, that there may come to rest upon me the blessing of Adam, Abel, and Seth, the blessings of Enoch, Noah, and Shem—all chosen individuals—as well as the blessings of Abraham, Isaac, and Jacob, the veritable "trees of the Lord's garden." Also, the blessings of Moses, Aaron, and all the prophets; the blessings of the Cherubim, the Seraphim, and all the heavenly Watchers (p. 18).

Of special interest is the inclusion, in two passages of their prayers (p. 22), of a potted biblical history, providing a kind of "Chain of Tradition" similar to that of the first chapter of the Ethics of the Fathers.

It contains some surprising and confused elements, as well as some unique traditions. Having referred to the creation of Adam and Eve, it continues, "And Abel and Seth and Yered were born." Yered was, of course, not a child of that generation, but a son of Mahalalel, the fourth generation from Seth (Genesis 5:16)! Why Yered should have been singled out is also mystifying. Jacob's ladder is said to have been made of gold; Elijah is described as "Elijah the Priest" and the duration of the drought in his day is stated to have been "three years and seven months" (cf. I Kings 18:1). Samuel is referred to as *ha-kohein ve-ha-navi* ("the priest and prophet"), and he is accredited with having written the Book of Judges, as well as his own book (p. 22), which accords exactly with the talmudic view.[1]

Isaiah is described as being "more exalted in his words than all the prophets of Israel, through the facility (literally, "sweetness") of his phraseology."

A rather confusing statement is that "Ezra and Setuel saw a vision, and when the city of Israel fell, and the children of Zion were taken captive, they wept and uttered lamentation over her" (p. 22). We have no tradition regarding a prophet by the name of Setuel, and the reference to Ezra living at the beginning of the Babylonian captivity cannot possibly be chronologically sustained. The father of the prophet Habakkuk is named as "Deker." The source of such a tradition is unknown.

The Messianic Era

The Ethiopian *Siddur* also contains an account of what is to occur in the messianic era:

> And when the epochs of this world will have been completed there will be a cataclysm on earth, bringing with it famine, drought, and plague. Sages and men of understanding will perish, the Fast Day will be abolished, and the new moons and special days, Sabbaths and festivals, will be altered. After this, Elijah will arrive and will set everything aright. He will proclaim a period of fifty-three years, after which the heavens and earth will come to an end, the sun, moon, and stars will fall from the heavens, and God will descend together with His angels.

> God will then say to Michael: Arise and sound the horn on Mount Sinai and on Mount Zion, the holy city. (With great awe the angels will glorify

Him. Their prince and leader, whose name is Michael, has dovelike eyes; his garments are lightning. He alone leads them.)

Then will the dead rise up in an instant, at the sound of Michael, and from afar they will worship the Holy One. The near angels will also worship the Lord and revere Him. God will then exchange heaven and earth, as one exchanges a garment, and gather together in an instant all the beings ever created.

They will be weeping bitterly as God separates the righteous from the wicked, and the pure from the impure.

They will then bring two bullocks, one from the east and one from the west. The name of the first is *chesed* (kindness), and the name of the second, *rachamim* (mercy). They will slaughter them with their own hands, and hew them in pieces for a blessing. King David will play on his harp and Ezra will offer a praise (from among his praises). Evildoers will then be annihilated, that they may not see the exaltedness of God. Then the righteous will enter for the heavenly banquet and for eternal life.

Numinous Hymns

A few compositions partake of that special mystical, rhythmic construction that we categorize as *numinous hymns.*[2] These may be defined as "irrational glorifications of God, whose sole purpose is to attempt to reproduce in words a formula that is calculated to induce emotionally an ecstatic state from which must automatically flow a keen sense of great mysterium."[3] Such poems "pulsate with a mesmeric rhythm, created by the unbroken regularity of the two stresses in each short line . . . and, when chanted against a background of drums and to the accompaniment of ritual dancing, was the type of song that would have been employed in biblical times by members of the prophetic guilds in order to engender a trance to aid their emotional climb toward a mystical experience."[4]

We know that the Ethiopian Jews used singing and dancing in their worship[5]; and, with their millennial African environment, the tribal dance genre would very likely have been appropriated.

The following quotation from their *Siddur* (p. 18) will convey the numinous spirit and rhythm infusing the composition, thereby putting it into the same genre as hymns like *Ha-adderet ve-ha-emunah*, and the six hymns that follow it, in our Yom Kippur prayer book.[6] Notwithstanding the fact that this hymn has been transcribed from Ge'ez into Halévy's Hebrew, the essential rhythm is unmistakable:

Gadol Ha-Shem, nora ha-shem, ram ha-shem,
Mekhubad ha-shem, adir ha-shem, chazak ha-shem,
Tahor ha-shem, tov ha-shem, tzaddik ha-shem,
Chay ha-shem, barukh ha-shem. . . .

A similar rhythmic beat underlies another numinous hymn (p. 11):

Ha-shem eloheinu, ha-shem echad;
Ha-shem malkeinu, ha-shem echad;
Ha-shem boreinu, ha-shem echad;
Ha-shem shomreinu, ha-shem echad;
Ha-shem roeinu, ha-shem echad. . . .

The section headed "Prayer at the offering of the sacrifice" (p. 25) is introduced by the following rubric:

After flaying the animal, they shall lift up the fat and cast it into the fire upon the altar; and as the flame ascends heavenwards the people shall all cry out, in unison, as follows:
Just as You accepted the sacrifice of Abel, so accept ours;
Just as You accepted the sacrifice of Eleazar, so accept ours;
Just as You heard the prayer of David, so hear ours;
Just as You delighted in the ministrations of Aaron, so delight in ours.[7]

There are great similarities between the liturgy of the Samaritans[8] and those of the Ethiopians, as might be expected from two traditions that trace their origins to the same early period of Israelite history and that have both remained immune to the mainstream trends and influences of talmudic Judaism and the literary stimuli—internal and external—that shaped the distinctive character of the medieval *piyyut*.

The above survey of some of the features of the Ethiopian *Siddur* is far from exhaustive. It is hoped, however, that it will provide some general idea of its main characteristics and themes, and perhaps encourage some further research into the liturgical expression of a segment of the Israelite nation whose mode of worship must surely help to shed light on the nature and spirit of early Jewish prayer—perhaps from the First Temple period—about which we have so little knowledge.

Part II

The Theology

8

Man's Dialogue with God

Does God Answer Prayer?

It is appropriate to open this section of our book by posing the perennial theological question: Does God answer prayer? Before it can be answered, however, another, far more basic, question must be put: Does God *answer*? Man expects answers to his questions, immediate answers. He assumes that, in matters of social intercourse, his preemptive role as the initiator of a question automatically puts him in the privileged position of master, whose summons demands a prompt response.

To ignore a question or request is grossly insulting because, primarily, it is antisocial. It is a rejection of an overture of communication. This cannot, obviously, be applied to God. He is not a social being. He cannot be *engaged* in conversation. He cannot be verbally preempted so that a response becomes expected of Him. He is not governed by, or tied to, the physical laws of cause and effect, thrust and parry, action and reaction, question and answer. Thus, when humans plead for their personal needs, it is naive to expect *a response*. God does not *respond* to man; He is always the initiator. He is aware of the crisis faced by the pleading individual even before the latter is plunged into it. And He determines its course even before the sufferer has opened his mouth in petition: "Before they call to me, I will answer" (Isaiah 65:24).

So the question "Does God answer prayer?" is a vain question, as vain as asking whether or not God exists, and, if He does, whether He is omniscient. The only possible reply, however perplexing, is, no, He does not answer *anything*. Yet—as we shall demonstrate later—this certainly does not mean that we should abandon the activity of prayer as a fruitless exercise.

But even according to the popularly understood expectation that God should accede to human petitions in His role of "Merciful and Gracious Lord," we still have to clarify the concept of God "answering" prayers. Presumably what is expected is that God should take into account the earnestness of our resolve and the merit of our righteousness, and that He should be moved to pity at the sight of our abject distress and anxiety, and alter, accordingly, whatever severe decree He had determined. This is, after all, the burden of our High Holyday expression of *teshuvah and tefillah*.

But let us test this logically. Are we entitled to assume that the person who enjoys a year of health and prosperity, from one Rosh Hashanah to the next, has been granted that exclusively on account of the impression made upon God by his prayers and repentance? Now say, one year, he is prevented, through illness, from praying or attending synagogue. Would he be forfeiting thereby his chance of a good year? Does God only "answer" when a "question" or "plea" is directed toward Him? Our comments above should already have disposed of that suggestion.

So, we may ask, what then *is* the purpose of prayer and petition? In an attempt to answer this, we would do well to take another look at a midrashic idea with which we are all familiar, that of God opening three books on Rosh Hashanah: one for the totally righteous, one for the totally wicked, and one for the average person.[1] The names in the first book are immediately inscribed for life; those in the second are immediately inscribed for dire punishment; and those in the third are granted a suspended sentence, until Yom Kippur, to see which side of the scale they will tip.

In the context of our particular discussion, this midrash raises an important question: If the righteous and the wicked are *immediately* inscribed, then surely we are neutralizing, if not negating, the efficacy of the High Holydays? Why does God not wait until after Yom Kippur to see if the wicked will be moved to remorse and sincere repentance through prayer?

Furthermore, the midrash seems to be suggesting that the truly righteous do not need the *teshuvah* and *tefillah* of the High Holydays, as they are inscribed for life *immediately!* Either way, prayer is relegated to a subsidiary role as a means of influencing God.

This midrash does truly place prayer in a position of minor importance in the context of our relationship with God. Prayer is of no use if it is merely a cry of despair, a call from fear, a sigh from a breaking heart, a lifeline to seize when crisis looms. That is not prayer; that is lamentation. Prayer can never be a final gasp. On the contrary, it has to be a token of awakening, an expression of a dawning sense of spiritual well-being, of peace and inner serenity, a sensitivity to the unity of all existence and its absorption in God. Prayer must flow from our lips, almost involuntarily, as a sigh of love and appreciation for all God's benefits to us. And perhaps this is how we may justify prayer in Hebrew for those who cannot understand the words.

Prayer is an emotion. The Hebrew formulae do have a significance, but that is secondary to their more basic purpose as a stimulus to our emotions, for which the words are mere husks. Like magical incantations or rhythmic beats, even if the words are unintelligible, they do generate spiritual sensations. Perhaps this is also how we justify the frequent experience of prayers unthinkingly gushing forth from the mouths of regular worshipers. Prayer is, indeed, a spontaneous activity; and if, amid all the welter of words, we are only aware, at the end of a service, of having expressed one emotion, the one enunciated on the very first page of the *Siddur*—"Lord, I love the habitation of Thy house, and the place where Thy glory dwelleth"—then we can still say we have truly prayed.

Is Prayer Really Necessary?

We have just hinted at the difficulty posed by the concept of God *answering* prayer, since a human call is certainly not required in order to rouse God to response and action.

From this line of thought flows the inevitable question: If God is always the initiator, if He decides, judges and acts, with perfect righteousness, independently of our prompting, what, then, is the point of prayer and petition?

The simple answer is that petition, or begging for mercy and forgiveness of sin, is only one facet of prayer. There are far higher forms, such as the praise that wells forth from the heart of one who longs to express his gratitude and love of God.

The latter kind of prayer does not wait upon any divine *response*. On the contrary: it is, itself, a response—to the stimuli of God's presence wooing the soul of the spiritually sensitive.

But there is also an intermediate rung between the latter, ideal prayer, on the one hand, and the purely self-centered prayer of petition and entreaty, on the other. Our tradition distinguishes between "love of God" *(ahavat ha-shem)* and "fear of God" *(yirat ha-shem)*.

Maimonides defines "love of God" in this way:

> When a man reflects upon God's wondrous and vast acts of creation, and perceives how unique and unlimited they are, he instinctively comes to love, praise, and glorify the Almighty, and to have a great yearning to know Him; just as King David said: "My soul thirsts for the living God."

On "fear of God," Maimonides continues:

> When a man studies those divine achievements analytically, he is immediately overwhelmed and overawed by the knowledge of how puny and lowly a creature he is, and how restricted is his own knowledge by comparison with the Omniscient One. As King David said: "When I see Your heavens, the work of Your fingers, what is man that Thou art mindful of him or the son of man that Thou takest account of him?"[2]

These two "responses" to God's existence and power have each generated their own respective genres of prayer. "Love of God" is responsible for having created the unsophisticated, spontaneous outpourings that characterize so many of the psalms, particularly the selection recited in the first part of our morning service, the *Pesukey Dezimrah* (verses of praise).

On the other hand, "fear of God"—as defined by Maimonides—has generated a genre of prayer characterized by an almost Kierkegaardian intensity of self-conscious restlessness and despairing self-deprecation, as the following passage from our early morning prayers will demonstrate:

> At all times let a man fear God, in private as well as in public. Let him acknowledge the truth . . . and say: Sovereign of all the worlds. . . . What are we? What is our life? What is our piety? What is our righteousness? What our success? What our strength? What our might? What shall we say before Thee, O Lord our God and God of our fathers? Are not all the mighty men as nought before Thee, the men of fame as though they had never existed, the wise as if without knowledge, and the men of understanding as if devoid of discernment? For most of their achievement

is inconsequential before Thee, and the preeminence of man over the beast is an illusion, for all its vanity.

Our initial difficulty is now, if not resolved, at least put into perspective. All prayer cannot be discredited merely because God's foreknowledge of our predicament ought to render any pleading on our part dilatory, if not superfluous.

We have seen that there is more to prayer than its utilitarian value. It is there to reflect our sense of *fear*, anger, and inadequacy, as well as our need of God's guidance. It is also there to express our *love* of God, our admiring praise of His handiwork and creative wisdom, as well as our thanksgiving.

But the above considerations have still not totally solved our initial problem. There are, after all, occasions when we *do* call upon God to reverse His harsh decree, to save us, to "allow His mercy to conquer His anger."

Might it not be suggested that the very expression of such a plea is not only vain, but an effrontery to the notion of the absolute righteousness of all God's decisions?

Can Prayer Help to Alter God's Just Verdict?

One answer to the above problem may be sought within the context of the biblical episodes of the Golden Calf, the spies, and the rebellion of Korach. On each of these occasions Moses petitioned God to set aside the grave verdict to destroy the people, and to deal mercifully.

Moses adduced various arguments in support of his plea for mitigation of sentence; and, in one instance, the Torah makes the rather surprising statement that, in response to Moses' pleading, "God *repented of the evil* which He had intended doing to His people" (Exodus 32:14).

Now, since it is obvious that the omniscient God knew in advance all the arguments Moses would adduce, we must conclude that God had not, in fact, decided upon an irrevocable sentence. His initial response had been intended merely to convey the gravity of the crime and to indicate the sentence that *ought* to be carried out in the absence of any plea of mitigation.

It was, from the outset, however, God's plan that Moses should act as counsel for the defense, representing, in effect, God's own attribute of mercy, which Moses was granted the privilege of activating.

Thus, even the prayer of petition has validity; for we know not the moment when the conditional divine decree becomes absolute. As long as reconciliation is still possible, petition will be efficacious.

No better argument could be offered for the value of regular worship. For if there *is* a moment when God is not only amenable to, but positively desirous of, our pleas for mercy, then it only makes sense to keep the lines of communication continually open.

A similar, philosophical approach to the question posed above — how can prayer help to alter God's just verdict? — is to argue that God's mind is never actually changed, since it is never categorically made up to punish man. God's absolute love for His children must mean that His delight and desire is to forgive them when they show signs of remorse and a sincere resolve to abandon their evil ways: "God desires those that fear Him, those that wait for His mercy" (Psalm 147:11). When the Talmud states that "a cry to God is of benefit to man both before as well as after the decree had been uttered," it is suggesting, in effect, that there simply cannot be an immutable divine decree to hurt His children.

God's "verdict" is never "altered" then. Prayer is a demonstration that *man* has altered. The "verdict" given was based exclusively upon the circumstances of the time, namely before prayer, before remorse, before the authentic realization of the sufferer that the fate he is now seeking to escape from had been imposed upon him because of his evil deeds that had distanced him from God.

But this turning toward God in prayer, this fluttering of con-science, means that *man* has altered, and the *circumstances* have also, consequently, altered. God now has before Him a person with a new heart, someone quite different from the one who elicited the original harsh decree. Thus, the answer to our problem is, quite simply, that prayer creates a new man, whereas God's verdict was imposed upon the old one. The man, not the verdict, has changed.

However, once the punishment has been activated — in the absence of any sincere change of heart, other than, perhaps, a mere prayer of anguish, like the cry of a drowning man for help — then divine mercy cannot be expected. "If someone, on approaching his home, hears the sound of tumult, and prays, 'May the trouble not be at *my* home' — that is a vain prayer."[3]

The rabbis offered a variety of explanations to account for the problem of why our matriarchs, Sarah, Rebekah, and Rachel — women of unsurpassing piety and faith — were subjected for so long to the psycho-logical traumas of barrenness, particularly in an age when that unfortunate state was regarded as the greatest curse, one that consequently justified divorce.

Of the several explanations offered, it was the statement of Rabbi Yochanan that is the most frequently quoted: "Why were the matriarchs afflicted with barrenness? – Because God yearned to hear their prayers and petitions."[4]

Rabbi Elimelech Bar Shaul, late chief rabbi of Rechovot, taking this explanation quite literally, amplifies Rabbi Yochanan's statement:

> God says, "If I give them children they will not pray to me." The barrenness comes only to bring out the prayers. This is like a king who greatly liked one of his servants. The king would summon him frequently, on the slightest pretext, so that he could enjoy his servant's company. The king was upset, however, by the realization that, once the servant had left his presence to go about his work, the latter never gave the king a thought. The king therefore ordered that all the servant's meals should be served at the royal table, so that whenever the servant was hungry he would, out of necessity, have to come to the king. And at that time the king would see him and be happy.[5]

This is a philosophically perplexing suggestion and analogy, for it implies that, somehow, God desperately needs to have man seek Him out. He needs man to be reliant upon Him; He needs to feel needed! We can hardly sustain a concept of a God who is unfulfilled without man's regular assurances, without acting the role of benefactor.

Without compromising Rabbi Yochanan's statement, we suggest that he was proposing a slightly more complex idea. He leaves us, in fact, to ask the question *why* God yearned to hear the prayers of the matriarchs.

And the answer to that question must be that God wants us to pray because only through that exercise do *we* reach spiritual fulfillment. Without prayer we will always remain insecure and isolated – even if surrounded by a brood of children. The servant in the parable behaved irresponsibly by his condescending attitude to his king. He didn't appreciate what the king's favor conferred, and what his displeasure might bring. But the king was great enough not to take the rebuff personally. It was, after all, in the nature of servants to become totally preoccupied with their heavy tasks. It was inevitable that the feelings could not be reciprocated, quite apart from the social chasm that divided them.

God craved for the matriarchs' prayers only because He desired them to achieve spiritual confidence and happiness, not because He *needed* their expressions of dependence. God needs nothing of man, though He demands much. And all His demands are predicated upon what will ultimately accrue to *our* well-being, *our* peace of mind, through the realization of *our* spiritual potential. Knowing that without His help we cannot attain our objectives – either temporal or spiritual – God insists that we "dine at His table," that we communicate frequently through prayer, so that God is enabled to be with us at all times. We cannot forget Him; we live our lives encompassed by His spirit. We converse with Him, and we gain confidence in the conviction that He will always answer.

God's Response

We referred above to the problem of whether or not it is vain for us to pray for mercy or deliverance, since God has certainly foreseen our predicament, and decided upon it with perfect justice, long before we ourselves were even aware of an impending crisis.

We offered the suggestion that the human cry for mercy in such circumstances is, indeed, an essential factor in the divine judicial process, and that God does allow His judgment to be influenced by it. It may be assumed, however, that God is not moved merely by the poignancy or extent of such pleas, but that He searches for some corresponding resolve and resolution underpinning the anguished appeal. God inevitably listens out for some deeper vibrations that will convince Him that the trials and crises have truly served to effect a spiritual transformation – and, with it, a new outlook on life – on the part of the suppliant. In such circumstances, God will be satisfied that the person's continued existence will be of positive value to himself, to society, and to those for whom his torment would provide an edifying example.

In the enigmatic area of the criteria God employs to grant or withhold mercy this point might well be noted; for it is possible that some, even undeserving, people are granted a release merely in order that they may serve as examples to preserve others from error and sin. After all, if all the unworthy were peremptorily consigned to an early grave, we would all become either saints through fear, or nihilists through despair. Neither of these, however, is in conformity with the divinely given challenge of a truly free choice, on the one hand, and the promise of salvation through optimistic faith, on the other. So we require the continued existence of those who have sinned, suffered, and been saved, so that their experiences may serve as a cautionary moral influence upon us as we determine whether to exercise our free will for good or evil.

Perhaps this is the real message of the episode of Jonah being swallowed up in the belly of the great fish. That is precisely where Jonah deserved to die for his defiance of God. But he was granted a release for the reason that others were going to be influenced to repentance through him. It is conceivable that the Ninevites' immediate repentance was occasioned by their reaction to the report of Jonah's awesome experience and his miraculous deliverance. Ironically, Jonah's rejection of his mission assured its ultimate success! Significantly, Jonah prayed to God from the belly of the fish. His prayer was answered, but not on his own account—rather because of a mission to others that he was ideally placed to fulfill.

We have hitherto been referring primarily to the prayers for life and mercy offered by, or on behalf of, a repentant sinner. Such prayers may be "answered" for very practical reasons, unrelated to the exclusive fate of the particular petitioner, but rather in order that he may live to become an agency for effecting God's wider purpose.

The idea that God may be constrained to save, not only an individual but even a nation, in order to carry out a wider purpose, is presupposed in the plea of Moses on behalf of the worshipers of the Golden Calf, and in the arguments adduced by Moses to secure divine mercy:

> And Moses interceded with God: "O Lord," he said, "why shouldst Thou vent Thy anger upon Thy people, whom Thou didst bring out of Egypt with great power and a strong hand? Why let the Egyptians say, 'So He meant to kill them in the mountains, and wipe them off the face of the earth, when He took them out'? . . . Remember Abraham, Isaac, and Israel, Thy servants, to whom Thou didst swear by Thine own self: 'I will make Thy posterity countless as the stars in the sky, and all this land, of which I have spoken, I will give to them, and they shall possess it for ever.' " So the Lord relented, and spared His people the evil with which He had threatened them.
>
> (Exodus 32:11-14)

Moses' plea for mercy is clearly predicated on the assumption that God could not possibly impose strict justice on the sinful nation because of wider, overriding, moral considerations.

Thus, the circumstances under which God "answers" prayer, and the motivation for doing so, emerge as complex and varied. Frequently,

He *has* to answer, because not to do so would either frustrate His own comprehensive plan for individual, national, or global destiny, or, simply, because the consequences of not answering would be to create a far greater moral outrage than that of saving one who is undeserving.

But how about prayers for purely personal wants, whereby no wider advantage could be envisaged? Does God answer prayers for wealth and good fortune, success in personal relationships, exams, and so on?

Striking biblical examples of purely personal prayers are those uttered by a number of our barren matriarchs when they prayed for children. One aspect of Hannah's plea for a child is especially noteworthy.

> Hannah made a vow in these words: "O Lord of Hosts . . . if Thou wilt not forget me, but grant me offspring, then I will give the child to the Lord for his whole life."
>
> (I Samuel 1:11)

Hannah was clearly attempting to strike a bargain with God, to convince Him that it was in His wider interests to answer her prayer. Any son born to her would be a man of God. He would be an exemplar to others; he would aid God's purpose on earth. The inference is that Hannah was constrained to make this offer; she did not think that, purely on her own merit, God would answer her prayer.

The answer to our question that now emerges is that purely personal requests are considered by God not merely in terms of whether or not to gratify our selfish desires, but rather in relation to their overall effect on us and, more especially, to the purpose to which they will be employed, if granted.

We must not forget that if we pray and do not have our prayer fulfilled, it is never because God does not answer, but rather because the answer is "no."

What Prayer Achieves

By means of our thrice-daily prayers we invest our workaday activity with a mantle of spirituality. *Shacharit* lays a sacred foundation for the day's tasks ahead; *Minchah* interrupts them in full swing, in early afternoon, cautioning us against total absorption with our material objectives. *Maariv* serves to climax the day's activity, emphasizing that we do not live to work, but rather work to live a happy and dignified life in the service of God.

Viewed in this light, daily prayer can also constitute a safety valve, to ensure that we do not lose our individuality in the face of the monotonous regimen of a working routine to which so many of us are subjected.

In this age of sophisticated automation, when so many people are constrained to undertake unimaginative, even "soul-destroying" employment, and when they can so easily be reduced to mere code numbers on a computer punch-out, or time check-in card, it becomes increasingly necessary to find some truly effective means of restoring their individuality and reviving their soul and their flagging spirit. Regular communication with the personal God can supply this urgent requirement.

But prayer interacts with our working lives at the philosophical level also. This may best be explained on the analogy with the *Birkot Ha-Nehenin,* the blessings we recite before enjoying the various gifts of nature. Before eating and drinking, for example, the *berakhah* we make serves to consecrate and elevate that basic physical activity so that the latter becomes subordinated to the higher purpose of providing us with a reason and stimulus for praising the Creator for His bounty.

Now, this bounty that we enjoy is by no means ours by right. This consideration underlies an interesting talmudic passage that draws attention to an apparent contradiction between two biblical verses:

The Psalmist states: "To *the Lord* belongs *the earth* and the fullness thereof" (Psalm 24:1). Yet in another verse he asserts that "the heavens are the Lord's heavens, but *the earth* he has given to the *children of men*" (Psalm 115:16).

The Talmud harmonizes these verses by stating that the first verse reflects the situation before man has uttered a *berakhah,* while the second verse refers to the situation which obtains after the recitation of a *berakhah.*[6] Thus, the *berakhah,* in some mystical way, serves as a combination to unlock to man the doors of the divine treasury. Our right to enjoy the fruits of God's earth is secured by means of the *berakhah,* perhaps because through it we are acknowledging that it *is* His earth and that we are merely tenants enjoying the usufruct.

That exegetical contradiction can also be extended to apply to the far more central concept of the Jewish way of life: Does the fact that "to the Lord belongs the earth" mean that we should spend our days on earth pursuing spiritual affairs and studying Torah? Or does the concession implied in the verse "the earth He has given to the children of men" allow us to immerse ourselves into worldly endeavors?

This issue was hotly debated in early talmudic times. The Yavneh school of Rabbi Yochanan ben Zaccai adopted an attitude of compromise toward the necessity for man to pursue a worldly occupation. They were fond of reciting the following formula, described by the Talmud as "a pearl in their mouths":

> I (who study Torah all day) am God's creature, and my fellow (out at work) is His creature. My work is in the city; his work is in the field. I rise early to my work, and he, likewise, rises early to his. Just as he cannot boast of being able to do my work, so I cannot boast of being able to do his. And in case you disciples ever say, "But I study much Torah while he studies little!"—have we not learnt that, whether you study much or little (reward is yours), providing you direct your heart to your Father in heaven.[7]

This approach was vehemently contested, however, by a later sage, Rabbi Shimeon bar Yochai, who maintained that to embrace a worldly occupation was a categorical rejection of the life of Torah. This sage could not conceive of any possible accommodation between the spiritual and temporal life. He even asserted that, had he been around at the time, he would have advised God to create man with two mouths, one of which would be reserved exclusively for Torah communication! One of Shimeon bar Yochai's most oft quoted statements is the one he uttered on emerging from the cave wherein he had taken refuge from the Romans for thirteen years. On seeing people active in the fields, sowing and reaping, he exclaimed, "They are deserting eternal life *(chayyey olam)* and occupying themselves with transient experiences *(chayyey shaah).*"[8]

If the great divide—between our worldly and materialistic lives, on the one hand, and the ideal Torah spirituality, on the other—can, in any sense, be bridged, it is by means of blessings and prayer. Prayer is the antidote to the drug of materialism; it is a red light to the workaholic. It restores the balance between the two opposing biblical concepts of "the earth being the Lord's" and "the earth being given to the children of men."

Just as, through the instrument of the blessings, our seizure and enjoyment of the fruits of God's earth is condoned, so, likewise, does prayer serve as a medium of justification for our having dedicated most of our waking hours to *chayyey shaah*, spiritually unproductive activity.

Regular *tefillah* interlaces our workaday activities with a web of holiness. It serves to superimpose a *chayyey olam* upon our mundane *chayyey shaah*:

> And in case you disciples ever say, "But I study much Torah while he studies little!"—have we not learnt that whether you study much or little (reward is yours), providing you direct your heart to your Father in heaven.

In prayer we fulfill this last condition. Prayer is the greatest spiritual equalizer.

9

Preparation for Prayer

Cleanliness Next to Godliness

Our religious codes have established many detailed regulations governing all aspects of worship, many of which have the sole purpose of facilitating *kavvanah*, religious concentration and meditation.

It was appreciated that no such concentration was possible if the worshiper was being distracted by any physical discomfort. Hence the ruling that an incontinent person may not pray, neither may one who requires to attend without delay to the needs of nature, nor one suffering from congestion of the lungs who requires constantly to expectorate.

The necessity for physical preparedness was inferred by one talmudic sage[1] from a literal rendering of Amos 4:12: "Prepare *your self* (i.e., your body) to meet your God." A clean body was regarded as a prerequisite for worship. Before the morning service, face, hands, and feet should be washed; before the afternoon and evening services, only the hands.

In many of our present-day synagogues a laver is provided in the foyer, though one rarely sees any queue to perform this prescribed ablution. We obviously require to be reminded of the truth of the maxim that "cleanliness is next to godliness." As far as the laws of preparation for worship are concerned, cleanliness is a prerequisite for godliness.

Ritual Immersion

This being the case, there is one intimate area that seems to represent an unusual exception to this rule, and that is in the freedom granted to those who have had marital relations to pray the next morning without either ritual immersion or even bathing.[2] According to Maimonides, it was only in Babylon and Spain that the communities adopted "the custom" of bathing the whole body, even though this was not required by law.

This lenient attitude is all the more surprising when viewed in relation to biblical law (Leviticus 15:16–18), which prescribed that after any nocturnal emission a person had to undergo *tevillah* (immersion), and wait until sunset before being regarded as pure.

An explanation of why the rabbis relaxed this law, shortly before the destruction of the Temple, may perhaps be sought in the context of a dispute between the Pharisees and the leaders of a pietistic sect called *Tovelei Shacharit*, Morning Bathers.[3] This sect laid inordinate emphasis upon ritual immersion as a prelude to every act of worship. They bitterly denounced the Pharisees for "mentioning God's name in prayer each morning without immersion."[4]

The talmudic references to this obscure sect disclose nothing of their origins, theology, or way of life. It is certain, however, that they were an Essene group; and their criticism of the Pharisees may have stemmed from their espousal of the traditions of those Essene communities that practiced sexual abstinence in an all-consuming desire to maintain themselves in a permanent state of purity.

We offer the suggestion, therefore, that mainstream Pharisaism, as part of a concerted effort to promote marriage—and to counter this sect's view that it was inimical to the state of purity—felt constrained to give official sanction to the already widely practiced relaxation of the biblical law. The average Jew was henceforth able to practice his daily religious duties within the context of a regular and uncomplicated marital association.

It should not be forgotten that it was at that period, in the middle of the 1st century C.E., that the institution of the synagogue assumed a dominant position in Jewish life, and attendance at public worship began to be regarded as the mark of a religious Jew.

Thus, a need must have been felt for legislation to enable people to attend synagogue every morning without having to disclose, by their absence, details of the frequency of their marital intimacies.

Clean Surroundings

Clean surroundings are rigidly prescribed as a prerequisite for prayer. Maimonides states that "if someone, after finishing his prayers, discovers there some dung, he has sinned in not examining the area beforehand, and he must repeat his prayers in a clean place."[5] The Talmud also relates that some sages would refuse to pray in a place that, although perfectly clean, was yet pervaded by any foul odor caused by fermenting food or drink.

The demanding standards of hygiene that Jews set themselves throughout the ages are axiomatic. It was these regulations, ensuring daily attention to physical cleanliness before engaging in prayer, that played a major part in molding our sensitivity in this area. Which other religion would ever have thought of making a religious ritual out of attending to the needs of nature, as did Judaism when it prescribed a ritual washing of the hands and a recitation of a special blessing thanking God for the intricate mechanism of the bodily functions?

Appropriate Attire

Appropriate attire during prayer was also insisted upon. One talmudic sage, Rav Kahana, took this to such lengths that he endeavored to dress for prayer in a manner that accurately reflected his state of mind. During periods of trouble or persecution he would wear simple, somber clothing, but during peaceful and happy interludes he would pray dressed in his finest robes.[6]

Maimonides recommends this policy of wearing the type of clothing that best serves to stimulate one's emotions:

One should prepare the garments one is to wear for prayer well in advance, with a view to making oneself appear as distinguished and good-looking as possible, in conformity with the verse, "Worship the Lord *in the beauty of holiness.*"[7]

Maimonides is clearly referring here to a period of peace and prosperity, and he follows Rav Kahana in recognizing the psychological boost to a person's spirit that the wearing of new or impressive clothing can provide. It was for this reason that Jewish Law prescribes that a man should buy for his wife and daughters fine new dresses for *Yom Tov,* so that they will be put into a happy frame of mind and better able to fulfill the *mitzvah* of *Simchat Yom Tov,* "rejoicing on a festival."

Those who are disposed to criticize our ladies' galleries, on occasions, for resembling a fashion parade, may now have to think again!

How Often Do We Really Pray?

If one were to ask a religious Jew how frequently he prayed, he would most certainly treat the question as an insult. "Obviously, three times a day!" would be his curt reply. But if a close confidant were to ask him candidly how frequently he *truly* prayed—how often, in synagogue, he really felt that he was communing with God, how often he was transported into higher realms of experience to the extent that he became oblivious to his surroundings, how often he came away exhausted, not by the length of the service, but by the emotional effort and concentration involved in the act of worship—it is doubtful whether he could give that same smug answer.

The truth is that it is on fairly rare occasions during the year that most people emerge from prayer with anything approximating the sensation of being truly moved spiritually. A midnight *Selichot* service, a *Shacharit* prayed at four in the morning following an all-night *Tikkun Leil Shavuot* study vigil, a *Kol Nidrei* or *Neilah* service, possibly a Friday night service—those occasions stand the best chance of penetrating the soul. The reason for this is that they take place at a time when we have been, or will be, divorced from the everyday routine of our workaday lives for a considerable period of time, and are therefore more able, psychologically, to liberate ourselves from the distracting preoccupation with the mundane in order to surrender ourselves to contemplation of ultimate and eternal values.

Kavvanah and Its Problems

It is well-nigh impossible to dive out of bed at the sound of the alarm each morning, have a quick wash, shave, dress, and be in *shul* a quarter of an hour later expecting to be transported into spiritual realms and able to conduct a meaningful dialogue with one's Maker. It is similarly impossible to "drop in" to synagogue on the way home from work, for "a quick *Minchah* and *Maariv*," and for that to make any lasting religious impression. Prayer declines to cast its spell when it has to compete with the genies of time and routine.

This is not, however, a weakness in the institution of daily prayer. It is a concomitant of our modern pace of living, in which "time" has become enemy number one, wherein leisure hours have to be "filled" with activities, socials, and entertainment. Prayer is the casualty of that philosophy; for who would think of using his leisure time for extending the period he devotes to his prayers and for walking to and from synagogue each evening in contemplative mood, instead of breaking the speed limit to arrive "in the nick of time?" Thrice-daily prayer was the invention of a bygone age when people had time to discover them-selves, their neighbor—and God!

But even in periods when people followed a more leisurely pace, and had more time for prayer, there were other factors—such as illness and business worries—that inevitably arose to distract them from achieving the desired spiritual state of mind. The Talmud appreciated the problem:

> When praying (the *Amidah*) one must concentrate one's mind fully on every single blessing. If, however, he is unable to do that, he should, at least, concentrate his mind upon *Avot*—the first blessing.[8]

Maimonides accepts this concessionary approach as law.[9] And this could well serve as a guide for the uneducated Jew who finds it difficult to keep pace with the *chazan* and congregation, or for one who finds difficulty concentrating his whole attention and achieving any spiritual elation. The message is, clearly, that if one is able to recite only one paragraph of his prayers with full comprehension, concentration, and devotion, he has still satisfied the basic precondition for worship. He should employ that particular blessing or passage for which he is able to muster *kavvanah* (religious concentration) as the launching pad for his own devotional thoughts and meditations.

The Talmud does not offer an explanation as to why, if it does have to come to a choice, it is just the first blessing of the central *Amidah* that takes priority. From a comment of Rashi, on a similar point in the same context, we may infer a rationale.

The Talmud observes that "if a person makes a mistake in that first blessing of the *Amidah*, it is a bad omen for him; and if he is leading the service at the time, it is a bad omen for the congregation." Rashi notes that because that is the very commencement of the prayer, his lack of concentration at the very outset is an indication of his indifference to the spiritual task confronting him.

We may infer from this that the attitude of mind with which one commences one's act of worship is of paramount importance as an indicator of devotion. Feelings speak louder than words, and once the appropriate frame of mind, and conditions for spiritual communication, have been established, then we have already achieved one of the main objectives of prayer—self-consecration and a reaching out to our Father in heaven. Indeed, the *Mishnah* codifies this as an essential prerequisite for prayer: "One may not commence praying unless one is mentally attuned."[10]

Early Chasidic Preparations

Correct mental preparedness for prayer was the cornerstone of a pietistic movement in early talmudic times. That same mishnah recalls some "early *chasidim* who used to repair to synagogue an hour before the morning service commenced in order to direct their hearts to God." Unfortunately, we are not told what they did in order to achieve that state of spiritual readiness. The instinctive assumption is that they sat in silent and reverent meditation. The indications are, however, that this was not the case. Rabbi Yosi said, "Would that my heavenly reward was as great as for those who complete the psalms each day."[11]

It seems that Rabbi Yosi had in mind those "early *chasidim*," and his reference discloses the precise nature of their preparations, namely the recitation of the whole Book of Psalms.

We can now understand why we recite the last six psalms in the Book of Psalms during the first part of our morning service; for, by the time the ordinary worshipers began arriving, at the normal time for *Shacharit*, those *chasidim* were just finishing off the last few psalms in the book. The newly arrived worshipers would join with them in reciting the last few psalms; and, in the course of time, this custom became the norm, and developed into our *Pesukey Dezimrah*. Thus, what began as a pietistic stimulus to devotion, later served, ironically, as an obstacle to devotional concentration by causing the statutory service to be extended, thus providing too much for the ordinary folk to have to recite in a limited time.

There is of course one solution to our problem, and that is to commence our services an hour earlier each morning! But then, we're not all *chasidim!*

The Right Frame of Mind

Our halakhic codes lay great emphasis upon the importance of being in the right frame of mind for prayer. This is how the *Shulchan Arukh* expresses it:

> When a person prays he must think deeply about the meaning of the words he is expressing. He should imagine that the Divine Presence is close to him, and he should consequently banish from his mind all distracting thoughts, so that his concentration and intentions are clear and pure.
>
> Let him consider well that if he was addressing an earthly monarch he would rehearse his words perfectly in order not to become confused. How much more should he do so when in the presence of the King of all Kings, the Holy One, Blessed be He, who probes all our thoughts.
>
> Pious and holy men in the past would sit in solitary meditation, focussing their minds so sharply upon the prayers they were about to utter that they were able to divest themselves of any self-awareness, to achieve a mental, spiritual, and emotional state that was almost at the level of the prophetic.[12]

Maimonides totally discounts the value of any prayer that is uttered without proper concentration *(kavvanah)* and demands that such a prayer be repeated. If a person is so preoccupied with worry that concentration on prayer becomes impossible, Maimonides declares it *forbidden* for such a person to embark upon prayer until he feels more relaxed: "Therefore, if one has returned from a long and arduous journey and he is exhausted, he may wait up to three days before resuming the exercise of prayer."[13] While Karo quotes this opinion in his

Shulchan Arukh, yet he adds the significant caveat, "But nowadays we do not keep to all this, because it is recognized that our generations are actually incapable of proper devotional concentration when we pray."[14]

The Nature of *Kavvanah*

The type of *kavvanah* that our medieval authorities recommended is far from what we could expect to achieve. It is not merely a devotional concentration, but is rather a cognitive affirmation of all the religious ideas and word associations that underlie the liturgical phrases being uttered. These deeper strata of meaning and allusion are meant to flood into our mind while we are uttering the respective word or phrase that relates to them.

An example of what is required is provided by the statement in the Palestinian Talmud[15] that the three biblical paragraphs which comprise the *Shema* were so chosen because they also encapsulate the entire Ten Commandments.[16] On the basis of this, the *Be'er Heiteiv*[17] insists that, while reciting the phrases of the *Shema* that are associated with those specific commandments, we must have the particular commandment in mind and undertake an exercise of self-scrutiny to determine whether or not we have transgressed any of them. Thus, in the opening line of the *Shema,* the words *ha-shem eloheinu* correspond to the opening verse of the Ten Commandments, *Anokhi ha-shem elohekha.* The continuation, *ha-shem echad* ("The Lord is one"), corresponds to the continuation of the first commandment, "Have no other gods before Me." The phrase *Ve-ahavta* ("And you shall love the Lord your God") is related to the second Commandment—its concomitant—"Do not take the Lord's name in vain." The phrase *u-khetavtam* ("And you shall write them upon the doorposts of *your house*") is related, albeit by loose association, to "You shall not covet your *neighbor's house.*" The phrase *ve-asafta deganekha* ("You shall gather in *your* corn") is associated with "You shall not steal" (namely, do not take someone else's corn), and *ve-lo taturu* ("You shall not go astray after your hearts and after your eyes") corresponds to "You shall not commit adultery."

Thus, *kavvanah* of this kind will be seen to require not merely devotion, concentration, and serious intention, but also knowledge of the background to each prayer, the significance of each phrase and allusion, and, more difficult, the ability to think instantaneously at various levels of meaning. No wonder, then, that Karo acknowledged the inability of people in his generation to achieve such a comprehensive *kavvanah!*

But if true *kavvanah* does elude modern man, perhaps by reason of the distractions induced by the complexities and tensions of our domestic, social, and business lives, then it is reasonable to ask, with what we are expected to replace *kavvanah.* Surely *some* specific state of mind, mood, or emotional attitude must be recommended! A. J. Heschel provides some guidance on this question:

> The quality of a speech is not judged by the good intention of the speaker but by the degree to which it succeeds to simplify an idea and to make it relevant to others. In contrast, the goal of prayer is to simplify the self and to make God relevant to oneself. Thus, prayer is judged not by standards of rhetoric but by the good intention, by the earnestness and intensity of the person.

> Ultimately the goal of prayer is not to translate a word but to translate the self; not to render an ancient vocabulary in modern terminology, but to transform our thoughts into thoughts of prayer.[18]

So, while Karo has admitted that we may no longer be capable of a *kavvanah* that probes the mystical, labyrinthine depths of meaning underlying, or associated with, the formulae of our prayers, yet we *are* capable of replacing the *Siddur*-orientated *kavvanah* with a soul-orientated *kavvanah.* We *are* capable of attaining the goal of prayer as conceived by Heschel, namely "to simplify the self." The new *kavvanah,* for modern, sophisticated man, is the exercise of shedding his external facade, his pseudosophistication, his macho image, and truly "simplifying the self," abasing himself before the One who, in any case, penetrates beneath the multilayered protective veneer with which we camouflage our inner emptiness, helplessness, and ignorance.

If a visit to synagogue and an act of worship are just another social exercise; if we are still acting out a social role in the house of God, still conscious of who we are, of our rank, and of the respect due to us in recognition of it, then our prayers are devoid of *kavvanah.* If, on the other hand, we can attain to a sincere feeling of social anonymity, if we can feel at one with every worshiper present in the synagogue, whatever his age or station in life, if we can detect our ego deflating through the clear recognition of our own unworthiness, if we can, indeed, "translate the self" and "transform our thoughts"—thoughts of ourselves—"into thoughts of prayer," then we have truly attained to that ideal soul-orientated *kavvanah* that may in fact be more acceptable to God than a *Siddur*-orientated degree of devotional concentration. Prayer is, therefore, the most complete act of human self-surrender and submission to the total will and embrace of God. Only when we lose ourselves do we find God.

A Prayerful Life

If we are quite capable of leaving our prayers, intentions, and *kavvanah* behind us when we quit the synagogue, then we may doubt whether we have truly prayed. Effective prayer must have an effect. It must condition all our daily activities, our thoughts and intentions, our behavior, our speech. "Prayer must always be related to a *prayerful life!*"[19] Thus, the Jew who prays regularly signs with his lips a detailed and wide-ranging covenant. Prayer becomes more than a mere communication of words and concepts. In the act of praying, one presents before one's Maker a program for spiritual activity and commitment.

And by fulfilling all the terms of that covenant, by translating the spirit of our prayers into honest endeavor and service of fellow man and society, we extend the sacred act of prayer throughout our working day. In this way we fulfill the otherwise impossible instruction that "this Law shall not depart from your mouth, but you shall meditate therein by day and by night" (Joshua 1:8). Pursuing our mundane, workaday activities in the spirit of the Torah becomes an act of worship. Love of one's wife and family is not only expressed through an embrace or words of endearment. Working hard to feed them and to support them in a dignified and comfortable manner is an equally valid expression of concern and love. So it is with God. Prayer is love of God expressed through word. Performance of *mitzvot*, integrity, charity, and moral living is love of God expressed through deed. Both are acts of worship.

The concomitant of prayer must be a prayerful life. Similarly, the predominant emotion of pleasure and joy, at the privilege of being able to worship the Almighty, should also infuse one's whole attitude to life itself, to become a philosophy of optimistic faith. Hence the duty of "receiving all men with a cheerful countenance."[20] Pessimism betokens a lack of faith; joy is an affirmation of gratitude. Thus, when the Psalmist asks us to "serve God with joy,"[21] he not only means that we should be joyful while we are serving God, while we are at worship, but that spiritual joy should be, in itself, an act of worship.

The concept of a "prayerful life" must embrace the Jewish home experience; and for synagogue prayer to have achieved its purpose it must also have succeeded in injecting a tangible religious quality of living into the home. Solomon Schechter expresses it most succinctly:

> If, after frequent visits to places of worship, you have experienced nothing of the nearness of God in your houses, then you may safely doubt whether you have really been in a house of God. It is the home which is the final and supreme test of the synagogue. A synagogue, for instance, that teaches a Judaism which finds no reverberating echo in the Jewish home, awakens there no distinctive, conscious Jewish life, has failed in its mission, and is sure sooner or later to disappear as a religious factor making for righteousness and holiness. It may serve as a lecture hall or lyceum, or as a place to which people in their *ennui* repair for "an intellectual treat"; but it will never become a place of worship, a real altar for acceptable sacrifices, bestowing that element of joy in God—the *simchah shel mitzvah* of our rabbis—which is the secret and strength of Judaism.[22]

10

The Framework of Prayer

The Informality of the Synagogue

Punctuality at synagogue is not an Orthodox Jewish characteristic. To the faithful of other religions, the spectacle of a Shabbat morning service—with people filing in intermittently throughout the morning, talking, gesticulating to their wives in the gallery, standing in prayer while the congregation is sitting, and sitting while the rest are standing—is more reminiscent of a marketplace than a house of God! To point out to them that it was precisely in the marketplaces of ancient Judea that the first public services, with public readings of the Torah, made their debut would do little to alter their opinion of Jews as an irreverent group, and of the synagogue ritual as an incomprehensible and chaotic system.

The Reform tradition is an exception. That movement owes its origin as much to the desire for a more decorous, disciplined, and formal mode of expression as to the need for a more progressive theology. Ironically, most Orthodox Jews who have cause to attend a Reform service return with one criticism: "It is too dignified, respectful, and formal for a *shul!*"

The Orthodox synagogue has truly preserved the spirit of the

119

ancient Temple from which it developed. The Temple was a bustling center, with officials busily and noisily going about their various tasks— the High Priest and his deputy, ordinary priests, Levites, choristers, musicians, gatekeepers, guards, and porters. There was also a hierarchy of permanent officials responsible for organizing the duty rotas of priests and Levites. All members of the priestly clan belonged to one or other of the twenty-four *Mishmarot*, on duty at the Temple for one full week twice a year.[1]

A permanent administration was clearly necessary to supervise the weekly arrival and departure of those officials, to attend to their board and lodging within the Temple precincts and to the equitable distribution of duties among the members of each *Mishmar*. The permanent staff was led by the *amarkalim* (administrators) and the *gizbarim* (treasurers). The former held the keys of the various stores, and aided the latter in the specialized task of assessing the amount of redemption that had to be paid by those who had dedicated the value of people, animals, or objects to the Temple. Much of their time was also taken up with the purchase and examination of animals and birds for the regular sacrifices, and the sale of these to the public for individual offerings. The treasurers also had to oversee the affairs of the Temple money changers; and the noise and commotion which this particular facility generated, as coins were weighed and people quibbled over exchange rates, can well be imagined.

There were also the sundry folk who thronged the Temple each day: the individual donors with their atonement or thanksgiving offerings, and the obligatory offerings brought by women after childbirth and Nazarites on the completion of their period of abstention, as well as the gift of each firstborn animal, and one animal in ten as a tithe. There were also those who came in order to be the recipients of the priestly blessing each day, and others who came merely as spectators, visitors, or tourists.

It goes without saying, then, that the Temple was hardly the place for quiet contemplation. It was, rather, a noisy place, with people chattering excitedly, priests calling ritual instructions to each other as animals were being dispatched and prepared for the altar, with oxen lowing, sheep bleating, children crying, Levites singing, vendors advertising their souvenirs, beggars importuning, and witnesses and litigants arguing loudly as they made their way to the Chamber of Hewn Stones to present their case before the Sanhedrin. On the occasions of the three pilgrim festivals, the atmosphere must have resembled a carnival. No wonder the rabbis had to issue an edict prohibiting those who had finished their paschal-lamb ritual from going on to an *afikomon*, a riotous revel.

The Temple did have some moments of awe and hushed expectancy, however, as when the High Priest entered the Holy of Holies on the Day of Atonement. It also provided a daily opportunity for individuals to prostrate themselves and utter a silent prayer for their personal needs. Generally, however, prayer was a public, choral demonstration, against a background hubbub of noise and activity.

This, then, was the legacy of the synagogue. Ours was not a heritage of silent meditation, but rather of *avodah*, activity and spiritual concourse. Significantly, the Torah refers to the pilgrim festival ritual as "appearing before the presence of God." It is not the ritualistic acts performed that are emphasized, but the fact of "appearing," the gesture of solidarity, fealty, and covenantal fellowship.

Dignified, formal, and stereotyped acts of worship—wherein each worshiper and officiant had a prearranged cue, a prerehearsed part, and a fixed pew to occupy—were kept to a minimum in the Temple tradition. They were viewed, indeed, as an impediment to the spontaneity that was then regarded as the most authentic expression of the religious emotion. And it is that informal, and mildly irreverent, spirit that has determined and molded the ethos of the traditional synagogue to this day.

Hillel once exclaimed, "Lord, if you come into my home, I will come into yours." This is the precise attitude toward the synagogue that we have traditionally adopted. When we visit synagogue, we are, in a sense, making a sociospiritual gesture of reciprocity. And we begin by doing what any appreciative guest would do: we admire our host's residence—"Lord, I love the habitation of Thy house, and the place where Thy glory dwelleth."[2]

We have to feel "at home." We have to be relaxed, natural, without inhibition. In synagogue, the dignity and decorum—even the dialogue—are of secondary consequence. It is the experience of Jewish fellowship underlying the concept of the *minyan* and the keen awareness of the Being before whom we are "appearing" and "assembling" (as conveyed by the term *Bet Kneset*, "house of assembling") that are the primary considerations and preconditions of Jewish prayer.

Facing *Mizrach*

The Jewish house of prayer faces east. The Ark, housing the Scrolls of the Law, stands against the eastern wall; and it is toward that direction that the congregation turns when reciting the central prayer, the *Amidah*.

It is not that there is anything particularly significant about the eastern direction. The primary consideration is, of course, that we should be facing Jerusalem and, in particular, the Temple, the matrix of Jewish spirituality. For this reason, when Jews in non-Western countries pray toward Jerusalem, they will obviously be facing directions of the compass other than the east. It was with this in mind that the standard Codes of Jewish Law refrained from referring specifically to the east *(mizrach)* when describing the position of the Ark. Hence Maimonides states, "We erect therein an Ark in which are placed the Scrolls of the Law, and we build this Ark in the direction toward which that city prays."

The only specific reference to the eastern wall of the synagogue found in our talmudic sources is, surprisingly, in relation to the main entrance to the synagogue chamber, which, it is specified, should be set in the eastern wall,[3] in conformity with the design of the desert sanctuary, the entrance of which was on the eastern side.

Karo explains that the purpose of siting the main door of the sanctuary on the eastern side was so that the Israelite worshipers could bow from the entrance straight ahead toward the Ark, which, in the sanctuary, was set against the *western* wall.[4] The *Mishnah Berurah* infers from this that "in our (Western) countries, where we pray and bow toward the east, we should build the synagogue's main entrance on the western side." This view has failed to become an established principle of synagogue architectural design, however, for we follow the view of those authorities[5] who assert that any regulation governing the siting of the entrance doors was intended to apply only to eastern countries.

When King Solomon built the first Temple, he seems to have already conceived of it as being efficacious not only for those who worshiped within its precincts, but also for those who merely faced toward it from a distance:

> But can God indeed dwell on earth? Heaven itself cannot contain Thee; how much less this house that I have built! Yet attend to the prayer and the supplication which Thy servant utters this day, that Thine eyes may ever be upon this house night and day. So mayest Thou hear Thy servant when he prays *toward this place.* Hear the supplication of Thy people Israel when they pray *toward this place.*[6]

This practice, of turning in the direction of the Temple, was followed by Daniel when King Darius proscribed the worship of the true God:

When Daniel learned that this decree had been issued, he went into his house. He had had windows made in his roof chamber looking *toward Jerusalem;* and there he knelt down three times a day and offered prayers and praises to his God as his custom had always been.[7]

Thus, from the very outset, the Temple was viewed not merely in the narrow sense of just another—albeit more grandiose—sacred site, but rather as a focus for the spiritual emotion of the whole nation, or, more accurately, as a kind of "transmitter" for the sound waves of prayer and petition that Israel wished to relay to the heavenly "Receiver."

The Temple served the function of a transmitter, transforming or encoding the raw messages or petitions into a form suitable for the channel. According to this analogy, we may say that just as during transmission radio signals can easily become changed or distorted, similarly in the transmission of prayer, and especially personal petition. If the raw message transmitted by individuals is inappropriate, selfish, ill considered, or unseemly, then it will create "interference" that will inevitably impair the effectiveness of the general communal signal. Thus, when Jews the world over face the Temple, to effect transmission of their personal prayers and petitions, all these messages are—as it were—being sent *through* the Temple—or, since its destruction, through the holy city of Jerusalem—in order to ensure that they are adequately and appropriately processed or "transformed."

Cumulatively, therefore, the petitionary sounds of Israel are correctly balanced there, and placed into an harmonious, interacting wave-pattern, so as to ensure a unified national plea, amid the granting of which the individual will likewise find relief, response, and blessing.

This theory, to account for our facing toward the Temple when reciting our central petitionary prayer, the *Amidah,* explains why we conclude this prayer by reciting the *Yehiy ratzon,* calling upon God to "rebuild the Temple speedily in our days," so that, once again, we will have the effective spiritual apparatus to secure for us a more immediate acceptance of our prayers, "as in the days of old and as in years gone by."

With the spread of Christianity, its explanation of the verse, "And his feet shall stand, on that day, upon the Mount of Olives" (Zechariah 14:4), as referring to the future "coming" of their savior, soon inspired the widespread practice of Christians to face Jerusalem in their prayers, in order to look out for that "coming" and to express their messianic expectations. This, accordingly, generated a strong reaction on the part of some sages, who promptly pressed for the abrogation of that original Jewish custom of facing toward the Temple. This attitude was supported by Rabbis Oshaia and Ishmael on the grounds that the Divine Presence is, in any case, located everywhere.[8] They were fortified in their opposition by the fact that sun worship and the elevation of light into a symbol of deity had become rampant not only in the East, in the Persian religion, as well as in Graeco-Roman communities, but also among Jewish sectarian groups, such as those of the Judean desert.[9] This was alluded to in a confession formula recited by the priestly marchers in the joyous *Simchat Bet Ha-Sho'evah* procession on Sukkot, as they reached the Eastern Gate: "Our fathers, when they were in this place, turned with their backs toward the Temple of the Lord and their faces toward the east, and worshiped the sun toward the east [see Ezekiel 8:16]; but as for us, our eyes are turned toward the Lord."[10]

Even though to face east might, accordingly, invite suspicion, yet there was not sufficient support to dislodge that already well-entrenched tradition; and facing toward the Temple remained an essential element in Jewish worship.

Hebrew—The Language of Prayer

Hebrew, the holy language, is an essential component of Jewish liturgy. The Hebrew language is a vessel of divine spirit, and by employing it in prayer we are recycling the sacred syllables uttered by God when communicating His will and spirit to our biblical ancestors. In a mystically symbolic sense, therefore, we are securing the effectiveness of our prayers by redirecting the sacred sounds—the raw material of spirituality that originated as God's manifested will—to their place of origin, to become, once again, ingredients of that same will, though newly directed toward the granting of our specific petitions.

But Hebrew is also the language of the Jewish people—its religion, culture, and civilization. It is, therefore, inextricably bound up with our national and religious experiences throughout the generations. The Hebrew language of our prayers links our petitions to those of countless generations of our coreligionists before us, and, in particular, those of our patriarchs and righteous forebears. Implicit in the act of prayer in our historic language, therefore, lies the question, "Well, Lord? How long more must we wait?"

The supreme significance of the Hebrew language, as the only effective vehicle of Jewish prayer, may be gauged from the opening chapter of Maimonides' section on the laws of prayer. There, in a brief introductory survey of the development of Jewish liturgy, he states categorically that standardized prayers—as opposed to spontaneous private prayer—were introduced into our tradition only in order to preserve the pristine purity of the Hebrew language of prayer against the incursions of neighboring dialects:

> After Israel went into exile, during the days of the wicked king Nebuchad-nezzar, they became intermingled with Persians, Greeks, and other peoples. Children were born to them in the lands of those nations, and the language of their children became mixed—an amalgam of many other languages. When they wished to express themselves, they could not do so effectively in any one language without errors, as it is written: "Half of their children spoke the language of Ashdod (Philistine) or of the other people, and could not speak the language of the Jews."[11] The result of this was that when any of them prayed, they were unable to make a personal petition or declare the praise of God in the holy tongue without interspersing it with foreign vocabulary.

> When Ezra and his Court (circa 440 B.C.E.) saw this situation, they immediately instituted a standardized order of eighteen blessings *(She-moneh Esrey)*, to be memorized and recited by all, so that those whose speech was confused would now be able to frame a prayer every bit as perfect as any created even by masters of a pure (Hebrew) style. Because of this requirement they introduced further blessings and prayers to be recited permanently by all Israel, so that every blessing would henceforth be clearly and effectively enunciated even by those with mixed dialects.[12]

If, as we have suggested, it is necessary for prayer to reflect the special ethos of our people, and to partake of the spirit of our national, historical experience, then it is easy to understand why Ezra was so insistent that the language of prayer should not lose its ability to convey all this as a result of the discordant intrusion of other languages. Such languages would have been invested with the residual echo of different national experiences, many of which were, in fact, at variance with—if not hostile to—the spiritual and national objectives of the Jewish people. Ezra was prepared to introduce draconian measures in order to restore the national, spiritual, and cultural cohesion of the nation. He banished all foreign influences from Judea, even including the many heathen wives that Jews had married. Prayer in the Hebrew language would, therefore, have been a most useful element in Ezra's program of reform. His new emphasis on the paramount importance of the national language would have served as a rallying call to symbolize the native Jewish traditions that he wished to restore and promote.

Ironically, that same Ezra was the one responsible for the actual introduction of the Aramaic dialect into one of our main rituals of public worship. During the public reading from the Torah he permitted each verse to be translated into the Aramaic vernacular so that the people—whose Hebrew had become rusty—would understand. This was a concession that he was unwilling to make, however, when it came to prayer, possibly for the reasons we have outlined above.

This might also explain why an exception to this rule was made in the case of just one composition, the *Shema*. Anyone unable to understand the *Shema* in Hebrew may recite it in his own native tongue. The reason is that the *Shema* is not, strictly speaking, prayer. It contains no petition and no praise of God. It is Torah, a section of Holy Writ. Torah is God's word to us; it is a symbol of *His* Unity. Prayer, on the other hand is our word to God; a symbol of *our* unity, our collective needs. The Hebrew language is necessary, therefore, only in the latter situation, as an expression and symbol of that unique national unity. *God's* unity is never in doubt; it can never be assailed. *Ours* can. And the Hebrew language of prayer is a potent medium through which we attempt to keep our unity intact.

Praying with a *Minyan*

The popular understanding of Judaism's concept of the *minyan* in public worship is that it reflects the essential nature of prayer as a social act wherein the worshiper identifies with his people and their struggles and aspirations. Group action, it is asserted, gives a sense of security and identity that a private act of worship can never achieve.

A. J. Heschel dubs this popular misconception "the sociological fallacy," according to which the individual has no reality except as a carrier of ideas and attitudes that are derived from group existence.[13]

It might be apposite, in the context of this attempt to define the relationship of the individual to the group in the sphere of public worship *(tefillah be-tzibbur)*, to note that we derive our concept of the nature of communal spirituality from the biblical episode of the rebellion of Korach, which focuses precisely on this very issue of the reality of the individual as a source or generator of spirituality *independently of his community*.

Korach resented the spiritual superiority of Moses and Aaron: "You have assumed too much personal authority, for all the congregation are holy, every one of them, and the Lord is among them: wherefore then do you exalt yourselves above the Lord's community?" (Numbers 16:3).

Korach believed that holiness *(kedushah)* was a "gift" bestowed by God and shared with absolute equality among the entire congregation. His conception was of a kind of spiritual communism, rather than that which was being promoted by Moses and Aaron: a form of religious capitalism, wherein the greater the investment—of heart, soul, faith, and mind—the larger the dividend of *kedushah,* and the more tangible the sense of God's proximity.

Korach's community was spiritually static; Moses' was dynamic. In Korach's system, no man could lay claim to having a qualitative spiritual edge over his fellow. They were identical in their attainment: spiritual clones.

Moses rejected that idea of the community. God did, indeed, select one particular tribe, he reminded Korach, because of its superior religious attainment and degree of loyalty. The other tribes had succumbed to worshiping the Golden Calf. Only the tribe of Levi had demonstrated an unswerving loyalty. They were consequently not "all equally holy." Some were holier than others.

And it is precisely this disparity in holiness that provides the essential tension at the nerve center of our national consciousness. The varying gradations of holiness act as a constant spur and challenge to those on the lower rungs to reach upward and achieve more. At the same time, those on the higher rungs are doubly challenged: first, to strive ever higher, as loftier and previously obscured rungs of holiness tantalizingly come into view, beckoning to be scaled; and, second, the challenge of reaching down to lend support and encouragement to those below who are finding the spiritual ascent too arduous.

This is perhaps what the rabbis had in mind when they stated that those important sections of the services when we affirm God's unique holiness—such as the *Kaddish,* the *Kedushah,* and *Borkhu*—can only be recited in the context of public worship. The rabbis found an allusion to this in the verse, "And my holiness shall be affirmed *(ve-nikdashti)* among the children of Israel," namely, in the context of community worship alone.[14]

The rationale for this is, however, as we have suggested: because for many individuals it is too much of a presumption to declare God's holiness independently, when they themselves are remote from any true perception of it. In the context of the community, however, we all stand together, mutually supportive, with our collective merit conferring upon us the mantle of holiness. The gradations are not obliterated— as Korach suggested—but, arm in arm, we demand to be regarded as a unity; we demand a hearing not only for those on our gradation, but for those below as well.

That we require just ten men to constitute a communal quorum is inferred by the Talmud from the episode of the twelve spies, ten of whom returned with a slanderous report of the Promised Land.[15] God referred to those ten as "an evil *congregation*,"[16] and that consequently became the numerical paradigm for the transition from individuality into community. Perhaps it was no coincidence, therefore, that when Abraham was pleading with God to save the cities of Sodom and Gomorrah for the sake of the righteous among them, as soon as it became apparent that there were not even ten righteous people—a *minyan*—able to testify to God's sanctity and to serve as a catalyst to promote and generate *kedushah*, Abraham realized that the cities were doomed, and he pleaded no further.[17]

Our concept of the *minyan* is mined from the strangest of quarries: the contexts of Korach and the spies. Yet, at a deeper level, this, itself, is supercharged with symbolic meaning, and serves to refute the existentialist doctrine that believes that the emotional state of sinful, mortal man, as he confronts his Maker in prayer, should be one of existential terror.

Quite the contrary. When we assemble as a *minyan* for prayer, we are, symbolically, establishing holy credentials. We are inviting God to contrast *our* devotion, humility, and loyalty to His commands with the wicked rebelliousness of Korach, the spies, and others who pursue such a philosophy.

By objective standards of holiness we know we must be found wanting in God's eyes. When measured by comparative standards, however—particularly by those of such rebel *minyanim* as those formed by Korach and the spies—we have a good chance of finding grace. The *minyan* is, therefore, a unique generator of encouragement and comfort. And this is another reason why public worship (*tefillah be-tzibbur*) is, conceptually and halakhically, so superior to private prayer. Our sense of merit, induced by the awareness of our degree of communal loyalty to God, is the sole consideration that will enable us to fulfill the Psalmist's instruction to "serve God with joy." Such pride and confidence in our corporate spiritual commitment should banish the terror we would, indeed, otherwise assuredly experience in presuming to address, and make demands of, the Master of the Universe.

Bar Mitzvah

We define an adult male, capable of being included in a *minyan*, as one who has attained the age of thirteen years and a day. The major criterion is not age, however, but rather physical development. By the age of thirteen, it could generally be assumed that most boys had attained the stage of pubescent maturity. That particular age was chosen, therefore, in order to establish a uniform and consistent practice for the transition to *Bar Mitzvah*, the moment of admission into adult religious responsibility.

There is a popular misconception that where there are nine men and a child present in synagogue the child may *always* be given a *Chumash* and construed thereby as an adult.

An examination of the talmudic source reveals that the admissibility of a minor in a *minyan* reflects merely the minority view of R. Joshua b. Levi, but that sage makes no reference to the minor having to hold a *Chumash*.[18] This precondition actually arose as a result of a confusion with a totally different ritual wherein a proper *Sefer Torah* scroll was employed to represent a missing scholar at the ceremony of intercalating the leap year. On the basis of this, the great *Rabbeinu Tam* — who permitted a synagogue (not his own!) to include a religiously minded minor, aged about nine or ten years, to make up a *minyan* — dubbed the custom of giving such a child a *Chumash* "a foolish practice."[19] Joseph Karo decides with the majority view that clearly prohibits the inclusion of a preadolescent child in a *minyan*.[20]

Since, according to the mechanics of halakhic decision making, *in the case of emergency* we may follow a minority view where it is a rabbinic (as opposed to a biblical) prohibition or institution, Rabbi Moshe Feinstein accordingly decides that a minor, provided he has already attained the age of twelve, may be included in a *minyan*. The *emergency* he envisages is, for example, the fear that, in a small community, the synagogue service might collapse entirely because people will tire of coming there and finding no *minyan*.[21]

Women and Prayer

Judaism relieved its womenfolk of the routine of daily synagogue attendance and protracted worship. There are a number of reasons for this. First, and foremost, spirituality is best and most naturally nourished within a family environment. So the woman's position as supervisor of the home, and prime generator of the spirit which infuses Jewish homelife, is regarded as one of great sanctity and responsibility.

In Jewish law we have a principle that "whoever is preoccupied with the performance of one *mitzvah*, is relieved from the duty of fulfilling another" *(ha-osek be-mitzvah patur min ha-mitzvah)*. Maintaining the *shalom bayit*, the harmony and smooth running of the home, and attending to the needs of one's children, is regarded as a most important *mitzvah*, one so absorbing as to render a woman halakhically absolved from other competing duties, such as *tefillin* and synagogue prayer. From a halakhic point of view, women are expected, however, to recite at least one *Amidah* per day.[22]

Another rationale for the rule that imposes exclusively upon men the burden of thrice-daily worship is that men may, in fact, *need* to pray more regularly than women. Exposed as men are to the aggressiveness and acquisitiveness of business life, to the temptation to speak falsely and act fraudulently in the course of their effort to keep ahead of their competitors, they need the regular regimen of prayer, and the spiritual stimuli it offers, in order to neutralize all those dangerous influences by which they are tested.

Women—at least until the 20th century—were cushioned from such tensions. The tranquillity and religious spirit that invests the Jewish home, making it a veritable extension of the synagogue itself, meant that the Jewish woman was actually surrounded by holiness throughout her day. She was reminded of her God and her faith as she walked from room to room, passing the *mezuzah* on her way. She was reminded of her religious responsibilities as she prepared her family's meals, observing the multifarious regulations of *kashrut*. And if her children were young, she spent hours of her day educating them in the theoretical and practical tenets of their faith. The life of the religious woman, as priestess of her home, was one uninterrupted act of symbolic worship.

Synagogue prayer—that is, public worship—is predicated upon the concept of the *minyan*. This involves the merging of one's independent identity and individuality into a larger corporate unit. The will and aspirations of the community become the priority, the dominant aspiration. This is possibly the reason why only men were deemed capable of "making up a *minyan*," for men are far more readily prepared to be regimented, to don a uniform, to dress identically to their fellow, to surrender their individuality, and become part of a team. Women are more private beings; they interact best in a one-to-one situation. Ten men become metamorphosized into a community, a *minyan*. Ten women, on the other hand, remain a disparate group, each with her own independent will and personality. Hence it is that men have the responsibility of forming themselves into minicommunities for daily prayer; and women, for whom it does not come so naturally, were absolved.

Mixed Pews

On Sukkot the great Temple celebration of *Bet Ha-Sho'evah*[23] took place in the spacious Court of the Women.

With the women occupying the main hall, the men were forced to crowd around the perimeter rampart *(chel)*, and fan out across the surrounding area of the Temple Mount. Although the sexes were kept separate by this arrangement, the four gates of the Women's Court were thrown open during the *Bet Ha-Sho'evah* so that the men outside could see through to the carnival being enacted in the elevated Court of the Israelites. One year the men surged forward into the women's section, and the improper crush led to some rather riotous behavior *(kallut rosh)*. In order to avoid a recurrence of this, the authorities insisted that a balcony be erected for the women and that the men should henceforth occupy the main area.[24] Separation of the sexes during worship has remained Jewish law to this day.

Rabbi Moshe Feinstein, in a responsum on the subject of synagogue galleries,[25] observes that where the design of a synagogue precludes a gallery, a *mechitzah* (partition) must be provided of sufficient height to prevent communication, contact, or *kallut rosh* flirtation. He decides that one of shoulder height is required.

It should be noted that even in Temple times, although the sexes were separated, there was no prohibition on women being visible. The balcony itself was merely a raised platform, and was not provided with a *mechitzah*. The sole objective was to avoid *kallut rosh;* and the inaccessibility of the women was sufficient to guarantee that, without their being out of sight.

While it is admitted that gazing at women, even in a gallery, may be a distraction for males—and the *halakhah* certainly condemns gazing at women sensuously—the institution of the gallery or *mechitzah* was not directed at that aspect of the problem. It was not intended as a means of furthering male concentration during worship, but exclusively, as we have seen, to prevent *kallut rosh*. That type of levity will not develop from seeing women at a distance, but only from the ability to communicate at close proximity

The issue of the gallery or *mechitzah* marks one of the main bones of contention between Orthodox and non-Orthodox Judaism, the former charging the latter with having abrogated a tradition that goes back well over 2,000 years, and the latter making the counterclaim that this is an outdated institution and a slur on the equality of the sexes.

One's attitude toward tradition will naturally determine which argument one believes carries the greater weight, though it must be said that a religion that is constrained regularly to change its institutions and traditions, merely to accord with each generation's susceptibilities and sociological conceptions, forfeits thereby its claim to being an "historic" religion, and surrenders the authority it enjoys as a concomitant of that status.

Even the exponents of non-Orthodox Judaism would not deny their rabbi, cantor, or executive officers a specially assigned place in synagogue, reflective of their dominant role in the proceedings. In the same way, the Orthodox seating arrangement, of males downstairs and women in the gallery, reflects the more active involvement of the former in the act of obligatory worship and in the performance of the ritual. It draws attention to nothing more than differing respective *functions* within the religious system, but certainly does not indicate a different relative *value* in the eyes of the tradition.

The gallery or *mechitzah* arose as a moral safeguard and is preserved as a timely symbol that the synagogue will steadfastly remain the final bastion of morality in an age of almost total permissiveness.

Those who attempt to justify mixed pews by adducing the "equality" argument might reflect upon the fact that it is the present generation's devaluation of woman into a sex object that has done most to deprive her of equality. The Orthodox synagogue tradition, by preserving a sense of respectful distance between the sexes, stands alone in attempting to restore to woman her equality.

Much is made of the pleasure of praying in synagogue surrounded by one's wife and family. This is not denied, though it fails to take account of the fact that one is also surrounded by one's neighbor's wife and family! Similarly, one's sons and daughters are also surrounded by members of the opposite sex. To suggest that this is not a distraction is absurd.

Mixed seating also focuses inordinately upon the domestic and social dimensions of the synagogue experience, rather than highlighting the centrality of its spiritual aura. In prayer we stand alone. That is the one time when it is appropriate to display our exclusive reliance upon God, rather than upon husband or wife. Here again, Orthodoxy demonstrates the equality of woman and the fact that her spiritual competence enables her to stand alone in prayer, determining her own depth of commitment, instead of, as in most other aspects of life, standing at her husband's side in either a supportive or sharing role.

11

Blessings

An Expression of Spiritual Wonderment

Blessings are a blessing. Through the medium of its brief *berakhot* formulae Judaism enables us to express a momentary flush of spiritual wonderment as a response to all the varied experiences of life. If our people have been hailed, justifiably, for their literary capability and intellectual creativity, the ritual of *berakhot* must be given its share of credit for having made us reflective, contemplative, and keenly sensitive to all the stimuli and phenomena of life and nature.

Not only do we offer a blessing to the Creator for our food and drink, but we also have specially prescribed and individually formulated *berakhot* when smelling fragrant trees and plants, fruits, spices, and oils, when seeing a flash of lightning or the rainbow, or when hearing thunder. There are also special blessings to be made when witnessing wonders of nature, such as high mountains, great deserts, rivers, and seas.

There is some dispute in our sources regarding which rivers and seas actually merit that special blessing. Although the *Mishnah* states that "over all seas and rivers we say the blessing *oseh maaseh bereishit*,"[1] later authorities restricted this blessing, in the case of rivers, to the Tigris and Euphrates (and the other two unknown rivers mentioned together with them in Genesis 2:11-14). This same *Mishnah* prescribes a special *berakhah* "on seeing the *yam ha-gadol*" (the Great Sea). While this term is generally applied to the Mediterranean,[2] one halakhic authority comes to the strange conclusion that the *Mishnah* here refers specifically to "the sea that surrounds the land of Angleterre."[3] Our major codes assume, however, that the *Mishnah* was, indeed, referring to the Mediterranean, which has a special blessing prescribed as a tribute to its significance for the Holy Land.

Shehecheyanu

The *Shehecheyanu* blessing is a formula of joyful thanksgiving for a variety of pleasures and joys, ranging from the spiritual pleasure induced by the onset of a festival, or the emotional happiness occasioned by a reunion with a dear friend whom one has not seen for some time, to the physical enjoyment of eating a fruit for the first time at the beginning of its annual season.

Shehecheyanu also expresses one's pleasure at acquiring a new home, new household items, or clothing. The *berakhah* over the latter should really be made in the shop immediately after purchase, since, says the *Shulchan Arukh*, "The purpose of the blessing is to emphasize our pleasure at *acquiring* them. Later, when wearing the clothes, one should say an additional blessing, *Barukh . . . malbish arumim* ('Blessed . . . who clothes the naked'), or, over household items, *ha-tov ve-ha-meitiv* ('Blessed . . . who is good and confers goodly benefits')."[4]

Shehecheyanu is expressive of human pleasure. However, in the context of Judaism's paramount concern for the welfare of animals, it was regarded as inappropriate to recite this blessing if our pleasure is being secured at the expense of the lesser forms of nature. Thus, a *shochet*, when performing the *mitzvah* of ritual slaughter for the first time in his career, must not recite *Shehecheyanu*, since he is, after all, taking a life.[5] For the same reason—although the *halakhah* never insisted upon it in this instance—popular opinion refrained from reciting this blessing when acquiring leather shoes.[6] Isserles tell us that ordinary folk would never wish each other "health to wear them."[7]

Blessing for Health, Wisdom, and Glory

We are encouraged to appreciate the intricacy of our own body and the blessing of good health. Hence the *berakhah* to be recited after attending to the needs of nature:

> Blessed art thou, O Lord our God, King of the universe, who has formed man in wisdom and created in him many orifices and organs. It is revealed and known before the throne of Thy glory that if one of these be opened that should be closed, or closed that should be opened, it would be impossible to exist and stand before Thee. Blessed art thou, O Lord, who healest all flesh and doest wondrous deeds.

But feelings of wonder and admiration are occasioned not only by the phenomena of nature. The divinely bestowed blessings of wisdom or glory upon certain individuals, which fill lesser mortals with awe and reverence, are also regarded as worthy of a *berakhah*. Hence those prescribed when beholding a king or head of state: "Blessed are you . . . who has given of His glory to flesh and blood."

A distinction is made in the wording of the *berakhah* to be recited when meeting sages distinguished in Torah and those (Jews or non-Jews) who have gained a world reputation in other branches of knowledge. For the former we say, "Blessed . . . who *has shared* Your wisdom with *those that fear You*"; for the latter we say, ". . . who *has given* of Your wisdom *to flesh and blood*." The blessing is not recited, however, over distinguished theologians of other religions.

The formulae of our blessings are accredited to Ezra the Scribe and have been hallowed by time and tradition. The rabbis strongly disapproved, therefore, of anyone "altering the mold that the sages have formed" by reciting any variant version of the accepted formula. A translation—even if freely rendered—providing it remains faithful to the intention of the original, is regarded as a valid *berakhah*.[8] This concession is extended however only to those who cannot read Hebrew.

Are These Blessings Really Offensive?

Rabbi Alan Henkin, of the Californian Synagogue for the Deaf,[9] has made a heartrending plea for a change of attitude toward the disabled.

He is especially sensitive to the offense that some of our early morning blessings might cause:

> I would also caution the representatives of the religious sector of Jewry to beware of such discomfitting prayers and rituals as for example, *"Blessed are You . . . who opens the eyes of the blind."*

He also objects to the following passage in the Reform *Gates of Prayer:*

> Can we imagine a world without color, a world without the grace of blue, the life of green? Can we imagine a world without sound?

Henkin asks us to consider how blind and deaf Jews must feel when they recite these sentiments.

The truth is that our *Shulchan Arukh* definitely is sensitive to this problem. Its considered view is that "anyone for whom these blessings are inappropriate, for example a deaf person who cannot 'hear' the cock crowing, or a blind man whose eyes are not 'opened' (this would, presumably, include one with a stoop, who is not 'raised up,' or a lame man, whose 'steps' are not 'made firm') should still recite the blessing, but with the omission of the divine name"[10] — a subtle fusion of praise and protest!

The latter restriction is contested by Moses Isserles, who adds the significant consideration: "If the blessings are inappropriate they should still be recited (with the inclusion of the divine name), for a blessing is not related exclusively to one's own circumstances. We bless God for fulfilling the needs of the whole world."[11]

If we analyze the wording of these blessings, we realize at the outset that the phraseology was never intended to be taken literally. The cock in no way merits to open the list of divine boons. It is obviously being employed figuratively as a thanksgiving for the daily restoration to us of our refreshed body and spirit, ready to face the manifold challenges that each new day brings.

Similarly, during sleep, we are, figuratively speaking, like the blind, with our power of vision neutralized. On awakening we bless God — *poke'ach ivrim* — for the restoration of this precious faculty. It may also be understood symbolically as thanksgiving for the new "insights" that come to us each day, helping us to see things in a different light. In similar vein, the "raising of them that are bowed down" is clearly a metaphor for the balm of comfort and tranquillity that each passing day regularly brings to those weighed down by care or bereavement. Time is the best healer.

But maybe Henkin does have a point. Perhaps this reference to the blind could cause them embarrassment.

There are several ways of approaching this problem. The first is to dismiss it dispassionately by noting that if we were to quibble at every biological reference, in case it offended a disabled person, then we should have to refrain from reciting large sections of our sacred law. Could not the reference in the *Shema* to the obligation of "hearing" ("*Hear* O Israel"), "seeing," and "remembering" ("And you shall *see* it and *remember* all the commandments of the Lord"), embarrass the deaf, blind, and mentally retarded, respectively? One could also argue that the reference to "teaching diligently to one's children" could cause pain to the childless! We may conclude, therefore, that the only answer is to tell the disabled not to be so sensitive!

. A more constructive approach might be to explain to them the actual relevance of the blessing "who opens the eyes of the blind." It would then be necessary to point out that the English translation of *berakhah* by "blessing"—with its connotation of joy and thanksgiving—is inaccurate. The *berakhah* is frequently merely an affirmation that God's wisdom, power, and mercy is activated on our behalf, or that its potential is available to us by indirect means, should we merit it. God certainly can, and frequently does, *open the eyes of the blind*, by blessing the hands of surgeons and the effectiveness of drugs. This *berakhah* may therefore be most appropriate as a petition for the restoration of sight.

But there is quite another way of approaching this problem. We cannot ignore the fact that our tradition does, at times, impose upon us the obligation of reciting certain blessings, and making declarations, which ordinarily would go against our natural disposition. The blessing *Barukh dayyan ha-emet* ("Blessed be the true judge") springs naturally to mind. Can this possibly be regarded as an accurate, ingenuous reaction of one who has just lost a beloved relative, especially at a tender age? Yet the *Mishnah* insists on such a blessing being articulated, according to the principle that "a man is obliged to bless God for the evil, in the same way that he blesses for the good."[12]

Blessings transcend the emotional individuality of the one uttering them. We bless as a community, "with our young and our old, with our sons and our daughters" (Exodus 10:9)—and, we may add, with our blind and our sighted, our deaf and our sound of hearing, our disabled and our healthy. We do not have a separate liturgy for either group. We assume that the gift of sight to the majority is also a source of satisfaction and blessing to the blind who, in consequence, are the recipients of our support and succor. The disabled may bemoan their condition; we do not, however, attribute to them any envy of the healthy on account of their good fortune. The blessing thus remains relevant. For the eyes of the blind *are* "opened"; they are given confidence and mobility through the professional help of our welfare agencies, and their experiences are broadened by Braille libraries, talking books, trained guide dogs, and other aids. Why should the blind not utter this blessing without inhibition for all the benefits which God, and a caring humanity, can confer upon them?

This particular point is actually enunciated clearly in the *Shulchan Arukh*, which states that "a blind man, who has never had sight of the luminaries, may still act as *chazan* to recite the blessing 'Creator of the luminaries' *(yotzer ha-me'orot)*, since he also benefits (indirectly) from the luminaries that others see, by which they are enabled to guide him along the road he wishes to walk" (*Orach Chayyim* 69:2).

A closer linguistic analysis of the phrase *poke'ach ivrim* ("who opens the eyes of the blind") yields two further possible interpretations. It is noteworthy that there is no Hebrew word here for "the eyes of." Furthermore, the verb *pakach* has the additional nuance of "being open-minded," "perceptive;" hence the noun *pike'ach*, "perceptive person." This is the sense in which *pakach* is used in Genesis 3:5,7, to explain how the eyes of Adam and Eve were, metaphorically, "opened" when they became conscious of their nakedness. In this sense of "perception" the blessing may be unashamedly pronounced by blind people as thanksgiving for the sharpening of some of their other faculties that occurs quite frequently in order to compensate, in some measure, for their impaired visual capacity. *Poke'ach ivrim* could therefore be loosely, though accurately, rendered, "who grants the blind greater awareness."

We may discover another area of contemporary relevance by focusing upon the word *ivrim*. This may not necessarily mean the totally blind, but can equally apply to anyone with impaired vision. Before the invention of the eyeglass in the 14th century, most people must have lived in a blurred, twilight world. Today we all have good reason to thank God for the availability of lenses to "correct our impaired vision"; and this is precisely how this blessing may be understood.

In the well-known talmudic account of the martyrdom of Rabbi Akivah there is a point of contact with the issue under consideration:

When Akivah was being tortured, the time for reciting the *Shema* arrived. He uttered it with a smile. The Roman guard cried out, "Old man, are you a sorcerer that you can mock at your suffering and smile at your pain?" "No," replied Akivah, "but all my life when I said the words, 'Thou shalt love the Lord thy God with all thy heart and soul and might,' I was saddened, for I thought, how is it possible that I might be able to fulfill such a command? I have loved God with all my heart and with all my possessions (might), but I could never conceive of how I might love Him with all my soul (i.e., my very life). Now that I am giving up my life, with my resolution as firm as ever, and the hour for saying the *Shema* has arrived, should I not smile?"

And as he spoke, his soul departed.[13]

Akivah here admitted that, throughout his life, he had recited Judaism's central affirmation of faith, the *Shema*, while being unable to fully comprehend, fulfill, or even associate himself with, the sentiments of one of its main elements, that of "loving God with all thy soul."

This particular sentiment was the exclusive preserve of the select fraternity of sainted martyrs. They alone can recite *u-ve-khol nafshekha* with any degree of authentic appreciation of, and commitment to, its import. And yet it is prescribed for recitation by *all Israel*, perhaps because we are all potential martyrs, given the hazardous nature of our sacred mission to mankind.

The same may be said for the blessing *poke'ach ivrim*, and the three blessings that follow it. Although they refer exclusively to the relieving of the specific predicaments of the unfortunate, yet they are equally relevant to the situation of *all Israel;* for we are *all* potential candidates for disability and suffering, given the weakness of our mortal frame and the frailty of the human condition.

Thus, the blind and the other disabled need feel no special sensitivity when the rest of us refer to their particular problem. It could so easily have been—and might yet become—our problem. And even if not, yet it cannot be a bad thing that we include the disabled at the very outset of our prayers, giving them the priority of our concern and reminding us so forcefully of our obligations toward them.

The Enigmatic Term, *Tefillah*

In order to discover the very basic and primary sense in which prayer was understood and expressed by our early ancestors, we have to discern the actual meaning of the root of the word *tefillah* ("prayer") and *le-hitpallel* ("to pray").

Zevi Karl[14] tells us that its basic root *(p-l)* means "to fall" (= *nafal*). Primitive man expressed his needs to God by merely "falling" on his face, without uttering any word. We find this even later, at a period when people were already accustomed to express their petitions in words. Hence, when the Israelites threatened, "Let us appoint a head and return to Egypt" (Numbers 14:5), Moses and Aaron "fell on their faces"—but without uttering any words. The act of "falling down" expressed, *as eloquently as any words*, their fear and their need of God's salvation. Again, in the face of Korach's rebellion, Moses "fell on his face" (Numbers 16:4)—in other words, he "prayed" for deliverance from the rebels. Since falling on one's face *(nefilah)* served as the original method of prayer, the Hebrew word for that act was used as the term of the later and more developed act of worship, *tefillah*, also derived from the basic root *p-l*.

Professor S. Zeitlin[15] makes the surprising assertion that "the word *tefillah* originally had the meaning of *argument;* the person who besought God argued with Him." Zeitlin attempts to prove this by referring to a few biblical passages where the verb *lehitpallel* ("to pray") occurs, but where the actual act performed is more *an argument* than a *prayer*. Thus, when the Israelites made the Golden Calf, and God threatened to destroy the nation, Moses immediately put up several *arguments* why they should be saved (Deuteronomy 9:26–29). These are introduced by the phrase *va-etpallel el ha-shem*, which Zeitlin would translate, "I put the arguments to God." While Zeitlin is obviously correct that Moses was here putting the case for Israel's deliverance, yet Moses commenced by offering *a prayer*—not an *argument*—as is made quite clear in the opening verse: "Lord God, do not destroy Your people and Your inheritance whom You have redeemed in Your greatness." This *prayer* is what Moses referred to by his phrase *va-etpallel el ha-shem*—"And I *prayed* to God."

Zeitlin refers to Jonah 4:2–3, where it is said of the frustrated prophet that *vay-yitpallel el ha-shem*. Yet what follows is essentially a complaint:

"Lord was not this my saying while I was yet in my own country? Therefore I fled beforehand to Tarshish. . . ."

Zeitlin has clearly overlooked the fact that the prayer proper comes at the end of Jonah's speech: "Now, therefore, Lord, take my life from me, I beseech thee, for it is better for me to die than to live." This was, indeed, his prayer and plea to God, and it is to this particular *prayer* that the introductory verb *vay-yitpallel* refers.

Zeitlin would have us believe that before the Second Jewish Commonwealth—"when the idea of God had become revolution-ized"[16]—our people had a primitive concept of prayer. They could only argue, bargain, or tempt God with gifts or vows. This is most surprising, in the light of the fact that Zeitlin has quoted Jonah as an example of the genre of primitive prayer, whereas the actual literary compilation of the biblical story of Jonah (as opposed to the period wherein the prophet actually lived and preached, which, according to II Kings 14:25, was during the First Temple period of King Jeroboam II, 8th century B.C.E.) is certainly a product of that "enlightened" period of the Second Commonwealth![17]

To create a theory purely on the basis of a few passages where a verb *(lehit)-pallel* occurs is most unscientific. Certainly some biblical prayers partook of the spirit of complaint, grievance, and argument. But others, such as the Prayer of Hannah (I Samuel 2:1–10)—introduced by the key phrase *va-titpallel*—are majestic outpourings of praise, joy, and thanksgiving. When the sentence of death was imposed on the Philistine King Abimelech, for seizing Sarah, God accepts his remorse and tells him that, if he returns her to Abraham, the latter, being a prophet, "will *pray (yitpallel)* for you that you might live" (Genesis 20:7). No "arguments" were required of Abraham in this situation. A simple prayer to save the king's life was all that God wished to hear, as proof that Abraham had forgiven the King for the seizure of his wife.

Zeitlin is patently in error in postulating a primitive conception of God, and a naive and self-centered approach in man's relationship to, and communication with, Him before the Second Commonwealth (500 B.C.E.). Indeed his theory makes nonsense of the very special and exalted relationship with God developed already by our patriarchs at the very dawn of our religious history.

S. R. Hirsch applies his inimitable philological-cum-philosophical approach to the meaning of the verb *palal*.[18] He relates *palal* with *balal*, since the Hebrew labial consonants (b/m/p) do interchange with each other. *Balal* means "to mix thoroughly together," "to unite," as in the recurring phrase *belulah ba-shemen* "mingled thoroughly with oil."[19]

In this way we can understand why the verb *palal* (= *balal*) also occurs in the Bible in the meaning of "to judge."[20] The judge takes the conflicting opinions, charges, arguments, and claims of contending parties or counsel; and, by giving a just decision, he quells the contention and restores harmony. By "mingling together," "synthesizing" *(balal)* all the evidence in his mind, he is able to administer justice *(palal)*.

According to Hirsch, all this underlies the applied meaning of *palal* in the sense of "prayer" *(tefillah)*. Hirsch doesn't like the translation "prayer," with its overtone of an "outflowing *from within* of that with which the heart is already filled." *Le-hitpallel* is "an act of *judging* oneself," in the sense we have expounded: allowing the elements of God's truth and power to work on us and to penetrate *from outside* all phases of our being and life, thereby conferring total peace and harmony upon our whole existence in God. By working on our inner self, to achieve the full "self-judgment" of the prayer experience, we are restored to "harmony" with God. All the conflict and turbulence of our life and nature is dissipated thereby, giving way to unity and identity with the "judge of the whole world."

Hirsch's concept of prayer, as a spirit working upon us from outside, is quite original. Indeed, this is the only way he feels he can justify our practice of having fixed times and prescribed forms of prayer. These surely presuppose that "periodically, at fixed times, the masses of a community are filled with one and the same state of feelings, one and the same trend of thoughts." If this were, indeed, the case, then prayer itself would be rendered superfluous, since "feelings and thoughts which are already lively within us have no need first to be expressed, and least of all in set phrases placed in our mouths. If the heart is truly full, mere words will never capture such a depth of feeling!"

Thus, for Hirsch,

> Our prescribed prayers do not enunciate facts, truths, which it is assumed we are already fully conscious of, but such that *they wish* to awaken, reanimate, and keep ever fresh in us. One can truly say then that the less we feel inclined to prayer, the greater our need for it, and the greater the importance, and the effect on us of the work which *we have to accomplish on ourselves by prayer*.[21]

It is a pity that Hirsch did not conclude his remarks by indicating just how comforting and helpful this approach might be to those who go through phases when prayer just doesn't seem to flow naturally from their lips or prove to be a meaningful or inspiring exercise. Hirsch's theory teaches that the forms, words, and times of prayer are not meant to be inspiring *per se*. The sentiments of the liturgy cannot possibly always coincide with our emotions, with "facts we are already fully conscious of." They are there as an ideal, a spur, and challenge to the heights to which prayer *is* capable of uplifting one, providing one truly "judges oneself," divests oneself of the tensions and conflicts which we so frequently self-induce, through our vain ambitions and materialistic obsessions. If we cannot achieve harmony and unity with God through the stimulus of prayer, it is very likely because we have not yet achieved harmony with life—and its true and enduring purpose.

If we allow ourselves some of the flexibility that Hirsch's philological and exegetical approach inspires, we may suggest a further extension of the scope of the root *palal*, to provide an interesting insight into the basic purpose of prayer.

If we analyze most the biblical roots whose kernel are the letters *p-l*—such as *pl* ("to be wonderful," "extraordinary," as in the noun *pele*, "*a wonder*"), *palag* ("to split," "separate," "divide"), *palah* ("to be dis-

tinct"), palach ("to cleave"), *palat* ("to escape")—we see that the basic underlying sense is "to mark something or someone off as a distinctive and detached element, with a frequent overtone of uniqueness, elevation, and wonder."

May we not, therefore, detect that same semantic strand within the verb *palal?* If the core letters *p-l* connote "wonder," and the final letter was originally merely the *lammed* of direction, then *pll* (= *pl el*) means "to attribute wonder, uniqueness, distinction *to* Someone," which is, after all, the essence and basic motivation of prayer.

Who Blesses Whom?

The very notion that mortal man can—either effectively or even ineffectively—"bless" God cannot seriously be entertained. To "bless" means to confer or transmit sanctity. It has an overtone of condescension, of a superior bestowing some of his own spiritual largess. So, although we can "praise" God, we can hardly employ the English verb "to bless" in relation to Him. If anything, it is *we* who become "blessed," in the sense of "spiritually elevated," when we indulge in the recitation of *berakhot* ("blessings").

It was recognition of this fact which was responsible for the original popularity of the expression *"to make a berakhah."* Man is no longer "blessing"; he is merely uttering a "blessed formula," one which—tradition promises—is meaningful to God. Perhaps this is why we do not commence our blessings with a condescending affirmation, such as "we bless You" *(Anachnu mevorakhim),* but rather with the words "You are (already) blessed" *(Barukh attah).*

The Hebrew verb root from which the noun *berakhah* is derived also furthers this idea. The basic meaning of the verb *barekh* is simply, "to bow," "to bend the knee" (hence the noun *berekh,* "a knee"). The *berakhah* is nothing more than an act of submission.

The actual syntax of the *berakhah* formula helps to promote this idea, by means of the sudden shift in the way God is referred to, from the second person: *Barukh attah* ("Blessed are *You*"), to the third person: *asher kidshanu be-mitzvotav* ("*He* who sanctified us by *His* commandments"). In other words, after having commenced by addressing God directly, we shrink away from this close encounter, and immediately acknowledge the great divide separating God and man, by breaking into the more respectfully detached third person mode of address. The *berakhah* thus asserts that God is, enigmatically, both immanent as well as transcendent, and that, either way, man is the recipient, not the donor.

Another approach to this problem of how man can actually "bless" God is to pay attention to the fact that the biblical verb *barekh* generally connotes more than "praise" or "adoration." The true objective of the biblical *berakhah* is to effect an "increase" and "augmentation" of the reserves of the recipient. This is the sense in which we are to understand the "blessing of the firstborn."[22] It served a practical objective: to confer an increase and augmentation of the firstborn's possessions by formally conferring upon him a major stake in the family estate.

This particular nuance of the root *barekh* explains why the noun *berakhah* is frequently used in biblical Hebrew to denote "a gift."[23] Similarly, the phrase *nefesh berakhah* occurs in Proverbs 11:25 in the sense of "a generous man"; and when the Torah states that "God will *bless (beirakh)* your bread and your water" (Exodus 23:25), it quite clearly means that He will bestow those gifts in abundance. Ibn Ezra explains the phrase "And God *blessed* the seventh day" (Genesis 2:3) in this identical sense:

> *Berakhah* means augmented benefits; namely, that on this day we are granted a feeling of physical regeneration and higher spiritual and intellectual perception.

So, "making a *berakhah*" does not necessarily imply that we are actually *blessing* God. The *berakhah* must be viewed merely as an acknowledgment of our good fortune at being the recipients of God's largess. Some *berakhot* connote the augmentation of our material requirements, for which we are expressing appreciation through the *berakhah;* others connote the augmentation of our spiritual and intellectual faculties, which prompt us to affirm the praiseworthy (or "blessed") qualities of God. In neither case do *we* bless *Him*. The *berakhah* merely affirms *our* augmented perception of just how indebted we are to God for all His gifts *(berakhot)*, and an expression of wonderment at how profoundly praiseworthy He is.

Now, instead of rendering the phrase *Barukh attah* as "You are blessed" or "We bless You," we may understand it in the sense of "You are the bestower of all blessings."

The *Berakhah* Prepositions *le* and *al*

In the basic formula of our *berakhot* we sometimes employ the simple infinitive *le* ("to"), as in *Barukh. . . . le-hadlik ner shel Shabbat*, whereas at other times we use the preposition *al* ("concerning"), as in *al netilat yadayim.* Even our most distinguished medieval authorities were unable to come up with a single explanation that could be applied with total consistency to all blessings to account for this variety.

Rabbi Jacob Tam suggested that the introductory formula *al* connotes a ritual that had to be performed immediately following the recitation of the blessing, without interruption, such as *Barukh . . . al ha-miylah* ("concerning circumcision"), *al biur chametz* ("on removal of unleaven bread"), *al mikra megillah* ("on reading the Megillah"). The infinitive *le,* on the other hand, refers to rituals of a more protracted nature, such as *le-hadlik ner shel Chanukah* (since, halakhically, the Chanukah lights may be lit at any time during the night, as long as people are still out on the streets to see them burning in the houses) and, *lishmo'a kol shofar* (since the *Shofar* is blown intermittently throughout the service).

The obvious flaw in this theory is that we recite *le-hadlik ner shel Shabbat* notwithstanding the fact that *Shabbat* commences *immediately* for the housewife! Maimonides therefore offered a different rationale: the infinitive *le* is used when it is a *mitzvah* that one is performing exclusively *for oneself,* whereas *al* is employed if it is solely on behalf of another. If it is being performed on behalf of oneself as well as for another, then the formula is *le.* Hence, when one affixes a *mezuzah* to one's home, the blessing is *likbo'a mezuzah;* on sitting in a succah *leishev ba-sukkah;* and on enwrapping onself in one's own *tallit* the blessing is *le-hitatef ba-tzitzit.* Thus, a *mohel,* circumcising the child of another, says *al ha-miylah,* whereas the father of the child says *le-hakhniso bi-vrito shel Avraham avinu.*

Where the activity is optional (such as taking a meal or slaughtering an animal) the formula is always *al.* Hence *al netilat yadayim* and *al ha-shechitah.*

This theory breaks down, however, in the face of *al akhilat matzah* and *al akhilat maror.* Eating is certainly performed by the person himself and the eating of these ritual foods is obligatory!

Another theory has it that *al* is reserved for any ritual that may be performed by others on our behalf, whereas *le* is used for those rituals that we must do ourselves. The objection that, by that token, we should recite *le-ekhol matzah* and *le-ekhol maror* (rather than *al akhilat*) is countered by pointing out that there is evidence to suggest that that, indeed, was the original talmudic formula.

This theory also makes the point that *le* ("to") has the specific connotation of a ritual which one has not yet embarked upon, whereas the more general preposition *al* ("concerning") may be applied to, and at, any stage of a *mitzvah.*

This insight will explain why, over the hand *tefillin,* we recite *le-haniach tefillin,* whereas over the head *tefillin* we say, *al mitzvat tefillin.* The *tefillin* ritual cannot be performed by another on our behalf, hence *le-haniach* is made at the outset. However, once one has already tied on his hand *tefillin,* the head *tefillin* is, in effect, merely the final stage of the same ritual. Since the head *tefillin* cannot, therefore, at that point, be designated a ritual that "one has not yet embarked upon," we recite over it the introductory formula *al,* which may be applied at any stage of a *mitzvah.*

The distinguished Spanish liturgist, David Avudarham (14th century), analyzes the various theories and discusses their flaws. Quite wisely, he refrains from offering his own theory, for fear of further complicating an area of great liturgical uncertainty.

Prayers to Angels and Departed Relatives

It is not an uncommon sight, particularly at cemeteries, to see emotional people directing prayers, pleas, and petitions *to* the souls of the departed, addressing them directly—even by name—and asking them to intercede with God on their behalf.

The religious propriety of such acts may be questioned; for should not all our feelings, needs, and petitions be channeled, through prayers, exclusively to God? Does not this communication with the departed smack of spiritualism, and is it not an infringement of the prohibition of "inquiring of the dead"?

To answer this question we have to widen the issue to take account of the general recognition of the existence and place of "intermediaries" in the transmission of our prayers.

The angels Michael and Gabriel were particularly believed to discharge this function. Standing on our right and left sides, respectively,[24] they act as intercessors with God on our behalf and as "presenters of our prayers" *(makhnisey tefillah)* before the divine throne.

Although the statutory prayers contained in our *Siddur* are generally free of such (some might say) gross allusions, they did succeed in infiltrating on occasions, and establishing thereby the validity of the concept. Thus, in the beautiful hymn, *Shalom Aleikhem,* sung by the family before the Friday night meal, the third stanza reads:

Bless me with peace, O angels of peace,
Angels of the Most High. . . .

The illustrious Rabbi Chaim of Volodzin objected to its recitation. "No petition should be addressed to angels," he insisted, "for they are impotent to act on their own volition. If a man is meritorious, they are forced to bless him; and if not, they must condemn. The interceding angel is merely a creative spirit brought into being by man's own good deeds." Notwithstanding this objection, the appeal to angels, that they should act as intercessors on our behalf, is a recurring theme, particularly in the *Selichot* liturgy.

Among the *Selichot* one particular composition stands out, not only for the bold confidence with which the author directs the angels to fulfill their role as intermediaries of prayer, but notably because its author was the renowned liturgical authority, Amram Gaon (9th century), who provided us with our first authorized *Siddur*, the *Seder Rav Amram*.

This composition is recited at the conclusion of the *Selichot* for each day during the week preceding Rosh Hashanah and for each of the Ten Days of Penitence:

Angels of mercy usher in (our petition for) mercy before the Lord of mercy.

Angels of prayer, cause our prayers to be heard before Him who hears prayer.

Angels of tears, bring in our tears before the King who is reconciled by tears.

The footnote in A. Rosenfeld's *Authorized Selichot for the Whole Year*[25] tells us that "many a commentator abstained from translating this prayer, objecting to the idea of praying to angels. They overlook the beautiful description of Jacob's ladder."

Perhaps Rosenfeld does those commentators an injustice. They were certainly aware of the symbolism of Jacob's dream. However, no inference can be made from that episode, since Jacob not only did not pray to the angels, but made no effort even to address them![26]

The great *Maharal* of Prague resorted to a slight emendation of the text in order to neutralize the charge that the above composition is a prayer to angels. In the opening line, he changed the imperative *hachnisu* to the future form *yachnisu*. The sense was now: "The angels of mercy *will usher in*. . . ." Significantly, he was not denying the angels their role in the process of prayer transmission. His objection was solely against addressing and petitioning them directly as if they possessed the power to act of their own volition in accepting or rejecting petitions. However, if the appeal to the angels is merely that they should discharge their allotted task of conveying our prayers or supporting our petition *to God*, then there is no objection.

Having established the religious validity of an appeal to angels or intermediaries as vehicles of prayer, it is but a minor extension of this concept to place our departed relatives into the angelic category. If the souls of the departed do, indeed, occupy a position of spiritual proximity to "the holy and pure who shine like the brightness of the firmament," then why should they be less effective than angels?

In the episode of the spies, the Torah states, "And *they* went up into the south, and *he* came to Hebron" (Numbers 13:22). The Talmud explains that the "he" refers to Caleb, who slipped away from the other spies and made his way to Hebron in order to prostrate himself at the tombs of the patriarchs at *Makhpelah*. He said to them, "My fathers, seek mercy on my behalf that I may be saved from the evil scheme of the spies."[27]

The Talmud also tells a quaint story of the son of Rav Mari who was being harassed by members of the patriarch's household. The young man thereupon went and prostrated himself over his father's grave, crying, "Father, father, they are causing me distress."[28]

Thus, there is a clear basis for the permissibility of addressing a direct plea to one's departed at the graveside, not that they should come to one's aid or answer one's prayers, but that they should, in turn, add their plea to the source of all blessing and the focus of all prayer.

Part III

The Synagogue

12

The Synagogue and Its Sanctity

A Spiritual Embassy

The synagogue is not merely a house of prayer, but a veritable extension of the Temple in Jerusalem, in much the same way as a country's diplomatic embassy constitutes a piece of the sovereign territory of the country represented by that special building and institution.

The Talmud anticipates the messianic moment when all those "spiritual embassies" all over the Jewish world will be restored to their assigned place in *Eretz Yisrael:* "All the synagogues and Academies of learning will one day be transplanted into the land of Israel."[1] Thus, the ground upon which each and every synagogue stands not only has the religious status of *admat kodesh,* the holy land of Israel, but is an essential parcel of the land itself.

There is a quaint talmudic record[2] of an occasion when Rabbi Yochanan was informed that there were people living in Babylon who had survived to old age. Rabbi Yochanan was astonished at that report, since the Torah states that the reward for keeping the *mitzvot* is that "your days may be multiplied . . . upon the land which the Lord swore to your fathers to give to them" (Deuteronomy 11:21). The implication is

151

that the only longevity that we can expect is on the soil of the holy land, but not in the Diaspora! When his informants proceeded to tell him that those old people are to be found attending synagogue early each morning and staying there late each evening, Rabbi Yochanan's perplexity was resolved: "That is what has secured their longevity!" he asserted.

The *Kli Yakar* finds this answer problematic. He cannot see Rabbi Yochanan's justification for extending the scope of that specific biblical verse, promising the reward of longevity *in* the holy land, to include synagogue attenders *outside* Israel. *Kli Yakar* looks in vain at the biblical verse for any hint that the reward promised can be so extended.

He then offers an ingenious rationale, taking into account the talmudic tradition, referred to above, that the ground of every Diaspora synagogue is to be regarded as a veritable piece of the territory of the holy land itself, being only temporarily sited outside of Israel. *Kli Yakar* suggests that we may consequently understand that the elderly of Babylon, by attending their synagogues on a daily basis, were, in essence, living out their lives on ground that was tantamount to the holy land itself. Thus, there was no conflict with that biblical verse which seems to confine the promise of long life to the land of Israel alone.[3]

This particular concept, of the mystical association of our Diaspora synagogues with the soil of Israel, underscored architecturally by means of the directional focus of our worship toward Jerusalem, reinforces the essential unity of Israel and *Klal Yisrael*, world Jewry. The synagogue has always been our most effective and inspirational unifying force, both spiritually and nationally. We pray for Israel, *toward* Israel, and, according to the *Kli Yakar*, *in* Israel.

Setting Up a Synagogue

A synagogue is a place that is designated as a permanent house of worship for ten or more people and has already been used for divine worship. These are the basic conditions that have to be fulfilled for a building to be regarded as possessing the sanctity of a synagogue.

Wherever ten Jews settle, they have a religious obligation to set up a synagogue. The *Zohar*[4] actually regards this as a biblical command, included in the verse, "And they shall make for me a sanctuary, and I shall dwell in their midst" (Exodus 25:8), a verse that is otherwise regarded as referring exclusively to the desert sanctuary, with no wider application.

According to *halakhah*, it is justifiable to exert pressure on one's coreligionists to contribute toward establishing a synagogue in a town.[5] If there is already a synagogue, however, and for any reason a need arises to establish another one, then it is not permitted to pressure would-be donors, since they have fulfilled their basic religious obligation through the presence of one house of worship in their midst. There is a view that it is, in fact, forbidden to set up a rival synagogue in a town if the existing one is sufficiently large to accommodate all the townspeople.[6] This is on account of the principle *berov am hadrat melekh*, "the greater the throng, the greater the glory to the King" (Proverbs 14:28).[7]

Breakaway Congregations

A breakaway congregation is tolerated, according to this view, only where dissension already exists, and to divide the warring factions into separate congregations, where they can implement their own ideas, will, in fact, help to lessen communal tension. Obviously, where people hail from different countries, where the form of worship was different from that of their new place of domicile, they are permitted to form a new congregation in order to perpetuate their own *minhagim* (traditions).

Another motive for creating a breakaway congregation forms the subject of a query that was submitted to the distinguished talmudist and halakhist, R. Jacob David ben Ze'ev Willowski (*Ridbaz*, 1845–1913), who, toward the end of his life, emigrated to Palestine and founded a large *yeshivah* in Safed.

The question was put to him by a community that, at its foundation, had made a formal agreement that the members would remain united within one synagogue and never split up, in accordance with the principle of *berov am hadrat melekh*. However, they had recently been joined by a large influx of unobservant settlers, and one group wished to break the original agreement and form a separatist synagogue in order that their children should not be influenced by the new arrivals. *Ridbaz* argues in his responsum that this is, indeed, another halakhically justifiable reason for cancelling the original agreement and forming a breakaway congregation, namely, in order to escape from circumstances or an environment that might be inimical to maintaining one's high religious standards.

He bases his opinion on an interesting analogy from the unlikely context of a widow's maintenance from the estate of her late husband who had children from his previous marriage. According to Jewish law, one of the terms specified in the *ketubah* (marriage contract) is that if her husband dies, then as long as the widow does not remarry she may remain in the marital home, and the heirs have a duty to provide "all that is necessary for her due sustenance." The *Mishnah*[8] discusses a situation where a (young) widow prefers to return to live at her father's home, and expects the heirs to bring her food there on a regular basis. The law, in this situation, is as follows: The heirs may say to her, "If you attend our home, you will be given food; if you do not come to join us, then you will not."[9] However, if she claims that her unwillingness to join the heirs at their table is motivated by moral and religious considerations—"since she is still a young woman, and they (the heirs, who are not her own children) are young men," under such circumstances "they must provide her with her sustenance at her father's home."

Ridbaz utilizes this analogy, where mishnaic law permits the letter of the *ketubah* to be set aside for moral reasons, to shed light on the issue put to him. Granted that there was an original agreement not to form a breakaway congregation. However, that was based on the assumption of a *status quo* situation. Where a religious threat is posed, however, by the uninhibited fraternization with antireligious elements, then this is no less valid a reason for breaking the agreement than the moral consideration that allows a young widow to extend the scope of her own *ketubah* agreement.[10]

A moral issue that frequently confronts—or ought to confront—synagogue authorities is whether or not to accept donations or gifts from sources of doubtful integrity. When King David sought a site on which to build an altar, he approached Aravnah the Jebusite with a request that he sell the king his threshing floor. Aravnah was honored, and pressed the king not only to have the site *gratis*, but also to accept "oxen for burnt offerings and threshing-sledges and the yokes of the oxen for the wood" (II Samuel 24:22). King David refused. "No, but I will buy it from you for a price" (II Samuel 24:24).

This passage is employed as a source for the law that no synagogue may be built upon land that has not been legally purchased or by means of donations that have been acquired unlawfully or earned through enterprises that infringe the ethical spirit of Judaism, as may be assumed in the case of the idolatrous Jebusite, Aravnah.

The Sanctity of the Synagogue

A synagogue is a building invested with *kedushah*, sanctity. This derives not from its bricks and mortar, its design or furnishings, nor even from the fact that it contains an Ark and scrolls. Its sanctity is inherent in the synagogue as a result of its role as an institution that is the heir to the Temple and partakes of the divine spirit that originally invested that mother institution.

The prophet Ezekiel discloses the divine promise that Israel in exile will still be in close proximity to the divine spirit, which, though originally concentrated upon the Jerusalem Temple, will now be focused upon a kindred source: "Therefore, thus said the Lord God: Although I have removed them far off among the nations, and scattered them among the countries, yet have I been to them as *a little sanctuary*" (Ezekiel 11:16). Rabbinic tradition interpreted the latter phrase to refer to "the synagogues and Torah academies of Babylon."[11] In other words, the synagogues and Torah academies of the Diaspora, where the spiritual exercises of prayer and study are promoted, are to be considered as institutions of holiness that have become repositories of the divine spirit that originally invested the Temple.

As regards the Temple, the Torah had warned, "You shall revere my sanctuary" (Leviticus 19:30). The *Mishnah*[12] clarifies precisely how this "reverence" is to be given practical expression: "One may not enter the Temple Mount carrying a staff, wearing shoes, or (just) a vest[13] or with dirt adhering to one's feet."

Since the synagogue is a "little sanctuary," it follows that similar regulations, to promote its reverence, also apply. Maimonides codifies these laws, as they are found in the Talmud:

> One must not behave there in an undignified manner, such as to express unbridled laughter, levity or idle chatter. One may not eat or drink therein, use it as a dressing room, an exercising area, or as a place to shelter from the hot sun in summer, or from the rain in winter.[14]

Rabbinic sources augment these examples with many other regulations, all aiming to enhance the honor of the synagogue. Thus, one may not use a synagogue precinct as a means of taking a shortcut to a place further afield. One should walk quickly *to* synagogue, but walk slowly on one's homeward journey, to indicate reluctance to leave the sacred place. A synagogue should be built on the highest level of a town, above the surrounding houses. One synagogue may not be demolished (if it is sound) until its replacement is ready (in case there is a delay in the building program, and the community is left with no synagogue to pray in). A synagogue must have windows, preferably twelve in number, to symbolize the twelve tribes—the entire house of Israel. One may not conduct or make financial calculations in a synagogue, unless they are in the interests of charity or to raise funds in order to ransom a fellow Jew from his captors.

Degrees of Sanctity

Though it is forbidden to eat, drink, or sleep in synagogue, an exception is made in the case of scholars and their disciples who use the synagogue as a place of learning, *Bet Ha-Midrash*. The synagogue is regarded as their home, since, if they have to return to their houses for each meal, much study time will be wasted.

While the synagogue and its appurtenances are sacred objects, yet there are relative degrees of sanctity. These have a practical application, as for example when it is necessary to sell either a synagogue building or some of its ritual objects. Since we have to follow the principle of "increasing holiness and not detracting therefrom" *(maalin ba-kodesh ve-ein moridin)*, we may only sell an object in order to buy with the proceeds something that is invested with a higher degree of sanctity.

The relative volume of holiness contained in each item of synagogal use is specified by the *Mishnah*.[15] The most sacred object is the *Sefer Torah*, followed, in descending order of sanctity, by *Chumashim* (books of the Pentateuch), scroll mantles, the *Aron Kodesh*, and, finally, the synagogue building. Thus, one may sell a synagogue building in order to purchase an Ark, scroll mantles, *Chumashim*, or *Sifrei Torah*, but one may not sell *Sifrei Torah* in order, say, to put the money toward the purchase of a new synagogue building or a new Ark.

On the issue of the permissibility or otherwise of selling a synagogue building, there are a number of halakhic considerations.[16] Suffice to say that we may sell a synagogue building—the lowest in the scale of degrees of holiness—though it will be put to secular use. The rationale is that we regard the holiness as becoming transferred to the money realized by the sale, which must, in turn, be applied, therefore, to another holy enterprise, such as to the building of another synagogue, the religious education of students, or to provide marriage dowries for orphans or poor brides. These are the purposes to which money realized from the sale of a *Sefer Torah* may also be applied.[17]

Weapons in a Synagogue

In the modern State of Israel, with so many Orthodox Jews on National Service or reserve duties *(milluim)* dressed in uniform and carrying weapons, a relevant halakhic issue is whether or not it is in keeping with the sanctity of the synagogue to enter there carrying one's weapons.

The *Shulchan Arukh* refers to this question, saying, "There are those who prohibit entry into a synagogue while carrying a long knife (sword) or with head uncovered *(rosh megulah)*."[18] The peculiar association between these two totally unconnected situations has baffled commentators, and the commonly held view is that the second situation (head uncovered) does not refer to bareheadedness, but to the exposed point ("head") of the weapon referred to in the same context. Hence the *Eliyahu Rabbah* permits a weapon to be brought into a synagogue if it is *concealed* either inside its holster or underneath one's clothing. This inference also explains the *Shulchan Arukh*'s specific reference to a "long knife," since the assumption is that a "short knife," or small weapon, can easily be concealed.

The reason for prohibiting a weapon to be on view in a synagogue is the same motivation that prompted the Torah to prohibit any stones that had been hewn with an iron implement to be used in connection with the altar, "for when your sword is lifted upon it, you profane it" (Exodus 20:22). The rabbis explain that the sword (and, by association, any weapon) is regularly used to shorten life, whereas the altar—whose sacrifices secure atonement for sin—prolongs life. They are therefore mutually incompatible. For the same reason weapons may not be exhibited in a synagogue—a place of prayer and Torah—which, like the altar, "prolongs life."

Microphones in the Synagogue?

Rav Shaul Yisraeli, writing in the halakhic journal *Barkai*,[19] seeks to permit the use of microphones in synagogues on Sabbaths and festivals, given certain safeguards, in the same way as we permit the widespread use of electrical time-switches (*Shabbat* clocks), hearing aids, and induction loop-systems.

The prohibition derives from a statement in the Talmud[20] that only that volume of wheat that may be completely ground before the onset of *Shabbat* may be fed into a water mill on Friday afternoon. In the subsequent discussion, one authority suggests that this restriction only accords with the view of Bet Shammai, whereas the school of Hillel would permit any activity that commenced prior to the onset of *Shabbat* to continue operating, under its own momentum, on *Shabbat* itself. Thus, providing the mill was loaded up before the onset of *Shabbat*,

Hillel, according to this reconstruction of his opinion, would allow the operation to continue under its own momentum on the *Shabbat* itself.

A dissenting authority has it that, in the case of a grinding mill, even Hillel would prohibit its continued automatic activity into the Sabbath, because of a new consideration: that of *hashmaat kol*, namely, that its loudly reverberating, grating sound would impair the sacred tranquility of the Sabbath.

In the *Shulchan Arukh*[21] we find Karo according with the first (and more lenient) interpretation of Hillel's view, which took no account of *hashmaat kol* as a prohibitive factor. Karo consequently rejects the notion that anything that creates a high frequency or amplified sound is prohibited on *Shabbat*. The *Remah* (R. Moses Isserles), on the other hand, agrees with the second interpretation, which suggested that Hillel might have taken a stricter line on the continued operation of a water mill, because of the fact that its noise factor might constitute a halakhic impediment. Thus the *Remah* prohibits amplified sound, "unless the prohibition involves financial (or other) loss."

Rav Yisraeli demonstrates that where the *halakhah* makes such allowances for financial or other loss, the same flexibility is also extended in order to forestall religious loss or neglect of Jewish observance. Thus, although amplified sound may, in general, impair the Sabbath tranquillity, yet, if its employment in the synagogue will actually facilitate attendance, enabling the elderly and hard of hearing better to hear the *chazan*, the reading of the Torah, and the rabbi's words of instruction, then its employment does not infringe *hashmaat kol*.

The issue of "suspicion" *(chashad)*—by those ignorant of the fact that the appliance has been properly programmed for permissible use on the Sabbath, and who may therefore come to suspect the user of infringing the *Shabbat* or *Yom Tov* law—is discounted. While the many passersby who see a water mill operating, and hear it grinding, may indeed suspect that it is being fed with wheat on the holy day, and are unlikely to go and seek clarification, yet it may safely be assumed that, in the close and sociable confines of a synagogue, such clarification will be sought and readily proffered by any member. It is for the same reason—that of ready clarification—that we discount the issue of suspicion in permitting the use of Sabbath lights in the home.

Yisraeli's preconditions for use are: (1) that the appliance is switched on before the *Shabbat* or *Yom Tov*, (2) that a time switch is employed for automatic switching on and off, and (3) that the on-off switch is sealed, and cannot be activated or adjusted by the speaker.

Rav Yisraeli concludes with an appeal to fellow halakhists to assess his findings and to establish, once and for all, a decision for communal implementation. Many will await that assessment with eager anticipation.

13

The Ark and the Bimah

The *Aron Kodesh*

The *Aron* (Ark) is a name borrowed from the Bible, where it refers primarily to the portable container which housed the two Tablets of Stone.[1] It is also applied to the coffin or sarcophagus containing the mummified body of Joseph,[2] as well as to the chest that served as the Temple charity box.[3] Its portable characteristic seems, therefore, to be the basic meaning of the root that underlies this noun. While Hebrew lexicographers list *aron* under the root *aran*—a verbal root whose meaning they cannot explain[4]—the present writer inclines to derive it from the root *arah*, "to pluck up, pick up," with its connotation of mobility and portability.[5] This explains why, in early talmudic times, when the Torah scrolls were housed in an anteroom and brought in only when required to be read, the name *Aron*, "Portable Ark," should have been the one most frequently employed.

When the change was introduced, and the scrolls were kept in a niche in the eastern wall of the synagogue chamber itself, the term *Aron* came to be regarded as an unworthy designation of the new permanent place of honor where the scrolls were housed. Not only was it no longer a portable carrying case, but, in addition, *aron* was the popular term applied to a "coffin" *(aron meitim)*. Both of these considerations must have been in the mind of R. Ishmael b. Eleazar who warned people in the strongest terms against "calling the *Aron Kodesh* simply *Aron*."[6] Other terms were therefore coined in the course of time, the most popular among Sephardim being *Teivah* (literally, "container"), a term already found in the *Mishnah*.[7] In oriental communities the more honorific term *Heikhal*, which occurs in the Bible as a designation of the "sanctuary," "palace," or "temple," was applied to the Ark.

No Arks have come to light among the excavations of early synagogues, though they are a common motif depicted on wall paintings and synagogue mosaics, as well as in catacombs. They appear consistently in the form of double-doored chests with a gabled or rounded top.

The *Parokhet*

The Ark curtain, or *Parokhet*, is intended to be reminiscent of the veil in the desert sanctuary (Exodus 26:31) and the Temple (II Chronicles 3:14). The veil totally partitioned off the Holy of Holies – containing the Ark, inside which was stored the two Tablets of Stone as well as the broken Tablets – from the rest of the sanctuary. It therefore serves the same function in the synagogue: to partition off the Ark containing the scrolls of the Law from the rest of the prayer hall.

The *Parokhet* of the desert sanctuary was made of blue, purple, and scarlet wool, and these have remained the traditional colors of the Ark curtain to the present day, with the exception of the High Holydays, when it is exchanged for a white curtain. As with the Ark itself, archaeology has yet to unearth a relic of an ancient *Parokhet*, though, once again, its use is clearly attested from floor mosaics at Bet She'an, Bet Alfa, and Hammat-Tiberias, where it is depicted as hanging in front of the Ark.

The distinction between Ashkenazi and Sephardi Ark curtains – in the former case the *Parokhet* hangs in front of the doors; in the latter it is inside, behind them, – might well reflect regional variety going back as far as talmudic times.

While our sources are not absolutely clear, Palestinian and Babylonian scholars seem to be referring to totally different objects and purposes in their respective references to the *Parokhet*. The Palestinian sage, R. Yose, implies that it is a kind of free-standing partition, positioned a few feet in front of the Ark and leaving sufficient room for the Torah scroll to be rolled up between it and the Ark, away from the gaze of the congregation.[8] The Babylonian Raba, on the other hand, refers to a multipurpose detachable curtain, hanging either on the inside or outside of the Ark doors, and used, folded, as a cover for the *Sefer Torah* when it lay on the reading desk, or as a cover for the reading desk itself when the Torah was placed on it.[9]

The decorative embroidery of lions and other animals and symbols upon the *Parokhet* is a custom hallowed by age, though one that has occasioned much unease among halakhists. As the excavation of early (4th century) synagogues has revealed, Jews believed that decorative art had a place in the house of God, in line with the principle, "This is my God and I shall *glorify* him" (Exodus 15:2). The latter verb, in Hebrew, is *ve-anveihu*, from the root *navah*, which the rabbis connect with the verb *naah*, "to be beautiful." This became transformed into a rabbinic plea to "beautify" God by using the most appealing ritual objects possible *(hiddur mitzvah)* for worship.[10]

The permissibility of introducing decorative art into the synagogue was enshrined in a most unlikely source, the Aramaic *Targum Yonatan (Pseudo-Jonathan)*. On the verse "Ye shall not place any figured stone in your land, to bow down to it" (Leviticus 26:1), the *Targum* observes, "But a flooring on which designs and likenesses are carved you may introduce into your sanctuaries, though not to prostrate yourselves on it."

Much license was taken in this area; and artists, with their traditional distaste for convention, regularly introduced pagan themes from Graeco-Roman mythology. While in the excavated synagogue at Bet Alfa biblical scenes were depicted, yet elsewhere we find mosaics representing the zodiacal wheel, with the sun-god in the center. At Chorazin a frieze depicted Hercules and human figures, at Hammat-Tiberias a representation of Helios supporting the globe with a whip in his hand, and at Capernaum figures of Eros carrying flowers!

The penetration of Greek aesthetics into Jewish life was regarded by some sages[11] as quite acceptable, indeed as the fulfillment of the biblical prophecy that "God would enlarge Japhet's beauty, and it shall dwell in the tents of Shem" (Genesis 9:27). On this basis, the Talmud[12] prohibits the Torah to be written in any foreign language other than Greek, the language of Japhet.

It seems that the patriarchs of Palestine were the patrons of those impressive early synagogues. Bearing in mind their need to fraternize with, and impress, the Roman occupiers, and the fact that they were also under considerable pressure from wealthy Hellenized families who constituted the diplomatic corps and played an important role in the

Roman civil administration, it is easy to understand why Graeco-Roman art should have gained such easy access into the synagogue. True piety resided in the schools of learning and in the small prayer houses. The lavish synagogues were rather opportunities for demonstrating that Rome was not alone in its ability to construct fine buildings, and that the Jews were also appreciative of wider culture and aesthetics.[13]

When excavated, many of those pagan symbols were found to have been defaced already, before the rubble of the ages had covered them. This suggests that there were already conscientious objectors who had demonstrated their feelings by means of iconoclastic activity. Their objections were based on the belief that such representations contravened the second Commandment. This was not a view that was shared, however, by some of the most distinguished talmudists of the age, such as _Rav_ and _Shemuel_, who did not shirk from praying in a synagogue in Nehardea, which had an imperial image.[14] As to the charge that they might be causing people to misconstrue their action, and suspect them of idolatrous inclinations _(chashada)_, they replied that such a fear does not exist where a crowd of people are openly visiting a public place.

Whether such artistic representations did or did not contravene the _halakhah_ was not the sole consideration, however; and a growing number of scholars expressed their opposition to it on the grounds that lavish ornamentation was indefensible when such excessive expenditure could have been better applied to the support of poor Torah students.[15]

This attitude ultimately won the day; and the tendency for plain walls and floors was nourished subsequently by the Arab invasion of Palestine, and the implacable opposition of Islam to the infiltration of pagan art into a house of God. But the urge to beautify the synagogue did not die out, though artistry henceforth assumed a lower profile and was channeled into exquisite design of the appurtenances rather than into the decoration of walls and floors.

The _Parokhet_ inevitably became the focus of artistic attention, and it became customary to endow it with richly colored embroidery, often embodying animal forms and symbols, particularly that of the lion, symbol of majesty and power. As such, its role on the Ark cover is to symbolize that the Ark houses the constitution of the "King of Kings." The lion is also the symbol of the tribe of Judah (Genesis 49:9), and, as such, was regarded as the emblem of Jewry, descendants of that tribe (and of Benjamin) when the remaining ten tribes were taken into captivity, and "lost," in 721 B.C.E. As a member of the feline species, the lion shared the former's association with immortality, which explains why felines appear so often on both pagan and Jewish sarcophagi. The association with the Ark lies in our belief that the Torah is the "key to immortality which God has implanted within us" *(va-chayyei olam nata be-tokheinu)*.

While the second Commandment clearly prohibits "any manner of *likeness* of anything that is in the heaven above or the earth beneath" (Exodus 20:4), the continuation of the verse makes it quite clear that the prohibition is purely in order to prevent the idolatrous worship of such symbols. The *Ran* states, therefore, that the fear of causing others to falsely suspect an act of idolatry *(chashada)* only applied in the case of objects which heathens did actually worship at that time. He therefore concludes that "nowadays, all kinds of representations are permitted."[16] Hence Karo permits designs, "even in relief, of animals, beasts, birds and fish, trees and plants."[17]

Shakh adds the significant gloss that "it would seem that all the forms that were forbidden are only prohibited if in complete form; for example, the likeness of a man with two eyes, a complete nose and entire body; but not if incomplete, as in the case of some artists who reproduce only a profile. This is not prohibited."[18] Most of the animal representations on our Ark cover are, indeed, merely in profile. Nevertheless, there are authorities who counsel against embroidering animals on the *Parokhet*, "so that it does not appear as if we are bowing toward them."[19] Other authorities object to such embroidery since it causes a distraction while praying, in the same way that the *Shulchan Arukh* objects to praying opposite a brightly embroidered wall or garment.

This question, of the propriety of having such a *Parokhet* embroidered with lions, is dealt with also in the responsa of contemporary halakhists. Rabbi Chaim David Ha-Levi, while reticent to declare prohibited a custom which great sages of previous generations have condoned, yet expresses firm inclination to discourage the practice.[20] Rabbi Ovadiah Yoseph, on the other hand, has no such qualms, and boldly asserts that "it is prohibited to hang a *Parokhet* that has lions embroidered on it, or to fix a bronze or marble form of a lion, or similar form, above the Ark."[21]

The Ark Maxim and the *Ner Tamid*

Above the *Parokhet*, near the top of the Ark, it is customary to inscribe a religious maxim or exhortation. The most popular choice was the verse from Psalm 16:8, *Shiviytiy ha-shem le-negdiy tamid*, "I have set the Lord continually before me." This Psalm-verse was hailed by one talmudist,

R. Shimon bar Shilat, as encapsulating the precise attitude of awe that should characterize one's frame of mind as one stands in prayer: "R. Shimon (the Pious) said: When praying, one should sense that the very Divine Presence is before one, as it is written, 'I have set the Lord continually before me.' "[22] So popular did this maxim become that, according to some commentators, R. Shimon was called *bar Shilat* not after his father, but as a tribute to his having promoted the cause of prayer. *Shilat*, they say, is a contraction based on the initial letters of the verse *Shiviytiy ha-shem le-negdiy tamid*.

The famous mystic, R. Isaac Luria, invested this verse with particular significance and a unique emphasis. He inferred from it the directive to "set *the word* 'the Lord' continually before one" during prayer. He therefore instructed his disciples to draw the four letter name of God on a card, and to suspend it in front of the cantor's *amud* (desk). These four letters of the Tetragrammaton were accompanied by the vowels *chirik (i)*, *shevah (e)*, and *kamatz (a)*, which are the vowels under the initial letters of the words *Shíviytiy lé-negdiy támid*.[23]

Besides its intrinsic message, there was also the association which the last word, *tamid*, suggests with the *Ner Tamid*, "the everlasting light," which is suspended in front of the *Parokhet*. In this way there was effected a reinforcement of the message of God's presence being "continually" in the fore of Israel's consciousness.

The *Ner Tamid* symbolizes that Presence, and is reminiscent of the seven-branched *Menorah*, whose lights had to burn continually *(tamid)*, in the sanctuary (Exodus 27:20-1) and the Temples. Indeed, the *Menorah* is referred to in I Samuel 3:3 as *ner elohim*, "the lamp of God," since light is a symbol of both God's presence and His Torah.[24]

Other communities preferred to inscribe a verse that was less self-confident. While King David could affirm that he had "set the Lord *at all times*" before him, it is hardly a testimony that the rest of us can so easily assert. An alternative, in the form of an exhortation, *Da lifnei miy attah omeid* ("Know before whom you are standing"), therefore became popular.

This verse presents a significant contrast to the maxim, "know *thyself*," which classical Greece inscribed at Delphi, the seat of its most famous oracle at the temple of Apollo. While the Greeks—and their cultural heirs—believed that a life spent in the cultivation of one's own emotional and physical potential was the *summum bonum*, the Jews believed that contemplation of *God* was the only constructive and beneficial human endeavor, one so comprehensive as to lead to knowledge of the *self* at one and the same time. Knowledge of God truly reveals knowledge of oneself.

But why do we use only a single lamp for the *Ner Tamid*, and not the seven as used in the Temple *Menorah?* It would seem that our single *Ner Tamid* actually corresponds to one particular lamp in the seven-branched *Menorah,* which, according to tradition, miraculously burned continuously and never went out, even if its oil was not replenished. This miracle is supposed to have ceased on the death of Shimon the Righteous, during the Second Temple period. The particular light is referred to in the *Mishnah*[25] as the *(Ner) Maaraviy,* "the Western Lamp," and was so called not because it was a separate light placed on the western side of the sanctuary, but simply because it was the second wick from the right, and, in relation to its neighbor (the extreme right-hand wick, which was closest to the *eastern* wall), it was a "western lamp."[26]

Because the *Ner Tamid* commemorates that miraculously ever-burning, "western" wick of the Temple *Menorah,* it was the original custom to place the *Ner Tamid* inside a niche in the western wall of the synagogue. It was later regarded as disrespectful to turn one's back to the lamp while facing east, and it was then given its permanent place, suspended in front of the Ark.

We have no evidence of the *Ner Tamid* as a synagogue symbol before the 16th century C.E.

The Rabbi's Seat

Next to the *Aron Kodesh* is the traditional place for the rabbi's seat. This special seat of honor, as a symbol of leadership, has a very long history. The Talmud[27] records that the famous Alexandrian synagogue had seventy-one such golden seats, or *cathedrae,* for members of the Sanhedrin.

The Midrash[28] calls such a seat by the name *Katedra de Mosheh,* "The Seat of Moses," a term well-known even outside the confines of the Jewish community:

> The Doctors of the Law and the Pharisees sit *in the seat of Moses.* Therefore do what they tell you; pay attention to their words." (Matthew 23:1–2)

The term is intended to imply that its occupant possesses the authority and prerogative of spiritual leadership as inherited from Moses.[29] Such a seat of honor for the leader of the community has, in fact, been discovered among the excavations of the synagogue at Dura.[30]

The "Sage's Seat" was also a feature of contemporary Samaritan tradition. In the 4th century C.E., the great Samaritan leader, Baba Rabbah, achieved an interlude of peace for his community. His first act was to rebuild its houses of prayer that had been destroyed:

> He took some of the stones of the Temple that had been destroyed by the men of King Saul . . . and set up seven of them as seven seats for his seven sages, and he took one great stone for himself to sit on.[31]

Significantly, Baba Rabbah regarded himself as a "second Moses"[32]; and the designation of the special seats, for himself and his appointed leaders, may owe its origin to the same common Palestinian tradition as reflected in Jewish—as well as Christian—sources. That such stone seats were a feature of Jewish synagogues has also been proved by archaeological finds at Chorazin and Hammat-Tiberias. Excavations at Sardis revealed that three tiers of concentric benches were provided at the front of the synagogue as seats for the elders, a tradition we were already aware of from the talmudic description of the great Alexandrian synagogue.

In most large, present-day synagogues there are two boxes, one on either side of the *Aron Kodesh;* and it has become a practice in some synagogues for the *chazan* to occupy the other box. This was not the case in the Middle Ages when the *chazan's* elevated seat was situated close to the place from where he conducted the services[33]; and in most synagogues the second seat next to the Ark is reserved for visiting clergy.

The *Bimah*

After the *Aron Kodesh,* the second focal point in a synagogue is the *Bimah,* also referred to as the *Almemar,* from the Arabic noun *Al minbar,* a dais or platform. Sephardim retain the talmudic term, *Teivah.*

Maimonides[34] states that the *Bimah* should be in the middle of the synagogue, "so that the one who is reading from the Torah, or giving a sermon of exhortation, may ascend thereon." This suggests that its central position is merely functional, to facilitate the official's voice being heard by all. Indeed, Maimonides' requirement of a central *Bimah* is based on the one talmudic source[35] that refers specifically to a gigantic synagogue in Alexandria, so vast that attendants had to wave flags to indicate to the throng that they should answer *Amen* to a blessing. Maimonides' reference to the *Bimah* being required for the sermon also proves, beyond doubt, that in his view its central location was not a halakhic imperative, but merely an acoustic benefit. Joseph Karo concurs with this, and adds that "in antiquity, when they had very large synagogues, it was necessary to place the *Bimah* in the center, so that all the people could hear; but in our times, when, as a result of our sins, our synagogues are small and everyone can hear, it is aesthetically preferable for the *Bimah* to be at one end rather than in the middle."[36]

A considerable web of legend seems to have been woven around that Alexandrian synagogue; and the Talmud—always a faithful recorder of traditions, though often leaving it to the student to make value judgments on their relevance and authority—even quotes a tradition that sometimes a congregation of over a million—"double the number of men who went out of Egypt"—was accommodated there! (Such a "tradition" is quoted in the Talmud by Rabbi Judah, who, it must not be forgotten, could never have personally seen that edifice, which was destroyed by the Emperor Trajan in 116 C.E., long before Judah was born.)

So, Alexandria apart, archaeological evidence has not yet provided corroboration of the existence of central *Bimahs* in ancient synagogues. We know that a *chazan's* reading desk, at the side of the Ark, was introduced around the 5th and 6th century C.E., but "the central *Bimah* or Almemor . . . apparently came into use considerably later."[37]

The question of whether a central *Bimah* is a halakhic imperative, or merely a recommendation, became a major issue among the many acrimonious controversies which widened the rift between Orthodoxy and Reform in the early 19th century. The Reform synagogues moved the *Bimah* from the center to just in the front of the Ark in order to parallel the Church arrangement where the importance of the altar is highlighted by its prominence at the front. When R. Moses Schreiber *(Chatam Sofer)* was asked by an Orthodox community whether, on rebuilding their synagogue, they could move the *Bimah* to the front, he gave a categorical ruling that this was not permitted. The central *Bimah* now became, as a matter of principle, the hallmark of the Orthodox synagogue; and this was underlined by a formal declaration issued in 1886 and subscribed to by a long and distinguished list of the leading rabbis of Hungary and Galicia.[38]

It must be admitted that the central *Bimah* has proved a boon for the cantor in his need to project his voice to all parts of the synagogue. Maimonides naturally made no reference to the *chazan* in delineating the purpose of the central *Bimah*, since it is only in comparatively recent centuries that the *Bimah* has come to be identified primarily as the place from which the *chazan* leads the services, rather than from where the Torah is read and the preacher gives exhortation.

From the point of view of Orthodox tradition, the raised *Bimah* is far from being the ideal place from which the *chazan* should lead the service. Quite the contrary: from the very beginning of the institution of prayer houses, the psalmist's sentiment, "Out of the depths have I called upon You" (Psalm 130:1), was taken literally. The regular term employed in the Talmud to describe the *chazan* is "the one who *descends* before the reader's stand" *(ha-yoreid lifnei ha-teivah)*. The *chazan's* desk was always placed in a low position, with the worshipers' seats rising in a tiered arrangement, as in a lecture hall, behind him.[39] The low position symbolized humility and total submission.

In the course of time this style of architecture was phased out, and the *chazan's* desk was placed on a level with, or at the foot of, the stairs leading up to the Ark. This was accepted as not being in conflict with a posture of humility. The Talmud is emphatic, however, that "one may not stand on a high spot and pray,"[40] for that is a symbol of haughtiness. Some of our halakhic authorities consequently come down very strongly against the use of the *Bimah* by *chazanim*.[41]

Some have attempted to justify the use of the *Bimah* by the *chazan* by citing once again the talmudic references to the Alexandrian synagogue where, "there was a *wooden Bimah*, in the center of which the *chazan ha-kneset* would stand with flags in his hand, and when the time to recite *Amen* arrived, he would wave the flag and all the people would respond." Such a source is no evidence, however, for the permissibility of the *chazan* to stand on the *Bimah*, since the *chazan ha-kneset* referred to there is not to be equated with the synagogue prayer leader, but rather the sexton or overseer. It was the latter, not the reader, who stood on the raised *Bimah* so that everyone could see him waving his flags as a signal. "Although the *chazan's* voice was not at all audible to vast numbers of worshipers, no attempt was made to rectify the situation by stationing him upon the raised *Bimah* rather than in his traditional position at the front of the synagogue."[42]

14

The Sefer Torah

Its Contents

The *Sefer Torah* – Scroll of the Law – contains the Pentateuch, or Five Books of Moses: a compound of history, law, symbolic ritual, and moral guidance, commencing with the Creation and tracing the development of the Hebrew nation from Abraham through to the slavery in Egypt, the Exodus, the giving of the Torah at Mount Sinai, and the forty years of wandering in the desert until the death of Moses.

Although passages from the other two main sections of the Hebrew Bible – the Prophets and the Sacred Writings – also provide texts for synagogue reading, they do not compare in importance or sanctity with the Pentateuch.

It is in the words of the Pentateuch that the Divine Revelation is described and the Divine Will communicated. It is from there that the spirit of Jewish nationalism draws its authentication, inspiration, and impetus, and it is in that source that Israel's mission and religious ideology is delineated.

The unique sanctity of the Pentateuch is also expressed by the reverence accorded to the handwritten Torah Scrolls, and the meticulous and detailed regulations that govern the preparation and writing of

169

the manuscript. These regulations were codified in a special tract of the Talmud written over 1,200 years ago and followed in every detail to the present day.

The *Sofer*

The preparation of the parchment as well as the writing is done by pious, skilled, and learned men called *soferim*, scribes. It is an art that calls for dedication as well as immense powers of concentration.

There are 5,888 verses and 79,976 words in the Torah, and it takes a skilled *sofer*, working about eight hours a day, some nine months to complete the writing of a scroll.

The *sofer* is not just an artistic scribe. He is primarily a uniquely pious individual who has devoted his life to the precise and exacting task of ensuring that *Torah, tefillin,* and *mezuzah* parchments are prepared and written with sacred intention and with strict adherence to their numerous and detailed regulations. Judaism has a proud boast that the text of the Torah has never been altered, neither has it suffered from the errors of scribal transmission which characterize most ancient texts and medieval manuscripts. We consequently refer to our Pentateuchal text as *masoretic* (literally, "as originally *handed down*"). A *sofer* was never permitted to write from memory. Though most of them inevitably knew the whole text by heart, they had to copy, word for word, from authorized master copies. And this law is still rigidly implemented.

Immunity to Scribal Errors

A number of laws provide an indication of how the Torah succeeded in immunizing itself from the otherwise inevitable infiltration and reproduction of errors, variant versions, and even sectarian glosses or readings, all of which were the lot of the early translations, such as the Greek renderings of Septuagint, Aquila, and Symmachos, the Latin Vulgate, and some Aramaic targumic fragments. The main factor is the necessity of immediately correcting any error in the public reading of the Torah, and insisting that the *baal korei* repeats the word correctly. This is necessary not only to ensure that the congregation hears every word of the authentic Torah, but also in order to detect any error in the scroll itself. Secondly, if any error reveals itself — even a minor spelling mistake or a single letter so faded that it makes it difficult for a sensible child of seven or eight to read the word — the scroll has to be removed immediately from the reading desk, even in the middle of a portion, and replaced with another scroll. To ensure that a faulty scroll does not somehow get mixed up with the other scrolls before it is corrected, it is the custom to wrap the binder[1] around the outside of the mantle of the scroll as a distinguishing sign.

Another law further ensures against the possibility of scribal errors becoming legitimated and popularized. This is the law that states that "a scroll that has not been corrected may not be kept in one's possession for longer than thirty days." It must be either corrected or put away in the *genizah*, the store for worn out and disqualified scrolls, books, and ritual appurtenances.[2] Furthermore, all scrolls have to be given to a *sofer* every few years for checking, since dampness or other atmospherical conditions can easily cause the writing to fade.

The Preparation of a Torah Scroll

The Torah is written with a quill pen obtained from goose or turkey feathers and an ink preparation containing gall nuts, copper sulphate crystals, and gum arabic. The parchment has to be made from the skin of a species of animal that is permitted for food. Even if that particular animal was *neveilah* or *terefah*, i.e., it died of its own accord, or the slaughtering was not performed correctly, or it had an organic disqualification, the skin may still be used for a *Sefer Torah*.

The skin of the animal is immersed in water for a day or two, and the flesh adhering to it is then scraped off. It is left for up to a week in a lime solution to get rid of all the hairs adhering to the skin, and is then treated, cleaned, bleached, and stretched on a special press, so that it is white and flat, before its edges are cut straight and square. The surface we write on is the one upon which the animal's hair originally grew, not the surface which adhered to the flesh.

The whole process of treating the hide — as well as the actual writing of the scroll — has to be performed *le-sheim mitzvah*, with a sacred intention to use it for a Torah scroll. The individual hides, called *yeriot* (literally "curtains"), are sewn together with threads of gut, called *gidin*.

In order that the text should be beautiful to look at, detailed regulations were established regarding layout. The text is set out in columns of 42 lines. This number is the numerical value of the Hebrew word *bam* in the phrase *ve-dibarta bam* ("And you shall speak *of them*") in the first paragraph of the *Shema*. Our custom is for each column to commence with the letter *vav*, a feature that is referred to, by a play on words, as *vavei ha-amudim* ("the *vavs* of the columns"), which occurs in Exodus 38:10. (Its literal meaning there, is "the hooks of the posts.")

There had to be at least one exception to this rule, as, quite obviously, the very first column of the Torah could not begin with a *vav*, since the first word of the Torah is *Bereishit*. This exception was extended to a total of five columns, whose exceptional initial letters are *bet, yod, hey, shin, mem*, making up the phrase *BeYaH SHeMo*—"His name is *Yah*."

There are rules governing the width of margin to be left around the text. The lower margin has to be greater than that along the upper edge of the scroll, since the hand comes into contact with the lower edge, and the *tallit* or sleeve of the one reading the Torah may rest on it and wear it away.

The precise method of writing each letter is prescribed, and is not left to individualistic style. In order to ensure straight lines, and ends of lines perfectly aligned on either side, the law prescribes a procedure called *sirtut*, "indentation," whereby the scribe lightly draws a sharp edge along each line and down each side of each column, providing an imprint to guide him.

To further enhance the beauty of the script, seven letters of the alphabet are adorned with decorative crowns or flourishes, called *taggin*, whenever they occur. These are the letters *shin, ayin, tet, nun, zayin, gimmel, tzadi*, popularly referred to by the mnemonic of their initial letters: *shaatnez gatz*.

There is a beautiful *Midrash*[3] in this connection, which states that when Moses died and arrived in heaven, he found God weaving the *taggin* on those letters. When he questioned God as to their purpose, he was told that, some time in the future, a unique teacher would arise in Israel by the name of Rabbi Akivah, and he would create mountains of religious traditions on every single flourish of the sacred text. In order to increase Akivah's scope, God was adding these extra flourishes to the text!

Apart from its intrinstic beauty, this midrash conveys the profound message that each generation has something to contribute toward the spiritual heritage. Each generation has new insights to disclose, and never can it be said of Torah that its last word has been uttered, that it has been entirely fathomed—even by Moses! It is ageless and eternal.

The *Atzei Chayyim*

Out of reverence for the Torah scrolls it was declared forbidden to touch the parchment with one's hand. The introduction of two wooden supportive staves, called *Atzei Chayyim* ("Trees of Life"), to which the beginning and end of the parchment roll is attached, was in order to ensure that the Torah could be opened, closed, and rolled to any part without the hands having to touch the parchment. The mantle that is placed over the scroll also ensures that even the back of the parchment is not handled while carrying the Torah.

In an obscure remark of Karo, in his *Bet Yoseph* commentary,[4] he seems to be criticizing the Ashkenazim for handling the *Atzei Chayyim* staves with bare hands while performing the *mitzvah* of *hagbahah*. Karo is taken to task for this by the distinguished and authoritative Ashkenazi halakhist, R. David ben Samuel HaLevi *(Taz)*, who asserts that the *Atzei Chayyim* may certainly be handled since they have no intrinsic sanctity, being merely in the category of *tashmish*, ritual accoutrements, to facilitate the performance of a *mitzvah*. He concludes by observing that "we have never seen, even among those who are ultra scrupulous in such matters, anyone recoiling from bringing their hands into direct contact with the staves."

Karo's comment was probably motivated by his feelings about the superior practice of the Sephardim, who housed their scrolls inside an arch-shaped wooden case, frequently decorated in leather, metal, or with silver platelets. The two halves of the Torah case are hinged so that they open out like a book to reveal the parchment inside. The open case is placed on the reading desk, and the Torah remains inside, standing upright, unlike the Ashkenazi scroll, which lies flat on the desk. Thus, the person performing the *mitzvah* of *hagbahah* with a Sephardi scroll merely takes hold of the Torah case, and opens it out to reveal the scroll inside. He does not hold the *Atzei Chayyim*, as do the Ashkenazim, a practice of which Karo disapproved.

The *Yad*

Since great concentration is required while performing the *Keriat ha-Torah* ("Reading of the Law"), to make sure that one is reading the unpointed and unpunctuated text accurately and with the correct and traditional musical notes (or *trop*, as the special system is called), it is necessary therefore to point to every word. As every word and phrase is sacred, having emanated from God on Sinai, we are not permitted to vary even a letter of the text. To ensure that we don't skip over a word, or omit a line, as can so easily happen when the eye moves swiftly from the end of one line to the beginning of another—frequently containing similar vocabulary—tradition insists that the *chazan*, or *baal korei*, points to every word as he recites it. Since, as we have observed, it is forbidden to run one's finger over the text itself, we use a *Yad*, a ritual pointer.

Yad means "a hand," and the end of the pointer is generally shaped like a hand with one finger protruding to enable the reader to use it to point to each word. They are usually made of silver, or wrought with silver filigree work, and sometimes set with semiprecious stones. In Israel, pointers made from olive wood are favored by less affluent congregations, schools, kibbutzim, and army prayer houses.

The Decorative Mantle and Binder

While the Sephardi parchment roll was totally encased, the Ashkenazim had recourse to another method of ensuring that hands did not touch even the back of the parchment when carrying the Torah. This was the provision of a decorative mantle. The mantle has two apertures in its top surface, and it is lifted above the scroll, and pulled down to completely enclose it, with the top of the two *Atzei Chayyim* staves protruding through the upper apertures. The *Atzei Chayyim* (singularly, *Etz Chayyim*) Trees of Life, are so named because these supportive staves are reminiscent of trees, which, in turn, are a symbol of the Torah itself, a metaphor employed in the verse, "She is a tree of life to those that hold fast to her" (Proverbs 3:18). Torah, like the fruitful tree, is constantly renewing its inspirational fruit.

The person carrying the Torah rests it against his right shoulder, and, with his right arm across the front of the mantle, he holds it firmly in his arms. The mantle is loose fitting, and does not really help to keep the parchment roll from coming undone or slipping down. In order to avoid this happening, particularly if it has not been rolled sufficiently tight, the Ashkenazim bind a long, wide linen wrapper tightly around the outside of the scroll, underneath the mantle.

In Germany and some Eastern European communities the binder, or *Wimpel*, used to be made out of a baby boy's swaddling cloth. This was cut into strips and the pieces were sewn together. It was then embroidered, generally with a design incorporating the child's Hebrew name, followed by the traditional blessing that "he should grow up to be a student of Torah; he should happily attain to the *chupah* ('marriage'), and perform *maasim tovim* ('deeds of kindness') all his life." Embroidered representations of these three facets of religious life were also frequently included. When the boy attained the age of *Bar Mitzvah*, the scroll from which he read was bound up with his personal binder.

The Torah Ornaments

The endowment of the Torah with fine ornaments to enhance its beauty seems to have been an ancient practice. The Talmud[5] preserves a stanza from a liturgical hymn, sung by the congregation as the portable Torah Ark was brought into the synagogue chamber. It is recorded by R. Isaac Nappacha, a 3rd-century C.E. Palestinian scholar:

> Sing, sing, O Ark of acacia wood,
> Be exalted in all your splendor.
> With golden weave they cover you,
> A palace resplendent with the Torah scrolls
> Adorned in the finest ornaments.

In another passage the Talmud[6] counsels: "Have a beautiful Torah scroll prepared, copied by a skilled scribe, with fine ink and calamus, *and wrapped in beautiful silk.*"

We have referred above to the silver *Yad*, which had a practical purpose. Other items of pure adornment were also provided: the two *Rimmonim*, the breastplate and the crown. By the 11th century these were established as the most appropriate adornment.

The *Rimmonim* are silver sheaths, or finials, that are placed on the top of each of the *Atzei Chayyim*. The word means, literally, "pomegranates," and is derived from the context of the High Priest's robe, which was embroidered at its hem with golden bells, and blue, purple, and scarlet balls shaped like pomegranates (Exodus 28:33). In rabbinic literature the pomegranate is used as a metaphor for Torah erudition. Like the pomegranate abounds in pips, so does the Torah scholar have a superabundance of knowledge.[7] Hence the appropriateness of the name as a Torah ornament.

The breastplate is also derived from the High Priestly context, it being one of his most important items of ritual apparel, referred to as "the breastplate of judgment." Into it were fixed the *Urim* and *Tumim*, used for ascertaining the divine will on matters of national importance. As a focus of the divine will, the breastplate is also an appropriate symbol, therefore, to adorn the Torah, the revealed will of God.

The most common design of the breastplate is consequently a representation of the twelve precious stones that were set into that of the High Priest. Each stone was engraved with the name of one of the tribes of Israel, and the stones were arranged in four rows of three stones.[8] The breastplate is suspended over the front of the mantle from above, by means of a heavy chain draped around the *Atzei Chayyim*.

It is suggested that the breastplate was originally introduced as a development from an original custom of hanging a tab over the Torah to indicate that that particular scroll was to be used on a particular Sabbath or festival, as it had already been rolled to the respective portion to be read on that occasion.

The ornamental *Keter Torah*, "Crown of the Torah," is a concrete representation of a common rabbinic concept. The crown of the Torah is one of three "crowns" in the world, the others being "the crown of kingdom" and "the crown of a good name."[9] It is also related to the fact that, as mentioned above, certain letters of the alphabet are artistically embellished with "crowns" as an adornment of the text.

The crown is generally an alternative ornament to the *Rimmonim*, and may originally have been used only on special occasions, such as at the presentation and consecration ceremony of the scroll, or on Simchat Torah. It fits completely over the two *Atzei Chayyim*, and rests above the flat top surface of the mantle. The crown is frequently encircled with silver bells. These again recall the (golden) bells on the hem of the High Priest's robe. Bells are frequently added also to the *Rimmonim* and the breastplate, thereby creating a distinctive and melodious ringing sound at the slightest movement of the scroll.

Touching a Torah—A Male Prerogative?

In all Orthodox synagogues the *Sefer Torah* is regarded as the exclusive preserve of the men. Men run to kiss the *Sefer* as it is carried in procession to and from the Ark, and men dance with the *Sefer* on Simchat Torah. Even in this age of sexual equality, few Orthodox women would press for the privilege of touching or holding a *Sefer Torah*. It is assumed that the laws governing the menstrual period *(niddah)* of women would, of necessity, preclude their physical contact with the holy scroll.

The Talmud states, however, that "words of Torah are not susceptible to uncleanliness,"[10] and on this basis Maimonides states categorically that "even a woman during her period of menstruation may hold the scroll of the Torah and read from it."[11]

The reticence of women to touch a *Sefer Torah* seems to have arisen as a result of the sole dissenting voice of Rabbi Moses Isserles, that distinguished authority of Ashkenazi tradition, who discouraged menstruating women from "entering a synagogue, praying, mentioning God's name or *touching a Sefer Torah*."[12] In a recent study,[13] Rabbi Avraham Weiss has drawn attention to some inconsistencies in Isserles' position, and he tells us, *inter alia*, that almost all other halakhic authorities consider it a mere stringency to prevent women from touching a scroll, even during their *niddah* period. Rabbi Weiss concludes, therefore, by posing the question whether the common practice of banning women from touching the Torah justifies the numerous benefits that would accrue from encouraging them to do so.[14]

Removing a *Sefer Torah*

As the repository of the word of God, the *Sefer Torah* obviously commands our greatest respect. There are many regulations that serve to promote this, such as the law that prohibits the removal of a scroll from its permanent place in the synagogue to another temporary location, even if the purpose of the move is in order to use the scroll for reading at a service. The situation referred to in the *Shulchan Arukh* is where Jews in a prison are granted permission to hold a service on Rosh Hashanah or Yom Kippur. It is still regarded as detracting from the honor of the *Sefer Torah* to transport it there for such an occasional use.[15]

In a situation where, by transporting the Torah from its permanent place, one is, in fact, enhancing the dignity of the Torah, talmudic law permits its removal. Hence it was the custom to take a scroll to the residence of the head of Babylonian Jewry, the Exilarch.

R. Moses Isserles opened the door to a more lenient practice by stating that if a special place is designated, and an Ark or receptacle provided, for the *Sefer Torah* to be housed in dignity in its temporary location for a day or two, then it may be removed there. While some halakhists refused to endorse this lenient view, it did, however, lend authority to what soon became the common practice of taking a scroll to a house of mourning to enable morning services with *Keriat ha-Torah* to take place there. Some are particular that the Torah should be read on at least three occasions in the house of mourning, so that an element of permanence or regularity *(chazakah)* may be said to justify having removed the Torah to a private house.

Removal of a *Sefer Torah* from its permanent place is similarly permitted by some authorities where the purpose of its removal is in order to do honor to the Torah, as, for example, to carry it in procession at the dedication ceremony of a new scroll, or to make up a complement of seven scrolls for the seven circuits of the *Bimah (hakkafot)* on Simchat Torah. The *Arukh Ha-Shulchan* strongly condemns, however, those who remove a *Sefer Torah* purely for their own convenience, to have a parallel reading in another room of the synagogue and to return it to the synagogue Ark after use. Apparently this was a practice of some communities on Rosh Hashanah, Yom Kippur, and Simchat Torah, when there was a desire to give more people *aliyot*.[16]

Division According to the Annual and Triennial Cycles

While the Torah scroll does not contain any commas, stresses, full stops, or subsidiary punctuation marks, such as are represented by the system of *neginot* (cantillations) provided in our printed *Chumashim*, yet our *Masorah*—tradition of textual transmission—does contain certain regulations that affect the nature of weekly divisions, paragraphs, and the way certain words or letters have to be transcribed.

As regards the division of the Pentateuch into weekly portions *(sidrot)*, from talmudic times there existed two different traditions: those of Babylon and Palestine. The Babylonian tradition divided up the Pentateuch into fifty-four *parashiyyot*, or *sedarim*, to accommodate an *annual* cycle of weekly readings, a system that has remained our universal practice. While Ashkenazim borrowed the name *parashah*, which originally signified the entire weekly reading, and applied it to denote each of the seven subsections into which the weekly portion is divided, they retained the alternative term, *seder*, for the weekly reading in its entirety, modifying it slightly into the cognate noun, *sidrah*. The Sephardim still employ the term *parashah* in its original sense.

In Palestine, however, they read a much shorter section each *Shabbat*, since they spread the reading of the Pentateuch over three years.[17] The objective of the Palestinian system (or, more accurately, *systems*, since a number of variant cycles seem to have been followed in different communities of Palestine during the talmudic period) was in order to ensure that the incidence of a festival or special occasion occurred on the actual week when the reading of the *parashah* either corresponded thematically, or, at least, was appropriate to it.

Thus, the Palestinian "Triennial Cycle" commenced (with the reading of the account of Creation) on the 1st of *Nisan*. Not only was this Spring month most appropriate as the beginning of the new year (Exodus 12:2), but also because, according to the view of R. Joshua in the Talmud,[18] the world was actually created in *Nisan*. This triennial system so arranged it that, in the second year of the cycle, the reading of Exodus, chapter 12, which describes the Exodus from Egypt and laws of Passover, coincided with the festival itself. Again, in that second year of the three-year cycle, the reading of the Ten Commandments (Exodus 20:1–14) coincided with Shavuot, the festival that commemorates the giving of the Torah; and the section of Leviticus, which describes the Day of Atonement sacrificial ritual also corresponded, in the second year of the cycle, precisely with that sacred occasion.

In the third year of the cycle, the Book of Numbers was always reached at the beginning of *Nisan*, so that the section commencing Numbers 6:22, which describes the inauguration of the sanctuary, was read at the very period (*Nisan* 1st–12th) when this biblical event actually occurred. Again, the last section of Deuteronomy, describing the death of Moses, always coincided, in the third year of the cycle, with the beginning of *Adar*, which, according to rabbinic tradition, was the period of Moses' death.

This triennial arrangement was also practiced in Egypt, having been brought there by a Palestinian expatriate community, and it continued to be practiced there, and in the homeland, until the 12th century C.E. This we learn from a most important and interesting source for medieval Jewish history, the diary of the Spanish globe-trotter, Benjamin of Tudela.

Benjamin records details of his visit to Cairo, around 1170. He tells of two large synagogues, following the respective *minhagim* of Palestine and Babylon:

> The Babylonian synagogue reads a section each week, corresponding to our Spanish practice, whereby they finish the entire reading of the Torah

each year; whereas the Palestinian community act differently, subdividing each section into three, so that they finish the Torah only after three years.[19]

The Palestinian Jews must have envied their coreligionists who were enabled to celebrate the joyous festival of Simchat Torah each year. Benjamin's account informs us of the way they overcame this obvious shortcoming in their system: "The two communities have an established custom, however, to unite and pray together on the day of the Rejoicing of the Torah, as well as on Shavuot."[20]

The Palestinian practice probably originated out of the necessity of accommodating, during the reading, an Aramaic translation and exposition of the biblical verses, though some have attributed its origin to a time of religious persecution when a hurried reading only allowed for a short section to be read each week. The Babylonian custom was, in any case, always the most popular and widespread, and ultimately totally displaced the Triennial Cycle.

Since our (Babylonian) system has fifty-four *sidrot*, and since the weekly *sidrah* is deferred for a week when a major festival falls on a Sabbath, it is inevitable that, in order to complete the fifty-four *sidrot* in less than fifty-two Sabbaths, there are some occasions when two *sidrot* have to be read. Traditionally, the *sidrot* so combined are *Va-yakhel/ Pekudei* (Exodus 35–40), *Tazria/Metzora* (Leviticus 12–15), *Acharei Mot/ Kedoshim* (Leviticus 16–20), *Behar/Bechukotai* (Leviticus 25–27), *Chukkat/ Balak* (Numbers 19–24), *Mattot/Masei* (Numbers 30–36), and *Nitzavim/Va-yelekh* (Deuteronomy 29–31). These combinations were chosen because each *sidrah* shares one or more mutual themes with its partner.

Petuchot and *Setumot*

We have explained the smaller divisions, within each of the seven *parashiyyot* of the weekly *sidrah*, as reflecting the Palestinian subdivision into smaller weekly reading units.

A glance at the opening thirty-one verses of the *sidrah Bereishit* will reveal that these are subdivided into six separate *parashiyyot*, each one followed by the letter *pey*. This is the initial letter of the word *petuchah*, "open," and serves to indicate that, at the end of this particular portion *(parashah)*, the remainder of the line in the *Sefer Torah* is to remain "open," and the succeeding section must begin on a new line.

Compare this with, for example, chapter three of the same *sidrah*. After verses 15, 16, and 21 the letter *pey* occurs again, but at the end of the last verse (v. 24) of the chapter there is a letter *samech*. This same letter marks off several sections within chapter five (vv. 5,8,11,14, 17,20,24,27,31). The *samech* stands for *(parashah) setumah*, "closed," indicating that the next chapter "closes up" the same line. This means that the scribe leaves a space of but nine letters on that line, and then begins the following chapter on the same line.

There is no logical or consistent reason why some chapters have been designated as *petuchah* and others *setumah*. The distinction is not altogether arbitrary however, for we can isolate one apparent criterion. It seems that where a chapter deals with, or ends on, an unpleasant topic, the preference is for a *setumah*, whereas if it is neutral, positive, or happy, the *petuchah* is employed. Thus, in Genesis chapter five, all the *setumot* follow sections ending with the word *va-yamot* ("And he died") or, "for God took him away" (Genesis 5:24). If we look at Genesis 9:29, however, the death of Noah is followed by a *petuchah*, thus proving the difficulty of sustaining a consistent theory. However, there might have been an original reason why such a reference was made an exception. Noah's death may not have been construed as a tragedy since he left progeny—particularly Shem—to continue the message of righteous living which he conveyed to mankind.

The problem of attempting to explain each and every occurrence is aggravated by the fact that there are many instances where considerable variety exists, within masoretic tradition, regarding the precise number of *petuchot* and *setumot*, and where exactly they occur. Our printed *Chumashim* have standardized these on the basis of Maimonides' preference for the Tiberian tradition of Aaron ben Moses Ben-Asher (10th century), though the masoretic variants of his contemporary, Ben-Naphtali, suggest that Ben-Asher's textual rules may not represent an uncontested, original tradition.

Chapters and Verses

The traditional text of our Torah, as we have observed, has no punctuation, and consequently no division into chapters and verses, other than the traditional masoretic divisions into *sedarim*, which were originally introduced in order to indicate how much was to be read each week during *keriat ha-Torah*.

If we open any printed *Chumash*, however, we will certainly see before us a text subdivided—in addition to the masoretic *petuchot* and *setumot*—into chapters and verses. It comes as a shock to many when they are told that this division was a Christian innovation, first introduced into the Vulgate, the Latin translation of the Bible, in the 13th century, in order to facilitate their public theological disputations with Jewry.

This division is attributed either to Stephen Langton, Archbishop of Canterbury (1150–1228) or one Hugo de Santo Caro (d. 1262); and it served as a preliminary exercise to facilitate the production of a Latin Concordance of the Vulgate text. It was henceforth easy for missionaries and disputants to find references and buttress their spurious arguments with a wealth of quotations. Rabbinic respondents, who did not possess the means of adducing all such sources, unless they possessed a photographic memory of the whole Bible, found themselves at a disadvantage. They were consequently constrained to utilize the same devices as their enemies, and to embody that selfsame chapter and verse division in order to recognize the sources being alluded to by such a reference and to rebut the Christian interpretation.

It was that same motive which prompted R. Isaac ben Natan, who produced the first Hebrew Concordance, *Meir Netiv*, in 1524, to employ the Christian chapter and verse division for his references. Another Concordance, edited by R. Elijah Bachur (1469–1549), actually excuses its adoption of that system by stating that "it was very useful, to disprove those who challenged our faith. They would quote a certain book by its chapter and verse numbers, and *one who had accustomed himself with its method* could do likewise!"

A similar apology was contained in the preface to the first edition of the Hebrew *Mikraot Gedolot* Bible, published by Daniel Bomberg in the year 1526. It is the Tunisian scholar, Jacob ben Chayyim, employed by Bomberg as proofreader, who makes this apology; but the popularity of this edition of the Bible helped to give the stamp of approval to the subsequent employment of this system. Indeed, later generations of printers, as well as rabbis and Hebrew scholars, seem to have been largely unaware of this Christian infiltration into the very heart and wellspring of Jewish spiritual inspiration.

15

The Reading of the Law

Aliyah

We popularly translate the term *aliyah* (literally, *"going up* to the *Bimah")* as "being called up." It is the act of being "called up," or officially invited, to read the Law (or have it read for one) that is being emphasized here, rather than the actual *mitzvah,* or honor, itself. This again has to be viewed in the context of the original custom of people having to read their own portion; and reflects halakhic concern that "no one should come forward to read the Torah without being previously ('called up') invited to do so."[1] This was an essential prerequisite, and it may be assumed that the "invitation" was extended at least a few days before *Shabbat* in order to give the person ample opportunity to prepare himself properly. The official Sabbath morning "calling up" *(yaamod, Reb . . . ben. . . .)* was merely a reminder to the person that the time had arrived for him to exercise his prerogative to come up and read from the Law. This invitation arrangement also ensured that no individual learned congregant would gain a monopoly in reading the Torah each week in the absence of anyone else who could read without adequate notice.

As we have seen, ritual practices are cherished even when changed circumstances deprive them of their original purpose and relevance; and hence the custom of formally extending an invitation, or "calling up," each person has still been maintained, even though the people "called up" do not themselves read from the Torah.

At the reading desk, on the *Bimah*, we are particular that there should be at least three people while the Torah is being read: namely, the *baal korei*, the one being called up, and the *gabbai*, or warden. The reason for this is to recall the tripartite manner in which the Torah was originally given: by God, to Israel, through the agency of Moses.

Since our custom is for the person who has been called up to stay at the reading desk until the one called up after him has completed his *aliyah*, there are generally four people around the Torah while it is being read. Delaying the return to one's seat in this way is merely a pious sign of reluctance to leave the Torah. This same sentiment underlies the custom of making our way up to the *Bimah* from our seat by the shortest possible route, to demonstrate eagerness to reach the Torah, and returning via the farther side of the *Bimah*, by the longer route. Shaking hands with the *gabbais*, on one's way back to one's seat, is also condoned as a demonstration not only of gratitude for the honor of being called up, but also as an excuse for extending the duration of the *aliyah* and the leave-taking of the Torah before returning to one's seat.

Blessings over the Torah

The above-mentioned, symbolic reminiscence of the giving of the Torah, alluded to by having three people at the reading desk, is reinforced by the two blessings which we make when being called up for an *aliyah*. Each blessing has twenty words, and the total of forty words is meant to recall the forty days that Moses spent on Mount Sinai to receive the Torah.[2]

Thus, when reciting these blessings we are challenged to ask ourselves whether the proportion of the Torah we are observing actually justifies Moses having remained on Sinai the entire forty days. Moses assumed that he would need to master the intricacies of *all* the Laws, since Israel would wish to adopt a total observance. His delay in returning actually prompted Israel to worship the Golden Calf. Moses could have avoided that, had he been realistic enough to confront his people as they were. But he naively put his faith in them, staying on until he had mastered the entirety of the religious tradition. The forty words of these blessings are meant, therefore, symbolically to assure Moses that his time on Sinai was well spent, and that our allegiance is to the entire heritage we received at his hands.

Before reading from the Law, the one called up recites the blessing:

Blessed art Thou, O Lord our God, King of the Universe, who hast *chosen us* from all peoples and *hast given us Thy Law.* Blessed art Thou, O Lord, who givest the Law.

The concept of Israel having been "chosen" by God is one of the most misunderstood ideas of any religion. It has frequently been noted that we do not regard ourselves as having been chosen for privileges, but for duties. And the juxtaposition of the phrase, "and hast given us Thy Law" provides clarification of this. We were *chosen* to accept "the yoke of the Torah" *(Ol Torah),* to be the embodiment and transmitters of God's spirit and word. We were given a code of moral discipline, ethical rectitude, and spiritual sensitivity to live by and to pass on to a world largely unwilling to be its recipients. This is the sense of the phrase, "who hast chosen us *from all peoples.*"

We have been condemned by theologians of other religions for our arrogance in claiming to be the "Chosen People." But this has never been a claim made out of a spirit of arrogance, but rather out of resignation. We never claimed that our virtue made us God's first choice. On the contrary, our own talmudic tradition asserts that, while in Egypt, our ancestors descended to the 49th degree of impurity, and, had God's grace not redeemed us "in the nick of time," we would have sunk to the 50th degree, beyond the point of redemption. Another tradition actually asserts that God first took the Torah to the other nations, encouraging them to adopt higher moral and spiritual standards. It was only when God made no headway with them that He turned to Israel, and coerced her to accept His Law.

These are hardly the traditions one would expect a nation that seeks to project a self-superior image to have enunciated! In the light of this, it will be appreciated that the concept of the Chosen People is not a value judgment on ourselves; it is a theological verity. It is also historically sound. For who can deny that Israel's Torah was *the* repository of the ethics and morals in which are enshrined the lofty principles and concepts borrowed by the main daughter religions, Christianity and Islam, which, together, have been the primary civilizing forces for mankind? For some reason it has always been acceptable for an athlete or conqueror to boast of his physical prowess and his victories. For Israel to merely allude to her spiritual achievements has been regarded however as the height of bad taste!

The blessing ends by hailing God as the One "who *givest* the Law." The present tense is used to convey the message that Torah was not "given" once and for all, a product of a bygone age and environment, but that its profound message and the way of life it maps out for its adherents is timeless and immortal. Its absorbing and enriching cultural and intellectual resources have enabled Jewish sages and students to discover in it new insights and new relevance for the problems that beset every age, as if the Almighty was, indeed, "giving" us His Law, over and over again, as often as we need it and as often as we desire it.

The concluding blessing, after the portion has been read, states:

> Blessed art Thou, O Lord our God, King of the Universe, who hast given us the *Law of truth*, and hast planted *everlasting life* in our midst. Blessed art Thou, O Lord, who givest the Law.

The "Law of Truth" is a reference to the Written Law, which is the only source of truth in the world that can be affirmed without hesitation, since it is the word of God, the source of all truth.

"Everlasting life" is a reference to the Oral Law, the traditional interpretation and supplementation of the Written text, which Moses conveyed orally to Aaron and the seventy Elders, and which they handed down, in turn, to their disciples; and so on down the ages into the rabbinic period when these were analyzed, clarified, and systematized in the Talmud and the subsequent Codes of Jewish Law.

For the Orthodox Jew, these two traditions, the Written and Oral Laws, are interwoven strands of the same mosaic. They form a unity which is the essential *raison d'être* of Judaism. Torah without Talmud is a body without a soul. Talmud divorced from an acceptance of the divine origin of the Written Torah, which it serves to clarify, is a tree whose roots have been severed. Torah is a "tree of life," and that presupposes both the Written and Oral Laws providing mutual nourishment and dual clarification and inspiration.

Hosafot—Extending the Number of *Aliyot*

According to the Talmud one may call up more, but not less, than the required number of *aliyot* on a *Shabbat* or *Yom Tov*.[3] This concession was not extended to Mondays and Thursdays or other midweek occasions such as Rosh Chodesh, Chanukah, and fast days, because of *bittul melakhah*, wasting the time of people who had to get to work. Our practice is not to call up more than the prescribed number of *aliyot* for each festival, a number that increases in relationship to the relative importance of that particular festival (see below), since to allow more than the prescribed number of *aliyot* on those occasions would obviously impair this whole arrangement of graduated *aliyot*.

Some authorities[4] believed that the talmudic permissibility of calling up more than seven people on a *Shabbat* only applied at that early period when the original practice obtained whereby the *first* person called to the Torah recited the opening blessing *(asher bachar banu)* and the *last* person called up recited the concluding blessing, after the entire weekly portion had been completed. In that situation, there was no fear that anyone called up over and above the statutory seven might be reciting an unnecessary blessing *(berakhah she-einah tzerikhah)*. However, according to the later practice, which obtains to this day, whereby each person called up recites two blessings over his portion, this fear certainly exists.

This view did not win much support however, since the changeover to each person reciting his own blessings was also talmudic, and most authorities believe that the talmudic permissibility of extending the numbers called up was given in the light of those later circumstances. Hence the Talmud itself had discounted, therefore, any problem of unnecessary blessings.

Joseph Karo takes this permissive ruling to extreme lengths, and decides that "it is permissible to call up *many aliyot* even if it means one person reading a portion that another has already read, and, consequently making additional blessings over that same portion. It matters not."[5] Understandably, other authorities disapproved of such an approach; and we avail ourselves of Karo's ruling but once a year on Simchat Torah, when it is our wish to call everyone present in synagogue to honor the Torah with an *aliyah* before we conclude the year's cycle of reading.

In some large congregations there are so many people who have a right to be called up, to mark a special occasion (for the order of precedence, see below) that the consequently protracted nature of the *keriat ha-Torah* makes it hard for the congregation to concentrate properly with so many intermittent breaks. Hence the *Arukh Ha-Shulchan* states: "Some have the custom not to add more than three extra *aliyot*, to make up the (significant) number of ten, though there are others who resolutely refuse to call up more than the prescribed seven; *and this is most proper and should be adopted, unless there is a wedding or circumcision."*[6] People who have *Yahrzeit* later in the week, and who could be called up on Monday or Thursday, should not, therefore, demand that they be called up on the previous *Shabbat* if it means having to extend the number of *aliyot* beyond an acceptable number.

Priorities for *Aliyot*

Bearing in mind the preference of most halakhic authorities for the number of *aliyot* to be restricted, it is obvious that some order of priorities was necessary in order to avoid dispute. Rightly or wrongly, being awarded an *aliyah* was regarded by most people as a personal honor; and the failure to be called up, particularly on an occasion when one felt it one's right, was deemed an insult and slight. In talmudic times this was particularly so, and people vied with each other, and brought pressure to bear on the synagogue wardens, in order to secure the privilege of being called up for the first few *aliyot*, which were obviously regarded as the most important. In order to stop this unworthy rivalry and pursuit of honor among people, it was decreed that these honors would not be given to laymen, but would in future be reserved for priests and Levites.[7]

Since squabbling over the *aliyot* continued, they were further restricted to people who really deserved to be called to the Torah for their spiritual merit. Hence the Talmud[8] prescribes that, following the Levite, one should call up sages who have been appointed to positions of communal leadership, followed by scholars whose knowledge makes them candidates for such positions, after which one should call the sons of those sages who are leaders of the community. They are to be followed by the heads of local synagogues,[9] after which ordinary laymen may be called for the remaining *aliyot*.

The preference for scholars and their families may also have been motivated by the wish to have an accurate reading of the Torah at a time when all those called up had to read their own portion in the Torah.

The exception to the above order of precedence was where a synagogue had the custom of selling the *aliyot* in order to raise necessary funds either for itself or for charity. In such circumstances the talmudic list may be set aside. R. Mordechai Jaffe insists, however, that, even then, the donors should be called up according to their seniority and status in the community.[10]

Nowadays, few synagogues have the custom of selling *aliyot*, and they are generally allocated on a rota basis, with priority being given—after *Kohein* and *Levi*—to *chiyyuvim*, people with a special right or "obligation" to be given an *aliyah*.

A trace of the talmudic order of priorities still remains though, underlying the status of *shelishiy*, the third *aliyah* (the one immediately following *Levi*) as the one most coveted, and still frequently allocated to a rabbi, scholar, or person of communal standing.

Next in importance comes *shishiy*, the sixth *aliyah*. According to the *halakhah* it is permitted to call up a priest and Levite twice during the course of the seven *aliyot*, providing that the traditional sequence of *Kohein, Levi, Yisrael* is maintained. It follows then, that *shishiy*, like *shelishiy*, is the first layman's *aliyah* in the repetition of the *(Kohein, Levi, Yisrael)* cycle, and hence its extra status.

The order of priorities applicable today for those celebrating family events to be called up for an *aliyah*, is as follows: (1) A bridegroom (other than a widower) on the day of his wedding, (2) a bridegroom on the Sabbath before his wedding, (3) a *Bar Mitzvah* boy, (4) a father celebrating the birth of a child, (5) a bridegroom on the Sabbath after his marriage, (6) a *Yahrzeit* occurring on that day, (7) the father of a boy on the Sabbath before circumcision, (8) a *Yahrzeit* occurring during the following week, (9) one who had recovered from an illness, (10) one who is leaving for, or had just returned from, a journey abroad, and (11) a visitor to synagogue.[11]

Shnoddering

The term *shnoddering* is the name applied to the practice of promising a donation of money to the synagogue or charity after being called up for an *aliyah*. The term *shnodder* is a contraction of a key phrase from the special prayer for the health and well-being of the donor and his family that accompanies, and relates to, the donation. The phrase so contracted is *ba-avur she-nadar* ("in recognition of that which he has promised to contribute").

Shnoddering is still practiced in many synagogues. It owes its origin to the custom we have already referred to of auctioning *aliyot* to raise money for charity. Since that was the only justification for setting aside the talmudic order of priorities, and as only the more affluent members could afford to compete in the auction, the less well-off must have been rather resentful. As a compromise, the sale itself was abandoned in most synagogues, to be replaced by a donation that people made according to their means. The justification for not reverting to the talmudic order of priorities was that this *shnoddering* was still construed as an offshoot of the original practice of selling *aliyot* to the highest bidder.

The Origin of *Keriat Ha-Torah*

Talmudic tradition credits Moses with having introduced the public Reading of the Law on Sabbaths and festivals, and Ezra the Scribe with having added midweek readings every Monday and Thursday mornings.[12]

Many people lived in isolated villages and farms where there was no opportunity of attending a local prayer meeting on *Shabbat*. These farmers traveled to the local towns, however, on Mondays and Thursdays when markets were held. Ezra therefore instituted public Torah readings on those days, at the markets, to give those incomers an opportunity of hearing Torah at least on those weekdays. Once introduced, the practice was adopted as binding even in places where they did have a regular Sabbath reading of the Torah.

Ezra's purpose in introducing a Sabbath afternoon reading was on account of the shopkeepers *(yoshvei keranot)*[13] who had to stay at their counters to guard their merchandise throughout the Mondays and Thursdays, and could not leave to hear the Torah being read. Ezra therefore introduced that extra reading as compensation for them. It is conceivable that at first it was only those shopkeepers who attended the *Shabbat* afternoon reading, but, as is the usual pattern, it subsequently became the common practice for all.

We referred above[14] to Ezra having accompanied the public reading by an Aramaic vernacular translation and explanation of each verse. This gave rise, many centuries later, to the *Targum Onkelos*, the official Aramaic version, authorized by the 1st-century Palestinian sages, R. Eliezer and R. Joshua. This *Targum* is printed next to the Torah text in most rabbinic Bibles.

Revising the *Sidrah*

We are advised to revise the *Sidrah* twice on *Shabbat* and to read through the *Targum* once *(shenayim mikra ve-echad Targum)*. The origin of this is not too clear, but it may have its roots in the original manner in which the Reading of the Torah was performed, namely that the person called up as one of the seven to make a blessing over the Torah was expected to read his own portion.

Inevitably it could be most embarrassing if someone was caught unprepared, and consequently made many mistakes in the reading and was frequently corrected. This must have occurred regularly; and there is one well-known case, recorded in the Talmud, where the great Rabbi Akivah actually refused the honor of being called up because he had had no time to revise the *Sidrah*. His colleagues approved of the explanation he offered on that occasion, namely that "it is forbidden to recite anything before the congregation unless one has revised it two or three times beforehand."[15]

It is easy to understand, therefore, why it became common practice, in talmudic times, that people would revise the *Sidrah* a few times so that, if called up, they could read the Torah with confidence.[16] The later halakhists recommended that this worthy practice be maintained even in the posttalmudic period, when the *chazan* took over the role of *baal korei* ("master of the reading"),[17] thereby relieving the layman of what, for many, must have been a considerable ordeal. With the dissemination of texts of *Targum*, the recommendation of revising the *Sidrah* twice was broadened to include a reading of that Aramaic translation in order to understand fully what was being read.

Seven *Aliyot*

On Shabbat we call up *seven* people for an *aliyah*. This is symbolic of the unique spiritual significance of this seventh day, and of its rich reserves of sanctity ("And God blessed the seventh day and sanctified it") which are *sevenfold*, in the sense that this day provides spiritual nourishment for the entire seven days of the week.

A halakhic explanation for calling up seven is closely linked to this idea. It is suggested that its purpose is to provide a compensation for anyone who might have been unable to attend synagogue for the whole of the previous week, and was consequently prevented from hearing *Borakhu*, that most important summons by the *chazan* to the congregation to join with him in "blessing God." By calling up seven people on a *Shabbat*, all of whom recite that *Borakhu* summons, such a worshiper is enabled to make up for all the occasions he has missed during the congregational prayers of the previous week.[18]

Separate *Sefer* for Each Reading

It is our custom to use a different scroll for every extra reading that is required on special occasions. Thus, on *Shabbat* Rosh Chodesh or festivals, we take out two scrolls. Sometimes we take out three scrolls, when there are three separate biblical sections to be read, as, for example, when *Shabbat* Chanukah also coincides with Rosh Chodesh *Tevet.* We then recite the ordinary weekly *sidrah (mikketz)* from the first scroll; from the second scroll we read the special portion for Rosh Chodesh, and from a third scroll we read, as *maftir*, the section for Chanukah.

The reason why we are required to use a separate scroll for each special reading, rather than use one scroll and merely roll it to the required passage each time, is because of the principle of *kevod ha-tzibbur*, having regard for the honor of the congregation.[19] It was regarded as demeaning for their honor to keep people waiting, "just sitting and observing in silence,"[20] while the scroll was being rolled and the required passage located. Maimonides, reflecting the practice of those who remain standing during the entire Reading of the Law, explains the requirement of separate scrolls as arising out of the principle of *tircha de-tzibbura*, avoiding imposing unnecessary burdens upon the community. The extra time spent in rolling the scroll to the required places is irksome to those who have to remain on their feet, in any case, such a long time.

Standing for *Keriat Ha-Torah*

In most synagogues there are a few people who have the custom to remain standing for the entire duration of the *keriat ha-Torah*, while the rest are seated. This practice is no more than a pietistic demonstration of honor toward the Torah. Halakhically this is not required, since the Torah while on the *Bimah* is regarded as being in a separate enclave, and consequently there is no disrespect in remaining seated. This is probably the reason why some authorities recommended that the *Bimah* should have at least three steps leading up to it, to reinforce its status as an independent area. The same reasoning applies to the *Aron Kodesh* itself. The scrolls are housed fairly high up inside the Ark, in order to mark this repository as an independent area *(mechitzah)*. For this reason it is permitted for the rabbi's box, or the people with seats along the eastern wall *(Mizrach)* to sit with their back to the scrolls of the Torah. The latter are considered as if in a separate room when the Ark is closed. During *hagbahah*, however, when the Torah is raised aloft for all to see, then obviously we have to stand in order to show it honor.

The Value of Mnemonics

Rabbinic scholars and students down the ages have rarely sought any leisure diversions unrelated to the Torah. Torah conditioned their entire outlook, thoughts, and emotions. Even their humor was rooted in, or at least colored by, the traditional lore. Thus, guided by the maxim "Turn Torah over, and turn it over again, for everything is in it,"[21] scholars frequently sought to discover "clever" or playful allusions to extraneous matters as underlying the text of the biblical verses. Hence the light-hearted suggestion that a reference to *Haman*, villain of the Book of Esther (who sought to destroy the Jews of Persia in the 5th century B.C.E.), may even be found at the beginning of Genesis. God asks Adam, "Have you eaten of the tree?"[22] which, in Hebrew, reads, *ha-min ha-etz . . . akhalta*. The first word of this phrase—*ha-min*—constitutes, according to one imaginative sage,[23] a Pentateuchal allusion to Haman, with a slight modification of but one vowel—with which surely no one will quibble!

The above is certainly intended to be taken in a lighthearted spirit. There are other examples, however, of a similar employment of biblical phrases, which were intended to serve the more serious and constructive purpose of acting as an aide-mémoire.

Mnemonic, constructed out of biblical words, is the most popular example of this genre, and this was employed by the famous *Chatam Sofer* in order to provide a biblical basis for one of the main rituals of the synagogue.

Reading from the Torah is a central feature of the synagogue service. The latter, as we have demonstrated, was patterned upon the ancient Temple and sanctuary ritual. Since "gold, silver, and brass" were the basic materials from which all the appurtenances of the desert sanctuary were fashioned, it follows logically that, to complete the "Sanctuary (Temple) = Synagogue" equation, we have to find a place for *zahav* (gold), *kesef* (silver), and *nechoshet* (brass) in the synagogue system.

The *Chatam Sofer* indeed finds that the individual letters of these three words contain an allusion to all the occasions during the year when we are obliged to read from the Torah. Beginning with the word *zahav*, he notes that the letter *zayin (za)* has the *Gematria* (numerical value) of *seven*, and refers, therefore, to *Shabbat*, the seventh day. *Hey (ha)* has the value of *five*, and *vet (v) two*, referring to the fifth and second days of the week (Thursday and Monday), respectively. So the first word *(zahav)* sets out our *weekly* obligation of reading from the Torah on those days.

Each letter of the succeeding two words—*kesef* and *nechoshek*—alludes to a particular festival day: *kaf (ke)* refers to *kippur* (the day of Atonement), *samech (se)* to Sukkot (Tabernacles), and the final letter, *pey*, to Pesach (Passover) and Purim. In the final word, *nechoshet*, the *nun* (ne) stands for *nerot* (lights), the symbol of the festival of Chanukah; the *chet (cho)* is for *chadash* (the *new* year) as well as for *chodesh*, the new moon. The *shin (she)* stands for Shavuot (Pentecost), as well as for Sheminiy Atzeret and Simchat Torah; and the last letter, *tav*, is for *taanit* (fast days).

The number of people called up to the Reading of the Law increases in proportion to the importance of the occasion. On Monday and Thursday mornings (and Shabbat afternoons) *three* are called up; on Rosh Chodesh and Chol Ha-Mo'ed (intermediate days of Passover and Tabernacles) *four*; on festivals, *five*; on Yom Kippur morning *six*, and on *Shabbat* morning, seven.[24]

Religious Eligibility for an *Aliyah*

An issue relevant to every Orthodox congregation seeking to cater for every shade of religious observance, is that of the participation in the services by *mechalelei Shabbat*, people who violate the Sabbath laws. Problems such as the propriety of calling such people up for *aliyot*, or allowing them to serve as *baal korei* (the one who reads from the Torah), or even as *chazan* (where a community cannot afford to employ the services of a full-time official), have exercised the minds of our halakhic authorities.

If we are honest we will admit that there does seem to be a blatant inconsistency in calling up to bless the Torah a person who consciously spurns one of its most important laws, such as Sabbath observance. The laws of *Shabbat* are emphasized twelve times in the Torah,[25] and Judaism regards it as such a central institution that denial of *Shabbat* is tantamount to rejection of the whole of the Torah.[26] The biblical punishment for profaning the Sabbath is, for that reason, the same as that prescribed for an idolator!

How then do we justify including Sabbath violators to make up the ten people required for a *minyan*? How do we justify giving them an *aliyah*, bearing in mind that the rest of the congregation is expected to recite *Amen* to their blessings?[27]

This is a complex issue, and a number of approaches to it have been presented in rabbinic sources down the ages. Scope for tolerance in this matter is already provided by the talmudic concept of *tinok she-nishbah le-bein ha-goyyim*, "a Jewish child snatched away into captivity by heathens." If such a person broke Sabbath frequently in his adult years, simply because he had been uprooted as a child from his religion and environment, and was, consequently, unaware of the importance or significance of *Shabbat*, "he only required, in Temple times, to bring *one* sin offering (though he had perpetrated numerous acts of desecration)." On the other hand, someone who was aware of the institution and significance of the Sabbath would require to bring a separate offering for each and every act of desecration, and for each Sabbath thus profaned.[28]

Maimonides broadens the whole concept of *tinok she-nishbah*, to include not only "physical captivity," but also "spiritual captivity." He refers specifically to Jews whose forebears were attracted to the Karaite heresy:

> The children and grandchildren of those defectors . . . are to be regarded as "children snatched away into captivity" . . . who are to be placed in the category of the coerced if they fail to follow the *mitzvot*. Even if such Karaites subsequently meet properly observant Jews, they keep the status of "coerced," since they have been reared under misguided influences. It is, therefore, right to encourage them to repentance and to attract them with welcoming words, so that they will take upon themselves the authentic observance of Torah.[29]

In another passage, Maimonides refers specifically to the tolerance to be extended to Sabbath-breakers:

> It is not right to keep aloof from Sabbath-breakers, or to spurn them. On the contrary, one should welcome them and inspire them to become observant. Our sages have already said that if a violator of Jewish law comes to synagogue to pray we should welcome him and not treat him disrespectfully.[30]

Maimonides' extension of the "child-captive" principle has also been applied to the unobservant of our day. It may be assumed that the Jew who breaks the Sabbath does not do so as a conscious act of defiance of his religion. It is rather to be attributed to a deficiency in his religious upbringing, or to the fact that the seductive values of an assimilationist or antireligious society and environment have captured his soul. The nonobservant today should not be classified, therefore, as apostates or heretics (*mumar* or *epikoros*), but rather as *tinok she-nishbah*, as spiritually immature and insensitive souls who have been captivated by influences inimical to Torah and who are truly unaware of the gravity of the prohibitions they are violating. Hence, as Maimonides has advised, such Sabbath breakers are to be welcomed and allowed to participate fully in synagogue ritual, including making up a *minyan* and being called to the Torah. It should be pointed out, however, that such leniency and tolerance may not be extended, from a halakhic point of view, to the *baal korei*, who reads the Torah for the congregation. We allow a Sabbath breaker to be called up since most halakhic authorities are of the view that the people called up are not reciting the blessings *on behalf of the congregation*. The congregation's obligation is merely to hear the Reading of the *Torah*. The *baal korei*, on the other hand, reads the *Torah* on behalf of the congregation, and, through his religious act, they fulfill their duty of hearing the *Torah* read. Thus, in the case of the *baal korei* — or a *chazan* — it would not be permitted to appoint someone who publicly desecrates the Sabbath and who has refused to abandon his sinful way of life![31]

Hagbahah and *Gelilah*

The Talmud does not appear to separate the two *mitzvot* of *hagbahah* and *gelilah*, but refers primarily to the latter honor, that of rolling up the Torah scroll.[32] Raising it aloft (*hagbahah*) was but a part — albeit the most important part — of the one ritual act of rolling it up.

R. Moses Isserles (1530–1572) implies that the subdivision of the *mitzvah* of *gelilah*, so that a separate person is deputed to raise the Torah aloft, was a comparatively recent innovation in his day.[33] It was probably introduced because of the difficulties encountered when but one person was attempting to hold the Torah in a dignified way, without the parchment slipping, while at the same time tying around the *mitpachat* or binder. Accidents must have been fairly commonplace before the decision to share the honor between two people. This situation explains why the Gaon Natronai (8th century) had advised that the Torah should be rolled up in a corner of the synagogue, away from the public gaze.[34] Indeed the *Sefer Ha-Eshkol* quotes an authority who wanted to ban the performance of *Gelilah* in public altogether.[35]

R. Joshua ben Levi (3rd-century Palestinian talmudist) stated: "Of the ten people who (form a *minyan* to) read in the Torah, the one who *rolls up* the scroll gains more merit than all of the rest put together."[36] Hence the Talmud[37] allocates the *mitzvah* of *gelilah* to the most distinguished person in the congregation. For the same reason it became common practice "to auction that *mitzvah* for a high price *in order to enhance its value*."[38] The implication of this is that its natural appeal was not too great, and consequently required to be buttressed! Indeed, nowadays *gelilah* is far from being regarded as the most coveted *mitzvah*, and is frequently allocated to minors.

It may well have been that R. Joshua's rather exaggerated praise of *gelilah* was merely an attempt to encourage the people of his own day, who may have felt that by being offered *gelilah* they were being palmed off with an inferior *mitzvah*. If this was not R. Joshua's motive, then it does seem strange that he should have elevated such a *mitzvah* over the *aliyot* proper, when the reading from the Torah—which is the essence of the *aliyot*—is an institution attributed to Moses, whereas the *gelilah* was only introduced in order to promote the honor of the scroll, which is impaired if the text is left exposed when the reading has been completed.[39]

The tradition which, taking Rabbi Joshua's statement at its face value, claims *gelilah* as "the most important *mitzvah*," certainly has to be revised in the light of the subsequent subdivision of that *mitzvah* into two, since it is the act of "raising the Torah aloft," for all to see the script, which, according to our halakhic authorities,[40] is the most important aspect of the *gelilah* ritual. This particular action, which is now reserved for the one performing *hagbahah*, not *gelilah*, must make the former the more coveted of the two! This view is, indeed, stated categorically by the *Mishnah Berurah*,[41] which infers, therefore, that "if someone is handed a *Sefer Torah* to perform both *hagbahah* and *gelilah*, and he cannot perform them both, he should rather choose the former and invite someone else to perform *gelilah*."

Among Western Sephardim, fear of people dropping the scroll or handling it in an undignified manner resulted in this *mitzvah* becoming the exclusive preserve of a brotherhood called *levantadores*, "Master lifters" of the scroll. While this elitist approach to *mitzvot* may well be resented by the noninitiated, it is in line with the spirit of the original talmudic practice of giving this honor to the most distinguished person present in synagogue. Furthermore, many Ashkenazi rabbis, on wit-

nessing with consternation the difficulties encountered by so many
people in attempting to lift a heavy scroll—particularly when it is
weighted on one side, when reading the *Sidrot* of the books of *Bereishit*
and *Devarim*—often wish that their synagogue also had such a system!

Ve-Zot Ha-Torah

When the Torah is raised aloft for *hagbahah* and *gelilah* the verse we
recite refers to a tripartite partnership: "And this is the law which *Moses
presented before the Children of Israel*, according to the word of *the Lord,
by the hand of Moses*."

The two references to Moses in this affirmation immediately strike
one as tautologous. R. Chaim of Volodzin[42] explains that it is actually
our omission of the middle of this verse which has created the tautology.
After affirming "And this is the Law which Moses presented before the
Children of Israel" *(ve-zot ha-Torah asher sam Mosheh lifnei benei yisrael)*, we
should really continue with the verse from Numbers 9:23, *"According to
the word of the Lord (al piy ha-shem) they encamped, and according to the
word of the Lord they journeyed; they kept the charge of the Lord, at
the commandment of the Lord by the hand of Moses (be-yad Mosheh)."* We
have merely culled the last phrase, instead of the whole sentence,
thereby creating an unnecessary repetition!

But, in drawing our attention to this verse, which we have
condensed, R. Chaim also explains the relationship of this affirmation to
the two other verses we recite, one when taking out the scrolls from the
Ark (Numbers 10:35) and the other (Numbers 10:36) when returning it
after reading.

When taking out the scroll we recite the verse, *Va-yehi binso'a
ha-aron* ("And it came to pass, when the Ark journeyed forward . . .");
on returning the Torah we say *Uve-nuchoh yomar* ("And when it rested,
he said . . .").

The latter two verses together with *Ve-zot ha-Torah* may now be
seen as a unity, recited as a symbolic description of the travels of the Ark
of the sanctuary at the head of Israel's tribes, "typifying God in front of
His people protecting and helping them, and leading them on to final
victory."[43] *Va-yehi binso'a* refers to the commencement of the Ark's
journeys at the beginning of the forty years of wandering; *Uve-nuchoh
yomar* alludes to its safe arrival at the promised land at the end of that
period; and *Ve-zot ha-Torah*, coupled with Numbers 9:23, highlights the

numerous occasions in between, when it was traveling from one place of encampment to the next. Thus, by reciting these verses, not only do we symbolically relive the experiences of our desert ancestors, but we also affirm our faith in the Torah's ability to lead our people through all the vicissitudes of a millennial exile, and provide us with the vision and promise of a safe return to the promised land. Bearing in mind that originally the scrolls were housed in a portable "Ark," in an adjoining room of the synagogue, the formal procession into the synagogue proper, bearing aloft the Ark, must, indeed, have been graphically reminiscent of the journeying of the original Ark of the sanctuary, containing the tablets of stone.

While the Torah is being raised aloft for *hagbahah*, the script must be shown to those present on all sides of the synagogue. The one lifting up the Torah *(magbiah)* exposes at least three columns before raising the Torah up as high as possible. He then slowly turns, showing the script first to those on his right, then to those on his left, those in front of him, and, finally, those behind the *Bimah*, so that everyone may catch a glimpse of the script. Some have adopted the pietistic practice of raising the edges of their *tallit* toward the script as it comes into view, and then kissing the *tallit*. The halakhic requirement,[44] however, is that we merely bow toward the open Torah as it faces in our direction. Technically, we should not commence reciting *Ve-zot ha-Torah* until the script comes into view and we are bowing toward it.

There are two basic differences between the Ashkenazi and the Sephardi methods of performing *hagbahah* and *gelilah*. The Sephardim perform this *mitzvah before* the Reading of the Law, immediately after it is taken out of the Ark, whereas the Ashkenazim wait until after the *Sidrah* has been read. Second, the Sephardim open out their scrolls, enclosed inside an ornamental carrier case, in such a way that the script is immediately facing the entire congregation, whereas the Ashkenazim raise the Torah with the script facing the one lifting it up *(magbiah)* and the *back* of the parchment facing most of the congregation.

The Sephardi method is based on the recommendation of *Massekhet Soferim*,[45] that the body of the one lifting it up should not interpose between the writing and the congregation. The Ashkenazim believed that their method did not contradict this, since it was lifted high above the head of the *magbiah*, and the congregation's view was in no way obstructed. It was also felt to be more respectful for the *magbiah* to have the script facing him, rather than to turn the scroll away from him as if spurning it.

The Sephardi custom of performing *hagbahah* immediately the scroll is taken out is based upon the view of their main authority, Karo's *Shulchan Arukh*,[46] which, in turn, followed the procedure exactly as recorded in *Massekhet Soferim*. While this source clearly reflects the original custom, it is by no means certain what was the precise purpose of showing everyone the script before commencing the reading. We may conjecture that it goes back to an early period when many different genres of literature in scroll form abounded in Judea. Some of those were sectarian, as, for example, the Dead Sea Scrolls; others were totally secular, even heretical, in nature. In order to reassure those about to be called up to read, as well as the rest of the congregation, that the text was the authentic sacred version, they held it aloft for all to examine[47] *before* commencing the reading.

The Ashkenazim, who are guided by the halakhic glosses of Moses Isserles, follow his statement that "it has become the custom to perform *hagbahah after* reading from the Torah." Isserles obviously did not feel as constrained as Karo to follow the letter of the law as contained in *Massekhet Soferim*, which, as a very late talmudic work, does not have binding authority. Perhaps Isserles saw greater logic in making the affirmation *Ve-zot ha-Torah* once we have already heard its laws, as a sort of promise that we will observe all that has just been asked of us.

Another significant difference between the Ashkenazim and Sephardim is that, after the Sephardim take the Torah out of the Ark, and, as we have stated, immediately open out their Torah case to display the parchment in an act of *hagbahah*, they then go in a procession, similar to that of the Ashkenazim, to take the *Sefer* to the *Bimah*, though with the Torah case in an open position so that the script is visible during the whole of the procession. The famous 16th-century mystic, Isaac Luria, used to peer closely and lengthily at the script as the Torah passed him, saying that he absorbed thereby a higher light of mystical perception.

A leading authority of the following century, R. Jacob Chagiz, who headed a *yeshivah* in Jerusalem, states, however, that the Sephardi ritual of taking the open scroll in procession was only introduced in Jerusalem for a very practical reason. Apparently the main synagogue of the Sephardim was extremely long (about three or four times its width), so that, particularly on festivals when there was an influx of visitors from other towns to celebrate the holy days at Jerusalem, it was impossible for them all to see the parchment of the Torah when raised aloft in the usual manner of *hagbahah*. To avoid the crush, many did not bother, therefore, to leave their seats in order to view it. Hence, as a concession to the circumstances, the custom was introduced of taking the open scroll around the synagogue.[48] In the typical manner of customs, however, this one quickly spread and took on the aura of authority. For subsequent generations, the original reasons or motives—whether practical, theological, or historical—are of little consequence in their eagerness to "maintain the customs of their fathers."

16

Synagogue Symbols

Self-Identification

A religion is no different than any other exclusive organization in its need to have a symbol or badge as a means of self-identification. The symbol also encapsulates a central or representative idea or teaching that helps to focus immediate attention or concentration upon the basic principles of the organization. In church, chapel, mosque, or synagogue, a distinctive architecture, combined with some sacred symbol, helps to promote the atmosphere of a house of worship and generate the required spirit of awe and reverence on the part of those who enter.

Judaism's distinctive symbols—freely displayed on the scroll mantles, ark curtains, and as architectural designs—are the *Magen David* ("Shield of David"), the *Menorah* (seven-branched candelabrum), and the Two Tablets of the Law.

While the last two of these three symbols are authentically Jewish in origin, they were nevertheless misappropriated by the church and became popular motifs in its representational art.

Chukkat Ha-Goy

Generally, our approach has always been to abandon customs that, though natively Jewish, were subsequently taken over by non-Jewish cults.[1] This is rooted in the biblical prohibition of *chukkat ha-goy*, not following the statutes of the other nations (Leviticus 18:3, 20:23). For this reason we abandoned the raising of hands heavenward during prayer, which was a common practice in biblical times.[2] Similarly, prostrations and kneeling were a common feature of worship in Temple times. Indeed, after each individual task—for example, after clearing out the altar ashes or trimming the wicks of the *Menorah*—the priest made a full prostration before withdrawing. When Christianity adopted prostrations as a central facet of church worship, these were abandoned by the synagogue, with the exception of on the High Holydays. It was, similarly, the custom for the Jewish bereaved to wear black garments as a symbol of mourning.[3] This practice was abandoned when it was taken over by the Church.

It is all the more surprising, therefore, that the *Magen David*, *Menorah*, and Two Tablets have been retained as cherished Jewish symbols even though, as we will presently demonstrate, they were invested with special significance, and frequently represented, in Christian religious tradition, both in plastic art and graphic design.

Judaism was never happy with attempts to employ art as a means of religious adornment and adoration. This was because it could so easily lead to a disregard of the second of the Ten Commandments, as well as because of its obvious association with the lavishly built and decorated Christian cathedrals and churches. And yet Jews felt the need for some simple sign, which would conveniently symbolize their own religion. With a surprising lack of artistic imagination, Jews utilized these three symbols in spite of the fact that church art regularly portrayed them when depicting—and at the same time deprecating—Judaism.

The *Magen David*

The *Magen David* is simply a hexagram, or six-pointed star, formed by two equilateral triangles placed within each other but in opposite directions. From the Bronze Age onward it had been used as a geometrical ornament or magical sign by many different civilizations. It was used as such in Christian and Muslim countries, and it appears as the royal seal of the Kings of Navarre in the 11th century, as well as being frequently employed by notaries in European countries on their official stamps.

The Talmud[4] refers to the ring, or seal, of King Solomon, possession of which enabled him to resist the hostility of Ashmedai, king of the demons, and his cohorts. While in Jewish sources, it is the divine name that was engraved on the ring, Christian writers and exponents of magical art identified its seal with the hexagram, to which they consequently applied the term "Seal of Solomon," a term commonly found on 6th-century Byzantine amulets, and widely used in Arabic magic.

It was probably the Arabs who first referred to it as the "Shield of David," as they had a tradition, preserved in the Koran, that King David was the first to introduce the protective shield. This might have some plausibility, as David refused King Saul's offer of armor before going out to fight Goliath. Not wishing to feel encumbered, he may well have chosen the shield as an alternative means of protection in other battles. There is absolutely no shred of evidence, however, to connect David's shields with the shape of the hexagram.

The ancient pagan or magical origin of the *Magen David* design prompted one scholar to offer the fanciful explanation that it evolved in Celtic tradition as a sign of the Druids. Their magicians are supposed to have used it as a charm against the Drudes, the demonic forces of the night. The word *Drude*, transliterated into Hebrew, is very close to the name *David* (with the mere addition of the letter *reish*), and, at a later period, when Jews and others knew little about Drudes and Druids, they read *Magen David* for *Magen Drude* ("Shield against the Drudes")!

Another theory has it that the interlocking triangles have a direct Davidic significance. The triangle, it is claimed, is, in fact, the Greek capital letter, *delta*, which bears that particular shape. The *delta* is simply an abbreviation, represented by the initial letter, of the name *David*. This was embossed on the shield of the Israelite soldiers in order to fire them with the same courage and fortitude of that great king and warrior, as well as with the messianic spirit of which King David is the symbol and embodiment. As there would have been no room for the full name of David to be emblazoned on the shield, the two *deltas*, which comprise the first and final letters of the name, were inscribed in an interlocking design.

Such attempts to relate the symbol to authentic Jewish history and tradition are brave but inaccurate. The hexagram clearly infiltrated Jewish circles from external sources, and its frequent appearance in early

Byzantine and medieval European churches and cathedrals suggests that the Jews who tolerated its introduction into the synagogue, as well as into their Hebrew Bible manuscripts, considered that the external connotations or associations that the *Magen David* possessed were a price they were prepared to pay for the convenience of having an artistic symbol of their faith. The fact that the emblem bore the names of David and Solomon would certainly have given them the confidence to ignore any earlier pagan or Christian association. They were fortified by the belief that they were merely claiming back what had originally been a proud Jewish symbol.

For the followers of the false messiah, Shabbetai Tzevi (17th century), the *Magen David* became the secret symbol of their movement and testimony to their belief in the messianic pretensions of its founder. The famous Rabbi Jonathan Eybeschuetz (1690–1764), who served as spiritual leader to the three communities of Altona, Hamburg, and Wanesbek, was charged with being a secret adherent of Shabbateanism after it was claimed that certain amulets, written and distributed by him, contained mystical Shabbatean formulae. They are all supposed to have been endowed with the *Magen David* symbol and the words "seal of Messiah son of David."

In the Nazi era Jews had to wear a *Magen David* as a symbol of shame. Hilter did not appreciate that this symbol had an equal historic significance in paganism and Christianity. He consequently overlooked the essential irony of his insult. It was as much a symbolic assessment of the bestial nature of his pagan philosophy, and of the responsibility for it borne by traditional Christian anti-Semitism, as it was of the hapless status of his victims.

In the modern period the *Magen David* is proudly displayed on the national flag of the State of Israel.

The *Menorah*

Another popular motif of synagogue art is the seven branched candelabra or *Menorah*, a prominent ritual object and sacred symbol of the desert Sanctuary and the Solomonic Temple. Light was the first element to be created by God (Genesis 1:3), and is itself a divine element—"Light dwelleth with Him" (Daniel 2:22). It is also a symbol of divinity: "The Lord is my light" (Psalm 27:1).

This is the kernel of the kabbalistic conception of Creation, and particularly the doctrine of divine emanations, or *Sefirot*, rays of generative light extending outward from the most intense light of the pure source of divinity, the *Ein Sof*, to beget the lower spheres of baser creativity in closer proximity to, and facilitating the creation of, the physical universe. Hence, in Jewish mystical tradition, the *Menorah* is the symbol of divine creativity, and the *Menorah's* various components are explained in the context of that symbolism. The oil of the *Menorah* thus signifies the dynamic stream or inner creative spirit which nourishes and infuses all existence. The oil of the *Menorah* was replenished each day, to ensure that "an everlasting light" (*ner tamid*, Exodus 27:20) was maintained. This, again, symbolizes God's uninterrupted supervision of the world.

The *Menorah* also symbolizes the Torah: "For the command is a lamp and Torah is the light" (Proverbs 6:23); and thus, by radiating its light to Israel, it is instrumental in symbolically facilitating the mystic unity of God, the Torah, and Israel.[5]

The original *Menorah*, exquisitely wrought in solid gold by the divinely inspired artist and craftsman, Bezalel, was placed in front of the curtain *(Parokhet)* partitioning off the Holy of Holies. This explains why some synagogues have a *Menorah*—that is, the eight-branched Chanukah *Menorah*—permanently positioned near the Ark.

In order to augment the illumination of his Temple, King Solomon had ten golden *Menorot* installed there; five on each side, flanking the *Menorah* of Bezalel. Sadly, all of these, as well as the other golden vessels of the Temple, were hewn in pieces by the Babylonians who laid siege to Jerusalem and sacked the Temple in the reign of King Jehoiachin (597 B.C.E.), completing its destruction at their second invasion of 586 B.C.E.

While Jeremiah lists the *Menorot* among the vessels destroyed by the enemy,[6] Ezekiel omits any reference to them in his vision of the restored Temple.[7] We may assume, therefore, that Bezalel's *Menorah* was either destroyed or lost during the siege of Jerusalem. Had it reached Babylon and been placed on view by the conquerors, Ezekiel would certainly have described it and looked forward to its restoration to its rightful place.

There is, however, a rabbinic tradition that, just before the Temple was destroyed, Bezalel's *Menorah* was hidden away and later retrieved by the returning exiles.[8] This has prompted the belief that it survived the whole of the second Jewish Commonwealth, until the destruction of the second Temple by Titus in the year 70 C.E., and that it is the original *Menorah*, which is depicted on the Arch of Titus in Rome. The logical inference is, therefore, that it may still have survived and is possibly lying in some underground vault of the Vatican.

It is very doubtful, however, that such a hypothesis can be sustained. Granted that in the Second Temple only one golden *Menorah* was used, but even if we assume that that was Bezalel's *Menorah*, yet the Book of Maccabees expressly states that Antiochus "entered the Temple presumptuously and seized the golden altar and the *candelabra* and all its vessels . . . and, having seized them all, he returned to his land."[9] This is consistent with the later statement in that book, that "the Maccabees made new sacred objects . . . the *Menorah*." This is, in turn, supported by a talmudic tradition that, due to lack of funds, the first replacement was made of iron, and when they grew richer it was replaced by a silver *Menorah*, and, at a later period of greater prosperity, it was replaced by one of gold.[10] It was most certainly the latter that was carried on Titus's triumphal procession as depicted on his Arch. This also explains why the *Menorah*, as depicted on the Arch, has a pedestal in the shape of two octagonal casings—similar to the one displayed on the emblem of the State of Israel, which was patterned on that of Titus's Arch. This conflicts with Jewish sources that describe a *Menorah* resting on a tripodal base.[11] Clearly the latter reflects the original design of Bezalel's, whereas the Arch depicts its last Maccabean replacement, which, out of deference to the original, would not have been made identical. The pedestal would have been the obvious choice for any distinction to be located.

The authenticity or otherwise of the Titus *Menorah* was hardly a subject that worried earlier generations; neither did this diminish the admiring attention that the Arch attracted, primarily on account of the *Menorah* depicted on it—so much so that throughout the Middle Ages the Arch was universally referred to as "the arch of the seven lamps," with no mention of Titus—an ironic example of a victor's glory becoming eclipsed by that which he vanquished!

Talmudic law[12] strictly forbids the making of a seven-branched *Menorah* out of any metal, since the Temple *Menorah* was not restricted to gold, but was made—as in Maccabean times—out of baser metals also. The propriety of making this the motif of the State of Israel—and the acceptance of a bronze seven-branched candelabra as a gift from Britain—may well be questioned. It was, after all, inevitable that artists and sculptors in Israel would be called upon to create representations of their national symbol! Obviously this prohibition does not extend to woven designs, and hence the popularity of this motif on the mantles of scrolls and on Ark curtains.

The *Menorah* is another example of a Jewish symbol being misappropriated by the Church. In the cathedral at Essen, Germany, stands a monumental gold-plated, bronze cast *Menorah*, presented at the beginning of the 11th century. This is the oldest of more than fifty seven-branched *Menorot* that are still in existence, or known to have been in existence, in Christian churches. On the marble pedestal of the *Menorah* in the Prague cathedral there is an inscription designating it as "Candelabrum of Solomon's Temple in Jerusalem"—a shameless acceptance of the fact that this was a Jewish sacred symbol, and part of the Christian propaganda exercise to demonstrate that the Church was the new and more perfect Temple of Solomon.[13]

The Two Tablets

The Two Tablets are almost universally displayed above the *Aron Kodesh*.[14] Their employment, in the distinctive form endowing each tablet with a rounded top, is perhaps the most astonishing example of a Church motif infiltrating the sanctum of Judaism.

The Tablets were never represented in synagogue art until the end of the 15th century, and it seems beyond doubt that it was only after the Church had popularized their representation as a symbol of Judaism, in numerous frescoes, that Jews followed suit.

England has been identified as the place of origin of the earliest extant example of representational round-topped tablets. An illustrated Bible, dated 1025–1050 and produced in Canterbury,[15] endows the episode of Moses receiving the Two Tablets (Exodus 31:18) with a drawing of a horned Moses carrying one round-topped Tablet in each hand. By the 12th century the round-topped Tablets cropped up all over Europe, in illustrated Bibles and on cathedral walls; and during the following two centuries they began to infiltrate Hebrew manuscripts, sometimes with the round-topped shape and at other times rectangular.

Two aspects of this are quite remarkable: first that Jews should have borrowed a motif that the Church had already popularized for anti-Semitic purposes, and, second, that Jewish artists should have been so willing to copy the round-topped shape of the Tablets when such a shape was a clear figment of Christian artistic imagination and—we suggest—malevolent theological propaganda, without the slightest echo in Jewish tradition.

The Babylonian Talmud states that the dimensions of the Tablets were six handbreadths in height by six handbreadths in breadth. The Palestinian Talmud quotes their measurements, however, as six handbreadths in height by *three* handbreadths in breadth.[16] *Tosafot*[17] plausibly harmonizes these two traditions by stating that the Babylonian source was describing them in their conjoint position, whereas the Palestinian Talmud was describing their separate dimensions. This must, indeed, be valid, since the latter source clearly states that "each individual Tablet *(Kol echad ve-echad)* was six by three handbreadths," whereas the Babylonian passage speaks merely of "the Tablets."

Thus, the traditional view is of two Tablets jointly forming a perfect square of approximately 60 cm × 60 cm. Indeed, the Palestinian source states categorically that the Tablets were *tetroga*, "square," from the Greek *tetra*. *Had there been any tradition of a rounded top, the Talmud would certainly have alluded to it.* It is beyond doubt, therefore, that the rounded-top Tablets are a Christian innovation that Jews unthinkingly borrowed!

When we consider the motivation and context of the Christian tendency to depict Moses and the Two Tablets we will be all the more surprised at this Jewish borrowing. The sole purpose of this portrayal was to present a contrasting image of the synagogue in decline and the church in ascendancy. "Church was shown as victorious, wearing a crown, holding a standard with flying banner in one hand, a chalice in another. By contrast, synagogue, from about the 12th century on, was frequently represented holding the Tablets of the Law (often portrayed upside down and slipping out of her hand), her eyes veiled, her crown falling, her staff broken, and her banner drooping."[18]

Frequently the round-topped Tablets are represented as broken, to indicate that Jewish law has been shattered, superseded by the New Testament. A host of other unsavory methods are also frequently employed to depict Jews and Judaism as out of grace, and to denigrate the synagogue. "In allegories dealing with the fall and redemption, Moses and the Tablets are grouped with Fall, Sin, Devil, Death, and Hell—opposed by the crucified and risen Savior who is grouped with Redemption, Grace, and Everlasting Life."[19]

Round-Topped Tablets

These humiliating contexts, wherein the round-topped Tablets are portrayed, prompt the question, why *did* the church introduce this novel shape? The only conclusion we can draw is that this was an essential element in the theological polemic which this genre of art served to promote.

We believe that the round top was an attempt to make the

Tablets—representative of Judaism—conform to the characteristic mold imposed by the church:

> During the four and a half centuries, from 1100 to 1550, arches were most widely used in European architecture, especially in churches and monastic buildings. . . . Churches of that period became veritable systems of arches. . . . It is only necessary to compare churches with secular and military buildings of the same period to recognize the extent to which arches were used to make churches different.[20]

It is surely no coincidence, therefore, that the church chose to alter the traditional square shape of the Tablets in order to give them a distinctive arched shape, thereby underscoring the basic teaching that Judaism is now totally subservient to Christianity and that the synagogue and the Jewish fate must conform to whatever mold the church determines for it. Perhaps the time has come for a return to square-shaped Tablets!

17

The Rabbi

Origin of the Title

The spiritual leader and guide on all matters of Jewish law and ritual is called the *rabbi*. The word actually means "my teacher" and was obviously applied originally as a personal mode of honorific address. The word should logically have been converted into the (Aramaic) plural, *rabban* ("*our* teacher") when it later became adopted as a title or designation of office. This was not done, however, because the title *rabban* had already become reserved for the scholars of unique distinction who were elected to the office of *Nasi*, Patriarch of Palestine.

The first sage to be given a title—that of *rabban*—was Gamliel (*Ha-Zakein*), the grandson of Hillel.[1] The historian I. H. Weiss states[2] simply that "we do not know the reason why such a title was introduced, but it is possible that there was no special reason other than that he was so universally loved and respected that people just could not refer to him by his first name without an honorific title; and from then on it came to be applied to all the patriarchs."

The title *rabbi* ("my teacher"), first accorded to Torah scholars ordained as graduates of the Palestinian talmudic academies, may have been introduced by Rabban Gamliel himself.[3] The greatness and hu-

211

mility of that sage was such that he may well have felt embarrassed to be the first and sole recipient of a title, and he very likely sanctioned, if not instigated, its more general application. Perhaps this is the background to the mishnaic comment that "from the time that Rabban Gamliel died, the true glory of Torah was lost"[4] – since henceforth every scholar, irrespective of distinction, bore the identical title of "Rabbi."

There may well have been a further motive, however, in his encouragement of the title *rabbi*. His period (30–50 C.E.) coincided with the rise and first wave of expansion of Christian missionary activity and the wider dissemination of its principles by the early disciples. Indeed, the New Testament actually claims that Paul was a disciple of Rabban Gamliel! In order to frustrate the sowing of confusion among the gullible masses, who might not easily have been able to distinguish an Orthodox teacher from one preaching adherence to the new faith, Gamliel may well have regarded the title *rabbi* as a useful label to mark the Torah-true sage. The followers of the new faith were scrupulous at that period to accord a title – that of "Master" or "Father" – only to their founder and mentor, so that it would be beyond doubt that anyone else bearing the newly introduced title of *rabbi* could only have been an authentic Torah sage.

While *rabbi* thus became a prefix to the scholar's name, which is always mentioned in the *Mishnah* and Talmud in the form "Rabbi so-and-so, son of so-and-so" (e.g., Rabbi Eleazar ben Azariah), one scholar, however, gained such authority and distinction that he is referred to frequently merely as "Rabbi," *The Master*. He is Rabbi Judah Ha-Nasi, Patriarch of Palestinian Jewry around 180–220 C.E., who was responsible for systematizing the whole of Jewish Oral Law in the form of the *Mishnah*. He is also known as *Rabbeinu Ha-Kadosh*, "Our saintly master." Babylon also had its counterpart, in the person of Abba bar Aivu (3rd century C.E.), founder of the academy of Sura, who is generally referred to simply as "Rav," *the* teacher (of the entire Diaspora).

Semikhah Ordination

The ceremony of ordination was, and still is, known as *Semikhah*. The term means, literally, "laying (of hands)," and derives from the divine command to Moses to install Joshua into office as his successor: "Take Joshua son of Nun, a man in whom the spirit resides, and lay (*ve-samakhta*) your hands upon him" (Numbers 27:18) . . . "And you shall put of your honor upon him" (Numbers 27:20).

So the granting of *Semikhah* is more than a certificate of graduation.

It is a most personal and spiritual act of sharing with another the sacred authority that one had hitherto jealously and safely inherited and preserved on trust from one's own teacher. It is consequently the most supreme act of personal generosity that a master can confer upon his pupil. It is tantamount to a parent bidding farewell to a son who has reached the stage when he must leave the family home to make his own way in the world. There is more than a touch of nostalgia, more than a pang of fear. Will the child be safe on his own? Is he well enough equipped to survive the hazards of life? The teacher has the same— perhaps even greater—misgivings as he gives his disciple the authority to teach and to make independent decisions on all matters of Jewish law. The teacher is putting unique trust in the "rabbi" he has ordained. He is trusting him to uphold Orthodox tradition and neither to deviate from it nor to misuse his new authority. He is also trusting him to quote his teacher accurately; for, indeed, it is so easy to misrepresent, albeit unwittingly, the teacher at whose feet one has sat for years, learning from, and discussing with, so many complex and varied topics of Jewish law.

Because a wrong decision by a newly ordained rabbi means, in effect, that someone will act contrary to Jewish law, contrary to the will of God, teachers have accordingly never been eager to confer *Semikhah*. After all, it is given to few individuals in a generation to really achieve total mastery of Torah. The teacher has to have confidence, therefore, that the ordinand will not only continue, throughout his life, to augment his knowledge, but that he will possess the humility to confer with senior colleagues when in doubt, and to consult, at all times, the traditional legal sources before giving decisions. *Semikhah* thus involves trust and confidence on the part of the teacher that his disciple is—and will continue to be—worthy and God-fearing.

Since the Holy Land was ever zealous to retain its rightful position as supreme authority in all religious matters over the Diaspora communities ("For out of Zion shall go forth the Law and the word of the Lord from Jerusalem"), the scope of *Semikhah* granted in talmudic times to scholars from abroad was restricted. The main restrictions were that the Babylonian sages could not share the title *rabbi*—they were called merely *rav*—and that they were not permitted to impose fixed fines as punishments *(ein danin dinei knasot be-bavel)*.

The latter restriction had serious repercussions, as, inevitably, it meant that the capacity of the Diaspora judges to punish evildoers was severely hampered. This problem was solved by the Palestinian authorities allowing their Babylonian colleagues to impose fines *"on the authority of, and as agents for, the Palestinian judges."*[5]

The determination of the Palestinian authorities to restrict the number of ordained rabbis in the Diaspora—in order to sustain Palestinian spiritual hegemony—is exemplified by the case of Shemuel, one of the most outstanding pupils of Rabbi Judah Ha-Nasi. He came from Babylon, and, after studying for years and achieving unique distinction in all branches of Jewish law, he wished to return to his home country in order to build up religious life, which was at very low ebb. He required *Semikhah* in order to carry weight and authority among his communities, but Rabbi Judah his teacher felt unable to grant it. He thus remained unordained all his life, notwithstanding the fact that he is among the leading authorities of the Babylonian Talmud!

This withholding of *Semikhah* is, indeed, puzzling,[6] and can only be explained in the context of the historic tensions between those two great centers of Jewish life. Babylon made some notable attempts to cut the umbilical cord that kept it subjected to the authority of Palestine, and Palestine felt accordingly obliged to ensure that its own traditional authority remained paramount. Shemuel's personal authority and brilliance, his drive and industry, could well have established Babylon as a rival center of Jewish learning—which it was, indeed, very soon to become. Together with his colleague Rav, they made a formidable combination, and the *yeshivot* they founded in Babylon attracted students and scholars in their thousands. Judah Ha-Nasi was perceptive enough to discern the unbounded capability of his disciples, and, for the honor of the Holy Land, he felt constrained therefore to clip the wings of a budding Diaspora, albeit by that merely symbolic gesture of withholding ordination from Shemuel. (It did, in effect, have a positive aspect, in that it enabled Rav to establish his own authority as paramount in Babylon, thus making for decisive action and swift progress in the reorganization of religious life in that country.)

Shemuel also happened to be a renowned astronomer,[7] and he may well have been the one who perfected the method of astronomical calculation that was later used to provide the basis for a fixed calendar to replace the original and unsatisfactory method of relying on the visual evidence of two witnesses testifying to the appearance of the new moon.[8] This being so, it would have constituted another understandable fear of Rabbi Judah, thereby convincing him beyond doubt that Shemuel was indeed capable of establishing Babylonian supremacy single-handed.

Essential Personal Qualities

In addition to competence in Jewish law, the scholar seeking *Semikhah* in talmudic times was expected to possess a large number of personal qualities and attainments. The Torah already enumerated some of these in the instruction to Moses that the judges he was to appoint should be "God-fearing men, honest and incorruptible" (Exodus 18:21), as well as "men of wisdom, understanding and repute" (Deuteronomy 1:13).

The last chapter of *Pirkei Avot* was originally known as *Perek Kinyan Torah*, "the chapter on the acquisition of Torah," and it contains the clearest statement on the qualities expected of a rabbi. The first prerequisite, in order to cultivate the idealism necessary to devote oneself single-mindedly for years to the acquisition of Torah, is the capacity to live frugally, since neither scholarships nor bursaries were available:

> This is the way that is becoming for the study of Torah: a morsel of bread with salt thou must eat, and water by measure thou must drink; thou must sleep on the ground, and live a life of hardship while you toil in the Torah.[9]

This source goes on to enumerate no less than forty-eight requirements and attributes necessary in order to acquire Torah:

> Audible study, distinct pronunciation, an understanding mind, and critical acumen; awe, reverence, meekness, and cheerfulness; the willingness to minister to the sages, to attach oneself to colleagues, to be ever available for discussion with disciples; sedateness; knowledge of the Scriptures and the *Mishnah*; moderation in business, in intercourse with the world, in pleasure, in sleep, in conversation, in laughter; the capacity to be long-suffering and goodhearted; possessing faith in the words of the sages, willing acceptance of chastisement, recognition of one's place and satisfaction with one's lot; limiting one's conversation; claiming no merit for one's achievements; being beloved, loving the All-present, loving mankind, loving just causes, uprightness and reproof; keeping away from honors, not boasting of one's learning, not delighting in giving decisions; sympathy with the suffering of a colleague, judging everyone charitably, leading people to truth and peace; being composed in one's study, constantly asking questions and not being reticent to answer, listening and offering suggestions (of one's own), learning with the object of practicing, making one's master wiser, preparing one's discourse with great thoroughness, always reporting a statement in the name of its author.[10]

Transferring Authority

While *Semikhah* is fundamentally the transference of rabbinic authority, yet authority is an elusive concept. The words "authority," "author," and "authentic" are semantically identical. One becomes an "authority" through intimate association with the "author," namely by being the "authentic" repository and expounder of a particular "author" or source of knowledge. So the *musmakh* (ordained) may become heir to the traditions of his *masmikh* (ordainer), and may, *in the eyes of the latter,* inherit his authority. Yet authority is meaningless unless a sufficient number of other people also acknowledge the fledgling authority as their expert and guide in the area covered by his expertise. The fact that the *masmikh* is an acknowledged "authority" is no guarantee that the community will accept his young *musmakh* and view him in the same light. So, in order to create spiritual leaders we require two criteria: halakhic expertise (presupposing also the special qualities of character and piety, as outlined above) and, equally important, men who are acceptable to the community as leaders. The *masmikh* should certainly have regard to the second criterion before awarding his *Semikhah.* The Talmud stresses the importance of the leader being well attuned to the needs of the community in its pithy maxim, *parnas le-fiy ha-dor,* "a leader must suit his particular generation."[11]

This second criterion is alluded to in a well-known talmudic passage, referring to the *Semikhah* conferred upon Rabbi Meir by Rabbi Judah ben Bava.[12] Among the repressive measures imposed upon Judea by the Roman emperor Hadrian was one prohibiting the ordination of rabbis, under penalty of death for the ordainer and the ordained, as well as the destruction of the town where the ceremony was performed. Five of the most distinguished young scholars decided to flee from Palestine to Babylon. R. Judah accompanied them into the open countryside and there conferred *Semikhah* upon them. As the Roman soldiers approached he urged the young scholars to flee and not to endanger their own lives, and the very future, uninterrupted chain of ordination, by staying behind with him. They thereupon escaped, and Rabbi Judah was apprehended and butchered.

The question posed by the Talmud is why it was necessary for Rabbi Judah to ordain at least one of the students, Rabbi Meir, when the latter had already obtained *Semikhah* from his first teacher, Rabbi Akivah. The answer is given that "although Akivah did ordain Meir, yet people did not accept Meir's authority." The reason for this, according to Rashi, was that Rabbi Meir was unmarried and still a mere youth. Hence it was necessary for Rabbi Judah ben Bava to award his own ordination.

Rabbi Shelomo Dichowsky[13] has pointed out that this begs the question; for, rather than endanger the life of R. Meir by ordaining him in such a situation, Rabbi Judah ben Bava should surely have relied on the *Semikhah* conferred by Akivah, which would certainly have been recognized by the communities once R. Meir had married and was eventually accepted as an authority! The answer suggested is that "one cannot escape from the conclusion that the agreement of the community constitutes an integral component of *Semikhah*, without which the ordination is *ab initio* void. For this reason a second act of ordination was required, notwithstanding the attendant danger."[14]

This accords fully with our observation above on the nature of "authority." A teacher may assure his student that he is "an authority," but it is the common consensus, the attitude of the community at large, which will determine whether or not his words and decisions will be invested with true authority. This is explicitly recognized in the talmudic prescription that "a community leader may not be appointed without first securing the agreement of the community."[15] Torah is very much "a tree of *life*"; it is not merely an academic pursuit. Its objective is *orthopraxis*, proper observance of *mitzvot*, leading to the establishment of a holy community *(kehillah kedoshah)*. The cloistered scholar does a disservice to the community if he does not put his learning and insights either directly at their disposal, or, indirectly, through the pupils he teaches and inspires.

The rabbi has a sacred responsibility to lead, to guide, to raise the religious quality of Jewish communal life. If he presumes to wield such authority over a community, it can only be done successfully if the community has such confidence in his wisdom, integrity, and capacity to relate the sacred traditions to the needs and conditions of the contemporary age, that they are prepared to accept his authority as binding upon them, whether or not his halakhic decisions prove popular. *Semikhah* is therefore also a contract entered into between the newly created rabbi and the Jewish community. The conferring authority is, in a real sense, also the agent of his people. It is his own acknowledged "authority" that gives him the right to assume such an agency, and to feel confident that it will meet with the approval of the community.

In the State of Israel this requirement of having communal acceptance of the rabbinic leader is fulfilled through the election procedure of rabbis, who are state officials rather than the appointees of individual synagogues, as in most other countries. Dichowsky[16] has complained that this has, in effect, pulled the pendulum to the other extreme, since the electing body for rabbinical posts is composed mainly of laymen, many of whom are not themselves religious and who have, consequently, no comprehension of the respective merits of candidates. Thus, while the precondition of "communal acceptance" is fulfilled, the first precondition, the agreement of Torah authorities, is disregarded. He also complains that the election of Israel's chief rabbis leaves much to be desired for the same reason. While the electoral college does constitute a coalition of laymen and rabbis, yet the proportion of the latter is so small as to ensure that the laymen's candidate will gain the majority vote. The rabbinic representation, according to the complainant, is too small to be said to represent the many Torah sages and the vast number of institutions, as well as members of Orthodox groups and synagogues, that have a direct interest in the appointment. Hence there is an inordinate emphasis on the "communal acceptance" aspect, and insufficient attention paid to "rabbinic agreement and allegiance."

Representative of God or the Community?

Bearing in mind the community's vested interest in the type of rabbinical leader to whom it grants and owes allegiance, the question has also been raised as to whether the rabbi is essentially the representative of God (*shelucha de-rachamana*) or the representative of the community (*shelucha di-dan*). This is an issue which the Talmud already raised[17] in connection with the role of the priest who, in Temple times, acted as spiritual leader and oracle of divine blessing, on the one hand, but also as representative at the altar on behalf of both the individual who brought a sacrifice as well as of the community at large.

Rabbi Shaul Yisraeli[18] believes that, unlike the priest who is regarded primarily as representative of God,[19] the rabbi must combine both sacred roles, even though they seem hardly capable of synthesis, and may even appear to be mutually conflicting. This, however, is precisely the unique challenge of the rabbinate.

The difficulty of becoming the embodiment of such a synthesis hardly needs to be stated. To be "the representative of the community" involves coming to terms with its spiritual apathy, abiding its espousal of a religion of convenience, tolerating its many shortcomings and excesses, and flattering and praising men and organizations that publicly flout the sacred tenets of the faith. One cannot be their representative or leader for long without one's own zeal for total commitment to letter, spirit, and ethic of *halakhah* becoming somewhat diluted or compromised.

The young rabbi's need—and the community's expectation of him—to provide an "appealing Judaism," his desperate desire to make them regard their religion with esteem, and not to view it as an uncompromising, outmoded system, inevitably preoccupy the mind of the leader and frequently move him to search for *heterim* (permissive rulings). Of course this can be justified on the basis of a well-established halakhic principle, *kocha de-hetera adif* ("the value of a lenient ruling is far more beneficial"). But this so frequently leads to his becoming "lenient" without the "ruling," adopting leniency as a matter of expediency, and ultimately as a philosophy. Compromise engenders further compromise. It is uniquely prolific. This is why the *yeshivot* generally do not encourage their students to enter the rabbinate. The *yeshivah* sees its task as that of producing the representative of God *(shelucha de-rachamana)*, not the leader who represents—and reflects—the community *(shelucha di-dan)*.

The rabbi who serves the typical, modern, nominally Orthodox community is frequently subjected by his members to considerable pressure for him to become a media personality, a controversialist, a public figure beyond the confines of his own congregation. Their rabbi's achievement of public recognition and stature must, so they believe, increase the status of his synagogue, and, accordingly, of all its members. The rabbi becomes the measuring rod of the vitality and vibrancy of his congregation. "In his light do *they* see light."

Add to this the desire of moderns to have everything in life raised to the status of the "meaningful," which is truly nothing more than the "with-it," the gimmicky, the well-packaged commodity. The contribution of the rabbi has also to be well packaged. Pulpit technique becomes more important than scholarship. As the large synagogues partake more and more of the spirit of the theatre auditorium, so the rabbi's "performance" must be equally dramatic and impressive. *What* he says is less important than *how* he says it. Content becomes subservient to form. This, in turn, easily expands degeneratively to become a veritable philosophy of religious expressionism.

Rabbi Yisraeli is acutely aware of such traps laid for the unsuspecting, and even the aware, young rabbi. Yet this distinguished sage is convinced that the synthesis of divine and human representative can still be achieved, not by compromise or condonation, but by unbounded love and deep sympathy. He uses the analogy of Moses, who is referred to in mystical writings as *raya meheimna*, "the faithful shepherd." This is rooted in the well-known midrash that, while Moses was tending Jethro's flock, a young lamb separated itself from the main herd. Moses followed it, unable to catch up with it, for a whole day. He never gave up following it to ensure that it came to no harm. At the end of the day he caught up with it as the young lamb lay exhausted, and Moses carried it back tenderly in his arms. God thereupon said to him, "You displayed such concern to tend the sheep. By your life, you shall tend *my* sheep, Israel, in the same way."[20]

This, according to Yisraeli, is the classical paradigm for the spiritual and communal leader—an indivisible entity. The rabbi's profound concern for "the sheep" should make him feel a personal sense of responsibility for their shortcomings and spiritual apathy. He does not have to regard compromise as a solution, for it truly is not. Compromise only preserves, nourishes, and compounds the problem. A judge may have a sympathetic feeling toward a wrongdoer who acted as a result of environmental or hereditary circumstances beyond his control. But that must not prevent the judge from reprimanding the accused and punishing him.

The rabbi's profound *ahavat yisrael*, love of Israel, must make him a tolerant shepherd who understands clearly the weaknesses of his flock. But being "tolerant" does not mean having "to tolerate." The rabbi must speak out and admonish fearlessly—but lovingly. He is precisely the *shelucha de-rachamana*; for, just as God is "One who dwells with them in the midst of their impurity" (Leviticus 16:16), so must His "representative" do likewise. The rabbi has to be "part" of his sinful community, yet "apart" from its sinfulness.

On the other hand, he is also *shelucha di-dan*, the representative of his flock. But one's representative does not have to be one's carbon copy. The rabbi is representative of the true mission of the Jewish community, not of the expedient standards and values of individuals within it. If a synagogue rabbi is invited to become a media disseminator of Jewish teaching to the wider community, it is not in the choice of "their" rabbi or in the "act" of dissemination that they should take pride, but in the message that he is conveying. Their delight should be, in fact, that the authentic will of God is being given an opportunity to be ventilated among a wider society so desperately in need of it.

The rabbi should be the "representative of the community" by standing in precisely the same relationship to it as the *chazan*. He should be the intercessor with God on their behalf. Like the prophets of old, he must inspire them with the will to raise standards, and he must point out where precisely the improvements have to be made, leading them, skillfully and persuasively, from the lower to the upper rungs of joyful observance.

Tribute may certainly be paid to the Lubavitch movement whose emissaries have gone out all over the world, to the farthest outposts of Jewish life, to reach down to Jews on the lowest rungs of religious apathy and ignorance in order to teach them, encourage them, and raise them and their children frequently to the dizziest heights of observance of Torah and *mitzvot*. It is, of course, much easier when one is one's own master, free to plan one's own missionary program. The community rabbi, whose varied pastoral and communal activities determine, to a large extent, the scope and limitations of his efforts, cannot so easily devote the lengthy hours and years required to cultivate and closely guide so many individuals and families. Nevertheless, if the communities are wise enough to understand the nature of the rabbinical office, they will enable their leader to achieve that subtle fusion of *shelucha de-rachamana* and *shelucha di-dan*.

Privileges of Office

The traditional concept of the rabbi has undergone many changes over the centuries. At first it was, as we have shown, a spiritual and academic accolade, whereby *rabbi* was synonymous with *talmid chakham* (literally "wise disciple"), "scholar." In talmudic times the bearer of such a title was entitled not only to respect, but also to certain prescribed privileges. He was expected, in turn, to conform to certain patterns of behavior and standards of propriety calculated to uphold the dignity of his office and the honor of the Torah.

The biblical command, "You shall rise up before the hoary head and honor the face of the old man *(zakein)*" (Leviticus 19:32), was applied to the scholar also. *Zakein* had that extra connotation and was popularly interpreted as a contraction of the Hebrew phrase *zeh she-kanah (chokhmah)* – "one who had acquired (wisdom)." It is thus regarded as a biblical law to stand up when a rabbinic scholar enters a room or passes by.

The first part of the sentence, which refers to the "hoary head," also makes it obligatory to show that same mark of respect to someone who had achieved the age of seventy, whether or not he is wise, but provided that he is not a wicked person to whom such a mark of esteem is unbecoming![21]

This biblical law is not confined to the sages or elderly of our own persuasion. The *halakhah* states that "even an elderly non-Jewish person must be shown honor by the respectful manner in which he is addressed, as well as by extending an arm to support him."[22]

Characteristically, the *halakhah* recognizes that achievement and merit in other spheres of life also merit the expression of esteem, even on the part of rabbis. Hence, "a sage, however celebrated for his wisdom, ought to stand up before *a man of great achievement (baal*

maasim).[23] This is left vague, as it will obviously be up to the discretion
of the sage as to whether or not the individual concerned truly merits
that mark of honor. "Great achievement" most certainly points to a
contribution, in any sphere of human endeavor, which brings lasting
benefit to society.

The privileges of office, extended in talmudic times to rabbinic
scholars who devoted themselves to Torah study full time *(toratam
omanutam),* included exemption from payment of certain taxes and
rates.[24] The scholar was also to be relieved of any menial work that the
municipality used to impose periodically as a civic responsibility on all
citizens, such as building operations or digging and draining the city
foundations. While the scholar was expected to make a contribution
toward certain other more essential services, such as the provision and
maintenance of the fresh water cisterns, he was to be exempted from
payment toward the city guard. The reason given is, significantly, that
"scholars do not need such protection, since their Torah protects
them!"[25]

The community was expected to take very seriously its obligation
to further the honor of scholars at all times. There was a special fine of
"a litra of gold"[26] or, in a case of extreme provocation, excommunication, imposed upon anyone who insulted a scholar. While Moses
Isserles (16th century) was of the opinion that the law absolving the
scholar from payment of taxes still applied in his day, he did not,
however, believe that the traditional fine could be exacted, since "we no
longer have any scholars of such repute as to be able to claim such a
compensation."[27] Nevertheless, he asserts, it is still an actionable
offense, for which the *Bet Din* may award suitable damages.

There were many rabbis in the talmudic period who, rather than be
supported by the community, preferred to undertake a little business for
part of the day so as to be self-supporting. The *halakhah* accorded them
a special token of recognition and privilege by insisting that other
traders, selling the same commodity, must not do so until the rabbi has
sold his stock![28] Another privilege, predicated upon the assumption of
the absolute integrity of rabbis, allowed the latter to claim a lost article
merely by declaring that the said article was theirs, while ordinary folk
had to describe the article in every detail before it would be released.

These special privileges were, for over a thousand years, the only
rewards a rabbi could expect for his scholarship, piety, and leadership;
for, until the 14th century, there was no such thing as a professional
rabbinate. Rabbis of communities supported themselves through business or, more commonly, the practice of medicine. This was one of the
few professions open to Jews in the medieval period, and was a
profession that was also regarded as possessing a spiritual dimension

that complemented their rabbinic vocation. Frequently this was augmented by the receipt of fees for officiating at specific religious functions, such as marriages and deaths. The reticence to make a full-time profession out of the rabbinate was motivated by the clear warning in the *Pirkei Avot* that "one should not make of the Torah a spade to dig with."[29] Torah must be studied for its own sake, not in order to secure personal reward or emolument.

The Professional Rabbinate

The professional rabbinate owes its origin to Christian persecutions in Spain toward the end of the 14th century. A number of distinguished rabbis—such as Simon ben Tzemach Duran *(Tashbetz)* and Isaac bar Sheshet *(Rivash)*—who had earned a living in Spain as doctors of medicine, fled to other countries where they found no opportunity to follow their own profession. They were consequently constrained to accept the offer of financial support from the community in return for their rabbinic services. Rabbi Isaac bar Sheshet consequently became chief rabbi of Algiers, and was succeeded, on his death, by R. Simon ben Tzemach Duran. Positions had to be found now for the many *yeshivah* students who could find no means of livelihood other than what could be provided by the community. Pressure thus built up for new rabbinic positions to be created, and so the profession expanded.

Leaders like *Tashbetz* and *Rivash*—and outstanding physicians, such as Maimonides and Isaac Israeli, who preceded them—personified an ideal combination of talmudic expertise and secular learning, of which the Spanish and Portuguese scholars were the chief exponents. It was largely as a result of the expulsion of these scholars from Spain in 1492 that new centers of learning were established in other European countries. They opened what were essentially Jewish colleges or universities. The medical school of Montpellier, for example, was founded by the Spanish refugees, and they also opened private fee-paying colleges where the curriculum included rabbinics, science, and medicine.

This concept of the "rabbi-scholar" underwent a metamorphosis in the middle of the 19th century, when westernized, cultured Jews began to expect not only that their rabbis should master secular scholarship, in addition to traditional learning, but that the traditional learning itself should be acquired in a critical, scholarly, and systematic manner. This involved broadening the curriculum to include such subjects as biblical studies, comparative grammar of Hebrew and other semitic languages, Jewish philosophy, history, liturgy, etc.

Rabbinical Seminaries

With the divisions into Orthodox, Conservative, and Reform groupings, came the demand for modern rabbinical seminaries to be established in order to provide that broad education, as well as to reflect the specific theology of each group. The Conservatives opened the first such seminary in Breslau, founded by Zechariah Frankel in 1854. In Berlin, 1872 saw the foundation of the Reform *Hochschule fuer die Wissenschaft des Judentums*. The Orthodox *Rabbiner Seminar* opened its doors the following year, under the direction of Azriel Hildesheimer.

In Eastern Europe there existed but one rabbinical seminary, the *Landesrabbinerschule*, founded in Budapest in 1877, whose doors remained open throughout the Communist era until the present. Its most distinguished student and teacher was Alexander Scheiber (b. 1913), appointed a professor in 1945, and director in 1950. With dogged determination he set out to ensure that his seminary served the purpose of keeping Judaism and the rabbinical traditions of Eastern Europe alive for the small remnant of Hungarian Jewry that survived the Holocaust. Scheiber was responsible for ordaining generations of rabbis who filled both official and unofficial positions in Eastern bloc countries. He was a scholar with an international reputation, who, in addition to his specialist fields of rabbinics and the history of Hungarian Jewry, also researched the *Genizah* collection at Cambridge and published some important fragments.

America, likewise, provided seminaries for its respective religious denominations. Isaac M. Wise (1819–1900), an immigrant rabbi from Bohemia, was the founding father, driving power, and administrative planner of Reform Judaism in America. He was instrumental in the establishment, in 1875, of the first rabbinical seminary in the United States, the Hebrew Union College of Cincinnati, Ohio, under the auspices of the Union of American Hebrew Congregations, a body that Wise also conceived and struggled to establish.

Wise was convinced that Orthodoxy would not survive in America (though a large Eastern European immigration soon refuted this premise) and his plan was, therefore, to establish a *Minhag America*, a unified and reformed religious tradition that blended the ideals of Judaism and Americanism, which for him were one and the same, leading to the creation of a universal faith.[30] The redemption of mankind, he believed, was to be effected through the agency of American Israel, an idea not too far removed from that of the Pilgrim Fathers in viewing their act of colonization as a significant reenactment of Israel's conquest of the Promised Land.

Wise retained a measure of respect for the Talmud, if only on the grounds that he believed it "had amended biblical laws, rescinded some, and invented others."[31] He was also in favor of a loose confederation of Reform congregations, allowing the expression of all shades and degrees of reform. He was consequently regarded as a moderate and denounced as a compromiser with Orthodoxy by his more radical colleague, David Einhorn.

On the other hand, there were those, spearheaded by Isaac Leeser, Sabato Morais, Alexander Kohut, Marcus Jastrow, and Benjamin Szold, who, while appreciating that a new approach to Jewish life and tradition in America was required, yet could not sympathize with the new radicalism. They, in greater or lesser measure, insisted upon the retention of Judaism's basic principles, affirming the relevance of the ancient tradition to contemporary life, as well as its compatibility with human reason and change.

This right wing of the Reform movement became known as the Historical School, to indicate their conviction that their ideas were a true continuation of historical Judaism. This was the forerunner of the twentieth-century American Conservative movement.

The founding fathers of the Historical School knew that if their movement was to develop in America, they could not continue to rely upon graduates of the European centers of Jewish learning. Hence the opening of the Jewish Theological Seminary in 1886. A major reorganization and relocation in 1902 was accompanied by an invitation to Professor Solomon Schechter, lecturer in rabbinics at Cambridge, founding director of research into the *Genizah* collection, and one of the world's leading Jewish scholars, to be the Seminary's new president. Schechter assembled a most illustrious faculty, including such names as Louis Ginzberg, Alexander Marx, and Israel Friedlaender. In 1909 Schechter established the Teachers Institute and appointed Dr. Mordecai M. Kaplan, who was to achieve renown as the founder of the Reconstructionist movement, as dean.

Successors to Schechter as president were Cyrus Adler (1915–1940), Louis Finkelstein (1940–1972; named as chancellor in 1951), Bernard Mandelbaum (1966–1972), Gerson D. Cohen (1972–1986), and Ismar Schorsch, who assumed the position of chancellor in 1986.

Mention should be made of Professor Saul Lieberman, a world-renowned giant of rabbinic literature and classical scholarship, who combined both disciplines to make a pioneering contribution toward the textual study of the Talmud, especially the hitherto-neglected Palestinian Talmud. Among numerous other works, he produced a critical edition of the *Tosefta*, and two major studies, *Greek in Jewish Palestine* (1942) and *Hellenism in Jewish Palestine* (1950), wherein he employed his mastery of Greek language and literature in order to trace the extent of Hellenistic influence on Jewish life and thought in the early centuries of the common era. In 1940 Lieberman joined the Seminary as professor of Palestinian literature and institutions; he was appointed as dean in 1949, and rector of the rabbinical school in 1958.

Another world-renowned scholar who graced the Seminary's faculty, as professor of Jewish ethics and mysticism (having previously taught at the Hebrew Union College), was Abraham Joshua Heschel, whose books on medieval Jewish philosophy, Chasidism, Kabbalah, and theology are, in addition to their intrinsic importance and originality, masterpieces of prose writing that have rightly become modern-day classics.

It was under Gerson D. Cohen's presidency that the *Masorti* (Traditional) movement was founded, to promote Conservative Jewish concerns and institutions in Israel. Cohen also removed the barriers to women's admission to the Seminary as candidates for rabbinic ordination. This movement has also made some modest inroads into Anglo-Jewry, where its acknowledged rabbinic authority is Rabbi Dr. Louis Jacobs of the New London Synagogue.

The foremost Orthodox rabbinical seminary is Yeshiva University in New York City, which developed from The Rabbi Isaac Elhanan (Spektor) Theological Seminary (RIETS), founded in 1897. This was the very first institution for the advanced study of rabbinics in the United States, and in religious philosophy and curriculum content it was the counterpart of the traditional *yeshivot* of Eastern Europe. The scope of the Seminary was expanded in the early decades of the 20th century to include an elementary and a high school, combining secular and talmudic studies, as well as a Teachers Institute, and, in 1928, Yeshiva College, an undergraduate college whose curriculum provides both Jewish studies and the regular courses of a secular university. Stern College, a counterpart for women of the men's Yeshiva College, was opened in 1954.

The greatest period of physical and academic expansion coincided with the presidency of Samuel Belkin, who succeeded Bernard Revel in 1940. Five years later it was elevated to university status, and adopted the title *Yeshiva University*.

In order to counter the claim that the *musmakhim* (rabbinical ordinands) at RIETS had a rather narrow, talmudically exclusive, education—notwithstanding the fact that entrance to the rabbinical faculty was restricted to graduates—the decision was taken, in 1955, that all rabbinical students must also pursue studies in such courses as Bible, Jewish history, philosophy, and Hebrew literature. These courses are taught at the nondenominational Bernard Revel Graduate School for Jewish and Semitic Studies.

The impact of Yeshiva University upon Orthodoxy in America has been profound, not only directly, in the hundreds of its graduates currently serving as congregational rabbis and educators, but also indirectly, through its religious influence upon the thousands of students who study at its secular, nonsectarian divisions. These include the Ferkauf Graduate School of Humanities and Social Sciences, the Belfer Graduate School of Science, and the most distinguished Albert Einstein College of Medicine and its affiliated College Hospital.

Illustrious rabbinic scholars have always headed the talmudical faculty of RIETS, men of the caliber of Joseph Dov Soloveitchik, who became professor of Talmud in 1941, while also occupying the chair of Jewish philosophy at the Bernard Revel Graduate School. His influence on successive generations of Yeshiva University has been paramount, and the nomenclature he has deservedly earned is, simply, *the Rav*. He was averse to publishing his most creative and profound ideas, preferring to communicate orally, which he did with rare oratorical power. Several of his students have published volumes of his thoughts, based upon recollections of or notes taken at his lectures.

The present professor of Talmud, J. David Bleich, has become universally known for his distillations, in the English language, of the most wide-ranging modern-day problems as treated in the halakhic responsa literature. These first appeared in the popular column, "Survey of Recent Halakhic Literature," in the journal *Tradition*, and have been collected in several volumes of his *Contemporary Halakhic Problems*.

Rabbi Norman Lamm (b. 1927) is professor of Jewish philosophy and the current president of Yeshiva University. A prolific author, he was the founder and first editor of *Tradition*. He is a champion of Centrist Orthodoxy, insisting—against the current tide of right-wing opinion that is gaining ground even within the faculty of his own institution—that *Torah im derekh eretz* means the harmonious synthesis of Torah and general culture. The prevailing view is that they are, in fact, parallel objectives that may, indeed, both be cultivated within a single mind, but can never fuse to become an integrated, personal program for a unified philosophy of Judaism.

It is this Centrist position that has exacerbated the traditional rift between the world of the traditional *yeshivot* and Lamm's Yeshiva University. Lamm himself has been the butt of some particularly unsavory personal abuse by those extremists who prefer invective to reasoned argument. To date he has stood his ground and has argued most eloquently for the position he holds, a position that, if surrendered, will assuredly result in the tragic demise of modern Orthodoxy, with wholesale defections to the progressive movements.

Echoes of the courage required to defend modern Orthodoxy at the present time may be detected in the address to the Centennial Chag Hasemikha (Ordination Ceremony) delivered by Professor Lamm on April 6th, 1986:

> I have been connected with Yeshiva for 40 of its 100 years. I know something of its previous history. The way that Drs. Revel and Belkin chose for us was often beset with pain and controversy. It was never easy. We were told by Jews who were authorities in the world of secular education that "yeshiva" and "university" were antonyms, that they could never coexist in one institution. And the rivals of Yeshiva in certain non-Orthodox camps, which today speak so admiringly of "pluralism," sneered at us, mocked us, wrote our obituaries. We were too Orthodox, too East European, too Old World.
>
> At the same time, other yeshivot refused to recognize our existence—they too believed that "yeshiva" and "university" could never live together. . . . For them we were too Modern, too American, too New World. . . .
>
> Yet the greatness of our Yeshiva is that we kept to our way with strength and with courage, that we conducted ourselves with individual and institutional dignity, that we refused to reciprocate petty insults and trade invectives, but continued to relate to others according to the principles of *Kevod habriyyot* and *kevod ha-Torah*. This will continue to be our policy—one from which we will not be deterred, neither by flattery nor by threats.

Norman Lamm's crusade to perpetuate a rabbinate committed to centrist Orthodoxy is being waged almost single-handed. The CLAL movement of Rabbi Yitz Greenberg has a quite different orientation, which is to build bridges between the Orthodox and the progressive camps. This approach is, perhaps understandably, suspect in the eyes of many Orthodox leaders who fear a dilution of religious standards in the wake of a philosophy of compromise.

As the rabbinate in Israel lurches more and more to the right, with few of its luminaries preaching a doctrine of tolerance, the future of modern Orthodoxy looks more and more bleak.

Jews' College is Britain's premier institution for the training of rabbis and teachers. Founded in 1855 by Chief Rabbi Nathan Marcus Adler, it has been the traditional supplier of clergy for the United Synagogue, the largest of three main synagogal bodies, providing religious facilities for a network of sixty-six synagogues, serving some 40,000 families. The other two bodies—the Federation of Synagogues and the Adath Yisroel—stand to the right and the far right, respectively, of the religious spectrum, each with their own independent *Bet Din* and synagogal and Kashrut administration. They look to the traditional *yeshivah* and *kollel* for their supply of rabbis, and would never consider a graduate of Jews' College.

The Federation services some thirty-four synagogues, most of them comprising a fairly low membership; and the Adath Yisroel, or Union of Orthodox Hebrew Congregations, is a loose federation of some 50 *shtibls*, representing the various chasidic traditions of Vizhnitz, Belz, Gur, Ryzin, Sanz-Klausenburg, Trisker, and Lubavitch, most of which are based in the Stamford Hill area of North London and in Hendon.

For the first one hundred years of its existence Jews' College provided pastor-preacher "Reverend Gentlemen" for the United Synagogue. Few wore beards, and their uniform was the clerical collar, rendering them outwardly indistinguishable from their Christian counterpart. Their rabbinic learning—and occasionally also their observance—was commensurate with the modest expectations of their Anglicized flock. They were primarily functionaries, whose mission was to preside with dignity over "hatches, matches, and dispatches." That attitude changed, however, due to the higher expectations of the immigrants who fled to Britain before and after the Second World War. Their perception of a rabbi, that they brought from their East European congregations, was based on the example of the graduates of the famous German rabbinical seminaries, who were, by and large, erudite scholars and talmudists.

The general raising of Jewish educational and religious standards that the refugees instigated, coupled with the expansion of the Jewish day school movement and the popularization of full-time *yeshivah* education, all necessitated a rabbinic leadership that could cope with the new demands. This was appreciated by Professor Isidore Epstein, appointed acting principal in 1945, who immediately introduced a *Semikhah* program under the direction of one of the most illustrious and internationally renowned talmudists (and authorities in Roman Law), Rabbi Kopel Kahana. The emphasis on Talmud at undergraduate level was intensified under the principalship of Rabbi Nachum Rabinovitch (1971–1983), resulting in the College becoming an attractive option for students who have already studied for a few years at Israeli *yeshivot*. The arrangement with Bar Ilan, whereby each year some of its professors spend a sabbatical at the College, and lead courses in talmudic studies, has been especially welcomed.

The College faculty has boasted many distinguished scholars of international repute. In addition to those referred to above, Michael Friedlander, Adolph Buechler, Israel Abrahams, H. J. Zimmels, Arthur Marmorstein, Cecil Roth, Naphtali Wieder, and Louis Jacobs are worthy of special mention.

The prestige of the College has been given a particular boost over the past four decades with the elevation of the last three chief rabbis from among the ranks of its graduates: Chief Rabbis Israel Brodie, Immanuel Jakobovits (formerly rabbi of the Fifth Avenue Synagogue, New York), and Jonathan Sacks (installed in 1991). Three principals— Isidore Epstein, Jonathan Sacks, and the current principal, Irving Jacobs—are also College graduates, as are most of the academic staff.

Given the history and traditions of Jews' College, and the essentially "middle-of-the-road" composition of the membership of the United Synagogue for which it caters, the struggle to maintain a Centrist religious standpoint is unlikely to be as keen or difficult as at Yeshiva University; though, in these religiously turbulent and uncertain times, no one can predict the future with any degree of certainty.

Seminary versus *Yeshivah*

Reference to rabbinical seminaries prompts a comment on the value of such an institution as contrasted with that of the traditional *yeshivah*. The *yeshivah* has never regarded its task as that of creating community rabbis. Its purpose is much wider: to teach Torah, and, in particular, *Talmud* and *halakhah*, to every Jewish young person who is prepared to acknowledge his duty to devote some years to an in-depth study of his religion, coupled with an earnest attempt to discover the right path to spiritual self-improvement or *yirat shamayim*. The *yeshivah* teaches *Torah lishma*, "study for its own sake"—for the *mitzvah*, not in order to graduate as a rabbi or teacher.

Thus, many young men, under the spell of the rarified atmosphere of "comradeship *(chavruta)*-in-Torah," which only a *yeshivah* can adequately generate, and totally enraptured by the deep fulfillment, the spiritual and intellectual exhilaration and preoccupation, which immersion in the labyrinthine complexities of talmudic inquiry inspires, become oblivious to the passing of the years. Some get married after five or six years at the *yeshivah*, and are encouraged to continue their full-time Torah studies in a *kolel*, or institute of higher rabbinical studies. Thus, even if, one day, the young *talmid chakham* wakes up to the need for a less cloistered and more comfortable life, he is generally too mature and unworldly to feel inclined to commence an undergraduate course at a university, and is unable to face the prospects of long years of study of another discipline.

He has no alternative, therefore, but to drift into the rabbinate out of necessity rather than choice. But, having made that decision, he soon realizes that what he expects to be *Avodat Ha-Kodesh*, "holy work," has more to do with "work" than "holiness." No one is interested in the subtle resolution of apparently conflicting decisions in the Code of Maimonides *(fahrenfer a Rambam)*, over which he enthused with his rebbe and colleagues at *yeshivah;* no one can appreciate his talmudic accomplishment, which is, after all, the whole reason why he has gained *Semikhah!* A pastoral rabbinate is the prospect that now looms over the profession to which he is to devote the next fifty years of his life! And that is before he comes up against so many aspects of his congregants' brand of Judaism that demonstrate so forcefully the size of the chasm that separates the *Yiddishkeit* of his *yeshivah* from that of his synagogue, a chasm frequently too great for him to bridge.

The seminary rabbi, on the other hand, opts for the profession with open eyes, knowing all the problems from firsthand experience and training, and well aware of the temperament and approach that will gain the best results, as well as the style of leadership that will have maximum impact.

The seminary rabbi has not led a cloistered student life. On the contrary: he has been a member of a student union and has probably lent his aid, and the benefit of his knowledge, to fellow Jewish students of other colleges in the regular campus struggles on behalf of Israel. He brushes shoulders in the seminary library with community rabbis and picks up useful hints. His lecturers have probably been, and some still are, rabbis of congregations. He will most certainly do some teaching in Hebrew School or outreach programs, thereby keeping up-to-date with trends in the community. The seminary rabbi is thus far better prepared for, and already enters with considerable experience of, the type of community he *wishes* to serve.

Role of the Rabbi

The role of the rabbi is far more complex and demanding in the modern period than ever before. He has to promote spirituality in the context of a pace of life that is constantly accelerating, values that are constantly changing, and human relationships that are becoming more and more tenuous, leading to widespread domestic and marital tensions. With their mother's milk youngsters imbibe the competitive, aggressive spirit and the absolute necessity of excelling. Discipline and morality are regarded as outmoded, and parental control is abdicated as soon as their offspring reach puberty.

The rabbi is frequently expected to put together the broken pieces of such social and moral fragmentation. But what is particularly galling for the rabbi is the fact that he is generally called in when it is too late, when all else has failed, when the breakdown between husband and wife, parents and children, has gone beyond the point of retrieval. One particular case in the present writer's experience exemplifies the problem. The phone rang, and the tearful voice on the other end pleaded for help as her son was going to marry out of the faith that very week. When asked how long the couple had been dating, the amazing reply was, "A few years." And not once during that period had the mother shared her problem with the rabbi! But the latter is expected, nonetheless, to wave a magic wand—or utter a kabbalistic formula—to make the problem disappear in an instant!

"The problem," in whatever guise it is presented, can generally be attributed to one cause: indifference to religious values. The home that exudes a religious spirit, on the other hand, will exert a strong influence upon its members, so that they will seek out as a marriage partner one who will sustain that way of life. The marriage partnership that is rooted in the concept of holiness—*taharat ha-mishpachah* (family purity)—keeps the relationship fresh and abiding, so that husband and wife cannot possibly take each other for granted or view each other merely as objects of sexual gratification. The example of such a partnership—where both parties relate to each other respectfully and lovingly—must provide a solid basis for a similar concept of "marriage for a lifetime" on the part of their children. And children brought up to value Torah as the most sacred will of God will be more likely to treat parents with respect, as so clearly and frequently enunciated in God's Law.

But how do you tell that to a couple who are merely entries in your synagogue membership list, and whom you do not see from one year to the next? You cannot be so heartless as to say "I told you so!" when they ask you to get their son off drugs or extricate their daughter from her non-Jewish fiancé!

This is one of the main dilemmas of the modern rabbi. He cannot wield halakhic authority over such families, as they neither understand the term nor respect its implication. He is therefore reduced to being merely an amateur social worker, or marriage counselor, who, by reason of his communal status, is called in to dabble as an auxiliary.

The rabbi is expected to fulfill the role of hospital visitor to any member who is indisposed. And the community is content to leave that "responsibility" to the rabbi, notwithstanding the fact that the *mitzvah* of *bikkur cholim* (visiting the sick) is equally incumbent on every Jew. The rabbi is also expected to be a fund-raiser, using the pulpit to make a succession of appeals throughout the year. He is also viewed as a kind of "Master of Ceremonies." His task is to know everyone and to make sure that they are all made to feel welcome in synagogue, with a friendly word and a smile. The friendliness or otherwise of a community is frequently gauged by whether or not the rabbi recognized a visitor (in large synagogues they could always be mistaken for "once-a-year members") and made a fuss of him.

The social role that the rabbi must play is also most demanding. It is gratifying, of course, if members want to call him by his first name and have him grace their dinner parties as personality and raconteur. But is it advisable? Ought there not to be, perhaps, a little "distance" in order that familiarity should not breed contempt? Each rabbi must search his conscience for the answer to this question. There is no decisive answer. The authority of some rabbis suffers as a result of familiarity; that of others remains inviolate.

The comment of one American writer suggests that most progressive rabbis have projected a predominantly social image. Abraham Karp writes that "whereas in former generations the rabbi served as a father figure, in our day he is more like a son-in-law figure—a nice young man, pleasant to have around, but not to take too seriously, not to lean upon too vigorously, not to look to for sustenance and guidance."[32]

Karp's critical assessment is not accurate, however, when applied to the Orthodox rabbinate in most countries. The Orthodox rabbi can perhaps be classified as an "older brother figure," an object of affection—even admiration—notwithstanding his faults, forever giving you advice on what you should or should not do, though knowing full well that you will please yourself anyway. And always there to lean on—even if you haven't seen him for years—when you're in need of support!

The American rabbi truly has to be "everyone's friend," since "life tenure" is not a natural feature of the position, as it is almost everywhere else. There, at least in the early years, his contract comes up every few years for renewal; and a rabbi who fails to please—one way or another—will soon find himself out of a job. It does mean, however, that congregations are not encumbered with leaders who are totally incompatible with the nature and spirit of their flock; but it inevitably has a more sinister facet in that they can easily dispense with the services of a rabbi who expects too much of them spiritually and, consequently, makes them feel uncomfortable. In this context they are more likely to forget that Judaism is not merely there to comfort the troubled, but, more importantly, to trouble the comfortable! In addition, the regular review of the rabbi's contract means that he is forced to become a politician, canvasing votes and support as much for himself, as for his spiritual mission.

One of the problems of the periodic review of the rabbi's performance is the issue of just how one is to assess a rabbi. If on his learning, then who is qualified to comment? If on his oratory and the quality of his sermons, who can possibly be consistently eloquent, inspiring, and challenging, week-in, week-out? Then again, a sermon is a matter of subjective taste. Some want the pulpit to teach Torah; others want it to address itself to topical issues. Some like fire and brimstone; others want calm and well-reasoned presentation of material. Of course, there are those who love a sermon; but there are others who think it achieves nothing. There are some who would replace it with a serious study circle after *davening;* and there are others who would replace it altogether with a shortened morning at synagogue, to leave more time for the afternoon *schloff!* The rabbi cannot win; and it is therefore by no means certain that he can carry a majority who share his overall approach and who will consequently wish to renew his contract.

The Rabbi's Dilemma

Some years ago a humorous presentation of the rabbi's dilemma appeared in an American Synagogue bulletin. Writing from memory, and with apologies to the author whose identity and the name of his journal is now lost in the mist of time, we can only paraphrase his thoughts:

> The rabbi has to be a man for all seasons. If he dresses in a modern way, they claim he is trying to be trendy; if he dons rabbinical garb, they say he is "old-fashioned." If he appears at every social and fund-raising function, they say a rabbi's place is in synagogue; if he confines his interests purely to matters spiritual, they say he is insular. If he doesn't burn the midnight oil in his study, they say he is lazy and ignorant; if he studies Torah with regularity, they claim he is neglecting his communal duties. If his sermons are related to modern issues, they claim he is aping the politicians and that the pulpit is the place for Torah alone. If he confines his addresses to Torah themes, they say he is out of touch with the problems of modern life. If he cracks jokes, they say it is unbecoming; if he doesn't, he's humorless. If he uses long words he is abstruse; if he keeps his vocabulary

simple, they say he is uneducated. If he attends every board meeting, they claim he is limiting members' free speech; if he doesn't attend, he is disinterested in the congregation's wider problems.

The rabbi truly cannot win; and he will fail if he tries too hard to do so. He will satisfy nobody if he attempts to ease himself into a preconceived mold, to project an image that is obviously contrived, one which he feels his community expects of him. He must have the courage of his own convictions, not the community's.

He must offer his own distinctive message, not a mere rehash of antiquated slogans. He must affirm the legitimacy of life in an age when its currency is cheap. He must be allowed to lead his community through the moral mine fields to the haven of the mountain of the Lord.

The famous Kotzker Rebbe observed that the initial letters of the Hebrew word *rabbi* can serve as an abbreviation for both *Rosh Benei Yisrael* ("leader of the Children of Israel") or, God forbid, for *Ra Be-eyney Ha-shem* ("unworthy in the eyes of God"). The rabbi is in the forefront of both Israel's gaze and God's scrutiny. To satisfy both is the incredible challenge of the rabbinate.

Stresses of Office

Only a rabbinical colleague can fully appreciate the enormous strains involved in being constantly "on view," with almost no free time or privacy. Only a colleague knows what it is like to have one's home constantly transformed into a place of work with the telephone incessantly ringing, to have a steady stream of people flowing in and out of one's life without any interlude of tranquillity, to have to be cheerful and sociable to everybody one meets, in whatever context—whether outside synagogue or in the local supermarket—knowing that if one fails to show the requisite recognition and interest, it will be reported to all and sundry and could immediately impact upon one's image, reputation, and ultimately upon one's very livelihood.

Only a rabbinical colleague, and his wife, can know and sympathize with the often unbearable pressure that being the spouse of a congregational rabbi entails. The perception of the rabbi's wife is that of an extension of her husband. Whatever her own qualifications or profession, her paramount title is *rabbanit* or *rebbitzen*, indicative of the role expected of her. Her protestations that she married a person, not a community, will be of no avail. She is her husband's congregational partner—whether she likes it or not. And the same communal sociability, concern, role awareness, and responsibility are expected of her.

The *rabbanit* is expected to be a counselor and a confidante, an organizer, a caterer, a religious authority in her own right, and a model of religious piety and virtue. She is expected to be a socialite, appearing at every major or minor congregational social or fund-raising event, while in no way neglecting her own manifold duties and responsibilities to her husband, parents, and family. She is expected to be figure and fashion conscious, to the extent that she projects a modern image to and on behalf of her congregation, yet not too attractive that she turns the heads of husbands. She is expected to be a source and oracle of information, yet at the same time a keeper of confidentiality. She has to stand with her husband on the pedestal, smiling serenely, never betraying the strains of her husband's office and her family life, remaining forever something of an enigma.

As for the children of the rabbinate, they are frequently the worst sufferers, and the most silent, because they are frequently unable or unwilling to identify and articulate the source of their anxiety.

Many and numerous can be the psychological effects of an upbringing grudgingly shared with hundreds of outsiders, all unfairly (from their perspective) jostling for their parents' time and attention. Their moments of crisis or need must, at times, coincide with parents' absence on official business. Help with homework, or simply to dry a tear with a kiss and a word of encouragement, may not be available just when required. There so easily develops a sense of insecurity, of having to fend for oneself, of lacking adequate support, of having no one present who is the ultimate arbiter and impartial protector in the natural, but stressful, domestic struggles with siblings.

Then there is the problem of the community's expectation. If, for example, the rabbi's son acquits himself admirably, say, in reading flawlessly the entire *Sidrah* and *haftarah* on his *Bar Mitzvah*, the probable reaction is, "Well, shouldn't he be able to do so; after all, he *is* the rabbi's son!" If, on the other hand, his dyslexia or his simple lack of ability or application results in his making mistakes, the likely comment is, "Hh! Not really a performance expected of a rabbi's son!" The result is that he is either deprived of the praise so necessary for child development or he feels a deep sense of having fallen short of an entire community's expectations.

Then there is the problem of being recognized wherever he or she goes. There is no possibility of merging with the crowd, of taking a comfortable flight into normality or anonymity. There is also the embarrassment of overhearing the inevitable criticism of aspects of their father's ministry that is occasionally bandied about. The rabbi's child dare not misbehave or play a prank, either in school, Hebrew class, or during leisure activities. After all, he constitutes an ambassador of his parents throughout his waking hours.

There may also be some serious religious problems involved in his or her role as a member and representative of the family whose religious standards serve as the model for so many. There is no allowance for the waxing and waning of religious fervor that is often a natural element in religious development. So doubts have to be suppressed, and standards imposed from without have to maintained. Even the choice of schooling and youth club is denied them. There are frequently the "accepted" institutions that they must attend, whether or not they wish to.

Of course the rabbinate has its compensations; and for all the problems, few rabbis, given their time all over again, would choose a different profession. It is certainly a "calling." And if one hears the "call" it is not something that can be ignored. It is, after all, a privilege to serve the Lord's people; and service necessarily involves sacrifice. One can only hope and pray that one's children will have the strength of character, the discipline, and the perception to come to appreciate the positive aspects and benefits of being brought up in such a spiritually rarified and constructive environment, and that they will eventually forgive their parents for any emotional shortcomings that they may lay at their door, and that they may come, indeed, if not to follow their calling, then at least to adopt their principles and values as a blueprint for their own lives.

18

The Chazan

The Need for Prayer Leaders

During the talmudic period, when the earliest synagogues made their appearance, the masses of Jews used only Aramaic, with an admixture of Greek vocabulary. It was only the learned, immersed in the language of the Bible, who were able to frame prayers in Hebrew. Hence the necessity for a *chazan* or *sheliach tzibbur* ("representative of the congregation") to recite the prayers on behalf of[1] the congregation, with the latter merely uttering the responses.[2]

During the 2nd century C.E., it was declared forbidden to write down blessings,[3] probably for fear that written formulae might be tampered with by Christian or sectarian devotees, or falsified and used by informers as evidence that the Jews were uttering seditious sentiments. Inevitably, therefore, particularly as the number of prayers began to increase, it became more and more difficult for the ordinary folk to memorize them, and a competent *chazan* became a necessity.

The further expansion of the liturgy, from the 4th to the 6th centuries C.E., as a result of the development of *piyyutim*, the poetic supplementation of the liturgical blessings, made the official *sheliach tzibbur* indispensable, particularly on festivals and High Holydays.

The paucity of laymen who were capable of leading a service competently in talmudic times is alluded to in a midrash based upon the verse "like a lily among thorns" (Song of Songs 2:2):

> The normal situation is that of the ten men who enter a synagogue, not one of them is capable of leading the recitation of the *Shema* or acting as reader for the *Amidah*. However, if one of them stands up and is able to perform this service, to what may he be compared?—to "a lily among thorns."

Ironically, the spread of the *piyyut* coincided with a period which witnessed a decline in general standards of Jewish learning and familiarity with Hebrew, which was another reason why the services of a professional *chazan*, capable of mastering the developing liturgy, became essential.

Chazan and *Sheliach Tzibbur*

The terms *chazan* and *sheliach tzibbur* were most popularly employed to describe those who led the services on a regular basis. The two terms are interchangeable, so that, today, when a *chazan* is called up to the Torah for an *aliyah*, his Hebrew name is prefaced by the title, *Ha-Shatz*, an abbreviation of the title *sheliach tzibbur*. A popular distinction, however, reserves the title *chazan* for a professional cantor, a true master of the art of *chazanut*, whereas *sheliach tzibbur* is, by contrast, one endowed with a pleasant voice who can lead a service competently, though not professionally.

The term *chazan* means, literally, "overseer" or "inspector," from the verb *chazah*, "to look closely"; and this is yet another example of the synagogue's penchant for preserving Temple titles, forms, and traditions. The term *chazan ha-kneset* was the title of one of the Temple administrators; and the first synagogue to borrow that title was probably the great synagogue in Alexandria, in early talmudic times. We referred above to the fact that the beadle who waved the flags on the *Bimah*, as a signal for the congregation in the vast auditorium to answer with *Amen*, was referred to, likewise, as the *chazan ha-kneset*.[4]

The primary application of the title *chazan* in talmudic times was to the one responsible for general synagogal duties. These included leading the service, reciting the blessings at marriages,[5] presiding at funerals,[6] comforting and blessing mourners and reciting *Kaddish* for their departed,[7] and reading from the Torah.[8] It would also seem from talmudic sources, that, by extension, anyone in the employ of the community—any civil servant—was also referred to by the general term of *chazan*. Hence, the (assistant) teacher, whose specific task was to help children with their reading, is called *chazan*,[9] as is the messenger of the *Bet Din* who is sent to summon litigants and witnesses to Court.[10] The same title is used for the attendants who helped dress the priests in their special ministerial robes;[11] and it is even applied, in one talmudic passage,[12] to members of the police force.

Since, in the course of time, special titles were coined for the above officials, as well as for others who discharged specific communal and religious functions, the scope of the term *chazan* inevitably came to be restricted, and was exclusively reserved for the professional synagogue prayer leader.

The association of the title *chazan* with the role of an intermediary in worship may well have been inspired by the biblical use of the verb *chazah* to denote "having a clear vision of God."[13] The cognate noun, *chazon* is also the common term employed to describe a prophetic vision. Hence, the prophecies of Isaiah commence with the words, "the vision *(chazon)* of Isaiah." Through the inspiration generated by his prayers, the *chazan* is expected to give his congregation a *chazon*, a vision, or at least an awareness, of the Supreme Being.

Traditional Qualities

The *Mishnah*[14] already lays down guidelines for the type of man worthy to discharge the office of *chazan:*

> He should be mature *(zakein)* and conversant with the prayers *(ragil)*; he should be a father of children, and one whose home is empty *(beito reikam)*, so that his heart will be wholehearted in prayer.

The Talmud[15] expanded upon these, by emphasizing certain desirable character and personality traits:

> He should be a well adjusted individual *(pirko na'eh)*, who has an unassuming demeanor *(shefal berekh)* and is popular among the people.

Musical talents and professional skills are also not overlooked:

> He should be able to chant competently, with a sweet voice. He should
> have a mastery of the reading of Torah, the Prophets, and the Sacred
> Writings. He should be conversant with *midrash*, *halakhot*, and *aggadot*,
> and know every single blessing.

While most of these terms and qualifications are self-explanatory,
the reference to his home having to be "empty" has baffled many
commentators, as has the precise definition of the phrase *pirko na'eh*.

An "empty house" suggests poverty. The poor man, who is most
in need of God's bounty, will pray with greater earnestness, fervor, and
personal involvement than one without that same sense of urgent
motivation. The Talmud explains it rather differently however, as a
symbol of ethical perfection. "Empty" means "empty of sin" (*reikam min
ha-aveirah*). In other words, his home must not contain anything
obtained by theft or in any other unworthy manner.

As regards the phrase *pirko na'eh*, the Talmud again prefers to
regard it as intimating an ethical or moral characteristic. The noun *perek*,
apart from its common meaning of "portion, division, section," has an
applied meaning of "period of maturity," "marriageable age." *Pirko na'eh*
is taken to mean, therefore, "an adulthood well attained," or, as clarified
by Abbaye, "a person who reached adulthood with nothing unworthy
being imputed to him in his childhood."[16]

The very first attribute referred to in the *Mishnah*, that the *chazan*
should be mature (*zakein*), was understood in the physical or biological
sense. Maturity, in antiquity, was identified with the ability to raise a
beard. Though Rabbi Judah states that a twenty-year-old, with or
without beard, may be assumed to have attained to the required age of
maturity,[17] yet the Geonim of Babylon were particular, however, that
their *chazanim* should be bearded.

Praying on Behalf of Others

The term *sheliach tzibbur*, "representative of the congregation," focusses
upon the original primary function of the *chazan*, which was to recite the
prayers—and particularly the central prayer, the *Amidah*—on behalf of
the congregation, who were largely unable to recite or memorize the
prayers themselves. Two religious principles underlie the *chazan's* ability

to discharge a prayer obligation *on behalf of* others: first, the concept that "all Israel have a responsibility, each toward his neighbor *(kol yisrael areivim zeh la-zeh)*. This means, essentially, that our identical national and spiritual aspirations, as well as our shared historical experiences, bond us all together as a single entity, so that when a fellow Jew prays on our (and his congregation's) behalf, his authentic and profound feelings for the common good even transcend his own personal desires, so that he is praying as effectively and sincerely for us as he is for himself. The corollary of this is that his prayers *on our behalf* are truly as effective as our own personal prayers.

The second, and related, principle is that of *shome'a ke'oneh,* "anyone responding with *Amen,* to a blessing or prayer made on his behalf, is on an equal footing with the one reciting it for him." Confirmation is as eloquent and effective as affirmation.

The confirmatory response, as a substitute for recitation of the sacred formula itself, has a long history, stretching back to the Torah itself where it is prescribed in several passages. When the blessings and curses were enumerated and affirmed by the nation in that dramatic ceremony on Mounts Ebal and Gerizim (Deuteronomy 27:11 ff.), the Levites alone recited aloud the catalogue of curses; and after each one, "the people responded with *Amen.*" Again, in the awesome ceremony of probing the suspected adulteress with the ordeal of the "bitter waters" (Numbers 5:11 ff.), the priest recited on behalf of the woman the "oath of purgation" which threatened dire punishment if she had indeed committed the adultery hitherto denied. The woman accepts the terms of the oath by merely responding with the one word, *Amen.*

One of the earliest examples of the priest discharging the role of *chazan,* in the sense of reciting a sacred formula *on behalf of* those unable to recite it themselves, occurs in relation to the ceremony of the presentation of first-fruits at the sanctuary (Deuteronomy, chap. 26). A special, quite lengthy, declaration has to be made by the donor as he presents his gift. The *Mishnah*[18] tells us that originally those able to recite it in Hebrew, as required, would recite it themselves, and those unable to do so would repeat the declaration word for word after the priest. It was soon discovered that, out of embarrassment, many people in the latter category were refraining from bringing their fruits and participating in the ceremony in order to avoid disclosing their ignorance. It was therefore enacted that, whether or not one was able to recite it, all must henceforth repeat the prayer after the priest. This concern for, and concession to, the uneducated was to set an important liturgical precedent, paving the way for the manner in which the *Amidah* later came to be recited aloud by the *chazan* for the benefit of those who were unable to pray unaided.

From a responsum of Rabbi Asher ben Yechiel, the *Rosh*,[19] leader of German Jewry until 1303, when he fled to Spain in the wake of the *Rindfleisch* massacres, we learn that the office of *chazan*—whether honorary or professional—was regarded by a number of Sephardi communities as unworthy for men of social standing to occupy:

> Regarding your letter, in which you write that in those places it is customary to appoint as *sheliach tzibbur* only people from families of low esteem, and that this is tantamount to despising a *mitzvah*, as if—like some menial job—it is not worthy enough to be discharged by upper class families, heaven forbid that the holy service should be regarded as "a job." It should rather be as a crown for one's head.

There is an ironical twist to this complaint that the task of *chazan* had become the exclusive preserve of lower-class families, for this is precisely the situation which the *Rosh* appears inadvertently to be encouraging through his ruling, expressed elsewhere,[20] that where there are two candidates for the honor of *chazan*, one from a lower class and the other from an upper class family, the former should be given preference, as his prayer will probably be the more earnest and plaintive. He sees this approach as underlying the verse, "welcome welcome, those that are far and those that are near" (Isaiah 57:19). Priority is clearly given to "those that are far," those who need the greatest encouragement.

The *Chazan* as a Performer

But it is in the continuation of Rabbi Asher's responsum that attention is drawn to one facet of the *chazan's* presentation that he regarded as most unbecoming, namely, the transmutation of *sheliach tzibbur*, "messenger of the congregation," into the role of cantor, or demonstrator of musical and vocal prowess:

> I have also been incensed, from the day I arrived here, about the *chazanim* of this country . . . whose sole objective is to provide a pleasant sound. People don't care if he is a thorough-going rascal, as long as he sings sweetly.

Joseph Karo quotes the distinguished 13th-century Spanish talmudist and halakhist, Solomon ben Adret (*Rashba*), who inveighs similarly against *"chazanim* who prolong the service so that people may hear their beautiful voice":

> If they do so purely because their hearts are joyful at the privilege of being able to offer lyrical thanksgiving to the Almighty, then they are deserving of blessing. If their intention is, however, to impress with their voice, and their pleasure rests entirely in that direction, that is disgraceful. However, *all* who prolong the service are not acting properly, for they are making it irksome for the congregation.[21]

Long before the time of Adret, *chazanut* had already developed its own unique musical tradition, the impetus to which had been provided by the popularity of *piyyutim*, the poetic supplements that, with their rhythm and rhyme, were tailor-made as sacred lyrics.

Inevitably, *chazanim* came to regard themselves also as artists and performers, and it was not long before they turned to contemporary secular music for added inspiration and for enhancement of the melodic beauty of their presentation. Thus, from the 11th century onward we find rabbis raising their voices in protest against the infiltration of foreign, non-Jewish, particularly Arabic, melodies.[22] One *chazan* was even threatened with dismissal from his post if he did not abandon his habit of adapting Arabic love songs.[23]

While the Geonim reiterated the ban on all secular music, a ban that had been operative, ostensibly, since, and on account of, the destruction of the Temple, Maimonides explains that their intention was really only to prohibit songs that aroused sinful sensuality, in order to protect the status of the Jews as a "holy nation." However, outside songs, which could aid in promoting spirituality, were never placed under the ban.[24]

It is very likely that it was Maimonides' tolerant attitude that really enabled cantorial music to tap the resources of secular music in the course of its development. Thus, the provenance of many famous operatic, aria-style, chazanic compositions cannot really be disguised!

Religious Standards

Many halakhic authorities emphasize the basic religious standards required of anyone who leads a service, even during weekdays. One who openly violates *Shabbat* is clearly an unworthy person to act as prayer leader. For this reason the law states that any member of the congregation can object to another acting as *chazan* if he has grounds for considering such a person unworthy.

It is recognized that there are small communities that might have only one person capable of leading a service, and insisting on certain religious standards would deprive such a community of the ability to hold a *minyan!* The *Magen Avraham* came to the rescue of such communities. He pointed out that objections to a *chazan* on religious grounds were only entertained in early talmudic times when the task of the *chazan* was to recite the *Amidah* aloud on behalf of the largely uneducated congregation. These days, however, when we all recite the *Amidah* silently for ourselves, the *chazan* is not discharging a religious obligation on our behalf. Hence, his religious standards need not be probed too critically, and the right of objection no longer applies.[25] It goes without saying, however, that there is no consensus opinion on this matter, and that "a worthy *chazan*" (*sheliach tzibbur hagun*) should always have priority.

The unpleasantness and discord that are created when people discuss whether or not one of their peers is worthy to lead a service — and particularly when this results in refusal to confer the honor — must have been a major contributory factor to the decision, in later medieval times, to appoint permanent, professional *chazanim*. Hence Karo states that "a paid *chazan* is to be preferred to one who gives his services voluntarily."[26] It was also felt that a paid official would generally be more competent, and, in order to keep his job, would also take greater care to maintain a consistently high standard.

Appointments

With the spread of professional *chazanim*, the *halakhah* was called upon to determine the rules governing such appointments. A *chazan* may not be appointed against the wishes of the majority of the congregation. His appointment must reflect the fact that he is "the representative *of the congregation*." Hence, no state appointment may be countenanced even if the particular nominee of the authorities does happen to meet with the approval of the majority of the congregation. It is the latter who must make the appointment.[27] Indeed, if anyone is foisted upon a congregation against its wishes, permission is granted for the members to refuse to recite *Amen* after his blessings.[28]

Different communities adopted different methods of funding the salary of the *chazan*. Karo recommends that it should be paid entirely from the general community chest, rather than by a donation for that specific purpose, since the poor, who cannot contribute as much, might feel that the *chazan* is not representing their spiritual needs as fully as he does those of the rich.[29] In Italy it was the practice to pay only part of his salary by direct contribution, from rich and poor alike, so that the poor would not feel at a disadvantage. The remainder came from the communal chest, so that "if the wealthy wished to attract a *chazan* with a better voice, they could contribute more toward that purpose."[30]

A professional *chazan* cannot be removed from office unless he is guilty of a proven moral indiscretion or religious shortcoming. A *chazan* who uses foul language is to be warned, and, if he persists in doing so, may be removed.

The *halakhah* recognizes a son's right of succession to the post of *chazan* occupied by his father where the latter has a life contract. If such a *chazan* is away, ill, or aged, he may appoint his son to take the service even if there is someone more competent in the community. He may also invite his son to assist him, and he may retire in favor of his son, even if this does not meet with the approval of the majority of the congregation.

The role of *chazan* was regarded as so important that the *halakhah* unashamedly states that "in a community that needs to appoint both a rabbi and a *chazan*, but cannot afford both, the appointment of a *chazan* takes priority, unless the rabbi happens to be a most illustrious Torah personality who has a mastery of halakhic decision-making."[31]

Unfair Jibes

The *chazan* has frequently been the butt of unfair ridicule and witticisms. Among the jibes that have become proverbial is the generalization that *chazanim zeinen naranim*, "cantors are naive," and a number of Yiddish songs are woven around that same theme.

With the emancipation of European Jewry and the evolution of the 19th-century liberal tradition of formal, cathedral-type synagogues, with organs and mixed choirs, and cantors dressed in special robes and performing the new melodies of such composers as Sulzer of Vienna, Naumbourg of Paris, and Lewandowski of Berlin—many of which were directly linked to the style of the church, and embodied secular trends and techniques—the reservoir of antichazanic Yiddish proverbs was augmented in order to express Orthodox dissatisfaction with this trend. Representative of this genre is the proverb, *Az der chazan ken kein ivreh nit, heisst er a kantor*—"when a *chazan* doesn't understand the Hebrew of the prayers he is reciting, he is called a *cantor.*"

Such sentiments were probably occasioned by more than a tincture of envy on the part of the luckless *baalei battim* of the *shtetl*, who slaved from dawn to dusk, six days a week, to provide the bare necessities for their large families. The dignified *chazan*—always formally attired, not subjected to their rushed, grinding, and menial routine, frequently well wined and dined at weddings and a variety of religious and quasireligious celebrations, the man who seemed to spend so much of his time socializing, with salary guaranteed, come fair weather or foul—must inevitably have convinced many congregants that he was hardly doing an honest day's work. Sarcastic jokes and proverbs are a time-honored method of attacking those whom one is unable—or it is unworthy—to assail by other means.

The *chazan*'s enigmatic role may also account for the fact that he was singled out for such treatment. He was called upon to discharge two incompatible roles, one as social and musical entertainer when off the *bimah*, at a variety of *simchahs* and events, and quite another as formal, dignified, spiritual representative of the community. Many congregants must have found it difficult to adjust to such a relationship. They were consequently unsure whether their *chazan* was at heart an entertainer, with the added ability of homing in to spirituality when the occasion demanded, or whether he was truly a man of the spirit who, by the nature of his profession, had, perforce, to entertain.

The Golden Age of *Chazanut*

The late 19th century ushered in an era of unprecedented popularity for *chazanim* and their art, which they were to enjoy at least until the Second World War.

This was the era of the great waves of immigration into the United States from Russia and Poland. Whether or not they maintained their religious standards, the immigrants generally retained a deep emotional attachment to the synagogue, an attachment which they expected the *chazan* to nourish. Thus, Eastern European *chazanut* was transplanted into the free world.

The large congregations of America vied with each other in their attempts to entice one of the "big names" from *der heim* to grace their *Bimah*. Large financial inducements were offered, and the *chazanim* became world celebrities, filling their own synagogues each week and making regular guest appearances at other synagogues, as well as at concert halls, before an ever growing circle of cognoscenti of *chazanut*. One of the most popular pastimes was to debate the comparative skills and vocal abilities of the respective *chazanim*.

This was also the era of the development of sound recordings, so that international reputations could be created before the artists had even journeyed forth from their hometowns. Among the names that became legendary—some for their compositions as well as their vocal and interpretive ability—are Israel Alter, Berele Chagy, Leib Glanz, Mordechai Herschman, Abraham Idelsohn (*chazan* and musicologist), Sholom Katz, Moshe Koussevitzky, Zavel Kwartin, Moishe Oisher, Pinchas Pinchik, David Roitman, Yossele Rosenblatt, Gershon Sirota (who was invited annually to sing for the czar), and Leibele Waldman. Some, like Jan Peerce and Richard Tucker, became renowned as leading operatic exponents, while, at the same time, retaining an active interest in cantorial expression. A few great exponents—and more of their offspring—were even wooed into the theatre and the world of motion pictures.

In Britain the situation was quite different. It is difficult to think of the name of even one English-born *chazan* who has gained an international repute. This may be accounted for by the same token that there are so few truly great English-born non-Jewish operatic tenors. Could it be the reserved nature of the English temperament, which feels inhibited when it comes to public demonstration of deep emotion? Perhaps it was also the comparative tranquillity of Anglo-Jewish history during the 17th and 18th centuries that, in contrast to the bitter vicissitudes of *shtetl* life, did not generate that sensitivity to the uncertainty of life, combined with the mellowness of personal, family, or communal suffering, that determined the emotional quality of Ashkenazi *chazanut*.

Cantor or Minister?

The United Synagogue in Britain never viewed its professional prayer leaders as exponents of the art of *chazanut*. They were to be virtually assistant rabbis, charged with the identical tasks as the rabbi himself outside of the synagogue, but with special responsibility for "reading" the service, while the rabbi preached the sermon. Men who had been reared in the traditions of Anglo-Jewry were satisfied to accept this situation which obtained until the arrival of the continental *chazanim*.

> The influx of foreign *chazanim* before and after World War II gave British Jews a synagogal experience which, in its way, created a minor revolution. Many shul-goers reveled in it, though, naturally, there was a proportion who just could not appreciate the depth of emotion which a good *chazan* could instill into his renderings, preferring the more calculated singing of the traditional "reader."
>
> The men who were fortunate to obtain posts in Britain were asked to undertake jobs for which they were totally unprepared, and frequently just as totally unfit. Most saw themselves as "performers" and resented the regimen of pastoral visitations, funerals and shivahs, cultural and educational work, which they were now expected to do as part of their contract. Since the *Goldene Medineh*, on the other side of the Atlantic, did not usually require these extra functions, many, who might have remained in England, went to the Americas where they could not only continue to fulfill their role as they had in Europe, but were also paid far more than they could ever earn in Britain. Among such star emigrants were the brothers Simcha, David and Jacob Koussevitzky, Ephraim Rosenberg, and Jacob Goldstein. In recent decades some other well-known *chazanim*—notably Joseph Malevany, Asher Hainovitz, and Naphtali Herstik—have also "tried out" the United Synagogue for brief periods.
>
> Since the war, *chazanim* who have been employed by the United Synagogue have, by and large, accepted their quasi-ministerial role, though with considerably varying degrees of willingness.[32]

This might explain why the profession has suffered a sharp decline over the past few decades, resulting in the closure of the Jews' College School of *Chazanut*. Many prestigious congregations in Britain are without *chazanim*—and, more significantly, do not even seem concerned about their inability to fill the positions. Appreciation of *chazanut* has largely died out as the TV and video can bring the greatest voices of the age into every living room at the press of a button.

To the majority of the younger generation of the modern Orthodox, the *chazan's* "performance," and the general formality of the large synagogue, is not to their liking, and in the current climate of polarization, the small *shtibls* are capturing more and more their affiliation. One of its benefits is that everyone is given the opportunity of acting as *sheliach tzibbur*. Perhaps this feature alone will, ironically, help to swing the pendulum back, and some young, vocally gifted men, having gained a taste for the *bretl,* might well be tempted back into the profession. But, in the meantime, most people believe that the *Bimahs* of large synagogues will be occupied more and more by part-timers or *kol-boniks* *(factota),* who will provide a comprehensive service, doubling up as *chazan,* preacher and teacher. If that is indeed to be the case, then it is the rabbis who will also have to look to their laurels!

Demise of *Chazanut*

There are, in fact, several factors that are responsible for the demise of *chazanut.* First, the spirit of traditional cantorial music has been identified as the natural expression of the tensions, agonies, and frustrations of Jewry's past ghetto experience. The traditional synagogue compositions are somber and restrained, slow in tempo, tense, repetitive, and suppliant. This impelled many cantors to freely punctuate the phrases of many of those compositions with the Yiddish interjectory sigh of lament—*oi.*

In the modern period, which has witnessed the rise and consolidation of a vital, lively, strong, and forward-looking Jewish homeland in Israel, with a Diaspora caught up in that selfsame optimistic national spirit, those sad, plaintive overtones of 19th-century synagogue music strike no receptive cords.

Indeed, it is the characteristic music of the modern State of Israel that has largely displaced the traditional synagogue melodies. The lively rhythmic beat of songs from the annual chasidic Pop Festival in Jerusalem, set to verses from the prayer book, as well as purely nationalistic or patriotic melodies, are heard with growing frequency these days in even the most formal of synagogues. The ordinary congregants want to sing. They want to express that new hope, confidence, and vitality that infuse their national and religious identity, rather than to listen to a performance that expresses an antiquated communal mood.

The second factor can also be attributed to Israel. More and more pre-university students—from Orthodox, traditional, or even nontraditional homes all over the Jewish world—are now taking a year or two to study in *yeshivot* (talmudic academies) or girls' seminaries in Israel. The emphasis in these ultra-Orthodox establishments is on the student developing a personal, direct, existential, fervent, and uninhibited dialogue with his Maker. There is clearly no sympathy in this context with any of the formal, artificial, and representative trappings of synagogue officialdom, which are construed as obstructions in the path of spiritual union.

A related factor in the demise of *chazanut* is that many of those *yeshivot* have veered in spirit toward the adoption of elements from the chasidic tradition. This is seen most clearly in the type of hat and black garb that is worn, the beards that are sported, and the *tzitzit* (fringes) that are worn outside their trousers. This is also true of their mode of prayer. The professional, or even amateur, cantor had no place in Chasidism. It was always the *rebbe*, the spiritual leader and mentor, who led his followers in prayer. Indeed, it was through prayer that the *rebbe* was believed to be able to wrest mercy from the Almighty. Chasidic music is that of the *nigun*, the impulsive and simple rhythmic tune, to the accompaniment of which the pietists would clap their hands and sway their bodies, singing aloud with joyful ecstasy. Those chasidic tunes, conceived in spontaneity and allegedly composed under the influence of the Holy Spirit by the *rebbes* themselves, constituted a totally independent and variant concept of prayer. It was a collective expression of joy in a higher union within which all the initiated were emotionally and spiritually interrelated. Quite obviously, there was no place within this system for an official cantor, singing formally, according to the rules and canons of secular composition. Furthermore, since so much of cantorial music was based upon existing operatic themes, the profession was also regarded with suspicion as being *chukkat ha-goy*, a parody of unacceptable non-Jewish practices.

The above two factors would explain why *chazanut* is still strong in the denominations to the left of Orthodoxy—particularly in the American Conservative tradition—which are not influenced by these particular trends. This had led, in recent years, to the defection of a few Anglo-Jewish cantors to the ranks of the Conservative movement.

A fourth factor takes account of simple economics. In the inflationary climate of the past few decades, few synagogues have found it possible to maintain two full-time officials. While there is some understanding of the ongoing, daily duties, commitments, and responsibilities of a rabbi, there is not the same appreciation of what a *chazan* has to do all day. Whatever pastoral duties he undertakes are regarded as a mere duplication of those of the rabbi, and, unlike the latter, who has a regimen of *shiurim*, lectures, and addresses, as well as the necessity of keeping up his learning and keeping abreast of modern halachic issues, the *chazan* is not regarded as having such preoccupations. (It has to be stated that in a number of large congregations such an attitude is clearly misplaced, and the cantor serves a most valuable role in the pastoral, educational, and welfare spheres.) In a commercial climate that is so sensitive to the importance of cost-effectiveness, the full-time, professional *chazan* has, regretfully, become an obvious casualty.

Finally, it must be said that the traditional rivalry between the rabbi and the *chazan* has not helped the situation. Some *chazanim* have tended to regard themselves as members of a uniquely gifted fraternity of celebrities who so enriched the community that their once-a-week performance more than justified their salary. The overworked and highly stressed rabbi, on the other hand, tended to envy his independent-minded, carefree colleague with so much more spare time on his hands. The rabbinate has also played its part, therefore, in undermining the status of the *chazan* and in concurring with those who have felt that it is a luxury that can no longer be afforded.

At the time of writing, there are no more than ten full-time *chazanim* in the whole of Britain, and the United Synagogue, London's main central synagogal organization, is now embarking on a covert policy to reduce all *chazanim* to part-time employment, if not to phase out the professional *chazan* entirely. Notwithstanding the financial difficulties of retaining the chazanic profession, and notwithstanding the changing communal tastes we have alluded to, it must certainly be lamented that such a historic source of synagogal inspiration and spiritual beauty and stimulation must, in time, be lost forever.

The Sephardi *Chazan*

The Sephardim have a totally different concept of the *chazan*. They have never regarded a fine voice as a necessary qualification for that office, and the nature of their liturgical music does not call for the wide vocal range of their Ashkenazi counterparts. Indeed, whereas the Ashkenazi *chazan* sings aloud the beginning and end of each prayer and psalm, with the congregation reciting them silently, the Sephardi congregation, on the other hand, chant aloud the entire service, word for word together with their *chazan*. The *chazan's* voice is expected to be heard leading the chant, a little louder than the congregation, but he is not expected to give a solo performance.

The Sephardi *chazan* has to be a learned man whom the congregation can respect, since he is looked upon as an assistant to the rabbi, and in many congregations he actually serves in both capacities. Whereas the Ashkenazi *chazan* frequently regards reading the Torah each week as outside the scope of his responsibility, or even damaging to his voice, it is a willingly accepted privilege to the Sephardi *chazan*, and it is an area where meticulous standards are generally attained, far higher than in most Ashkenazi synagogues.

Oriental *Chazanut*

Much variety exists in the cantorial style and the nature of the respective compositions of the Spanish and Portuguese and the Oriental Sephardim. Wide differences also separate the liturgical traditions of these, on the one hand, and the Yemenite or *Teimani* communities, on the other. The latter brought to the State of Israel a very ancient tradition and style of prayer rendition which had suffered far less foreign infiltration than any other *nusach*. The Yemenites have never had the concept of a professional *chazan*. It is a most honored and sacred function to discharge, and to pay someone to do it would in their eyes demean its importance.

Persian Jewry has, alas, been deprived of the knowledge of their authentic *nusach*, and today represents a mere variety of the Spanish and Portuguese tradition. As a once great center of Jewish life, a refuge for exiles from the holy land and a satellite of the prestigious Babylonian community on its western flank in the medieval period of the latter's heyday, Persian Jewry certainly had its own *nusach* and musical tradition. We may surmise that this represented a synthesis of those of ancient Palestine and Babylon.

Persian Jewry apparently fell victim to a powerful campaign on the part of some 15th-century Spanish zealots, who were determined to spread the Spanish prayer rite further afield in their belief that it represented the single authentic tradition. Their delegation to Persia was led by the Moroccan *chakham*, Yoseph ben Mosheh Maman. Seeing their "peculiar" *nusach*, he convinced them that they had also originally hailed from Spain, and that they were doing wrong in not keeping to their ancestral prayer rite. He thereupon distributed *Siddurim* and *Machzorim* printed in Venice and Livorna, and, before long, the Persian liturgical heritage was lost.

Having done his work in Persia, *Chakham* Maman proceeded in a north-northeastern direction to the community of Bukhara (north of Afghanistan, in Russian Central Asia), where he succeeded in convincing the Bukharans that their tradition, that they hailed from the Ten Lost Tribes, was erroneous, and that they, like the Persian Jews, are descendants of Spanish exiles and must return to the synagogal traditions of Spain.

An *aliyah* of Bukharan Jews to Israel began in 1870. They formed their own independent community at Rechovot in 1892, and to this day they have retained some remnants of their original *nusach*, which was largely forgotten when they adopted the Spanish version imposed by *Chakham* Maman. The most significant of these are their melodies for the half-*Kaddish* preceeding *Borakhu*, their prolonged singing of *Nishmat*, and their special melody for the *Yotzer* blessings.

The Israeli Melting Pot

These, and other, unique traditions, which were proudly observed and preserved in the synagogues of Israel founded by immigrants from the far-flung Diaspora communities, make up a fascinating, varied, vibrant, and rich cultural and spiritual tapestry which must not be allowed to fade into the mist of time. It is for this reason that such opposition greeted the efforts of those who, with misplaced nationalism, worked toward the establishment of a unified *Minhag Eretz Yisrael*, involving the surrender of all that makes Israel's religious complexion so fascinatingly vital from an emotional and historical point of view, in order to replace it with a slavish conformity to an artificial *nusach achid* that is the heritage of neither Ashkenazim, Sephardim, nor any other group.

This misguided objective, of creating a unified "Israeli" prayer tradition, was spelled out in a book entitled *Bet Ha-Kneset*, issued in 1955 by the Israeli Ministry of Religious Affairs:

> A great and important task confronts Jerusalem, the mother of all sacred music, and that is to synthesize all the *chazanut* of the Diaspora and to create out of it a single, unified, national *chazanut* to serve all the communities. Just as God, Israel and the Torah are a unity, so should *chazanut* in Israel be a unity. . . . It is totally unacceptable that Diaspora *chazanim* should come here and constrain us to listen to their foreign traditions, riddled with all their shortcomings and errors, as well as being deficient in the essential harmony between verbal expression and musical interpretation.[33]

Most unfortunately, in the decades that have elapsed since this gauntlet was first thrown down, its protagonists can claim much success. Apart from Jerusalem's two leading virtuosi, cantors Naphtali

Herstik and Asher Hainovitz, and Aryeh Brown, chief cantor of the Israel Defense Forces, *chazanut* is almost dead in an Israel, where its ability to stir people to spiritual emotion and to inject humility and awe into the headstrong, is much needed. In most synagogues—particularly of the Ashkenazim—the services are gabbled in a most uninspiring manner, creating attendant problems of decorum. Prayer itself has largely become perfunctory in the very country that so lovingly created it.

19

The Shammash

Duties of the *Shammash*

The *shammash* (generally pronounced *shammas*[1]), or sexton, completes the "threefold cord" of salaried officialdom that maintains the organizational and spiritual efficiency of the synagogue. Whereas the rabbi and, to a lesser extent, the *chazan* occupy an office of leadership that tends to distance them somewhat from the "man in the pew," the *shammash*, by contrast, is ubiquitous and readily accessible. He opens the synagogue early in the morning and locks it up at night; he frequently oversees its heating and lighting, its repairs and cleaning; and he sets out and collects in the *Siddurim* and *Chumashim* before and after the service. He ensures that the Torah scrolls are rolled to the right place in readiness for the next day's service, and that the right cards are slotted into the wall display boards. These remind worshipers of the *sidrah* being read that week, or special prayers, liturgical insertions, or Torah readings being added, and, during the *Omer* period, the precise day that has just been counted. The *shammash* – at least until the modern period – was indispensable.

Israel Abrahams succeeds in conveying the special character of the *shammash's* position in the medieval *kehillah:*

The most powerful officer of all was the *shammash* or beadle. This functionary rapidly became ruler of the synagogue. His functions were so varied, his duties placed him in possession of such detailed information of private affairs, his presence so permeated the synagogue and the home on public and private occasions, that, instead of serving the congregation, he became its master. Unlike the parish beadle, the characteristic of the *shammash* was not pompousness so much as overfamiliarity. He did not exaggerate his own importance, but minimized the importance of everyone else.[2]

One of the functions the *shammash* had to discharge in the *shtetls* of Eastern Europe was that of *shulklapper* ("the knocker who summons people to worship"). In the freezing Russian and Polish winter mornings he had to get up at an unearthly hour, and, treading his way through the thick snow and ice, had to make the rounds of the town knocking on the front doors of each home in order to rouse the men for prayer.

Since constant knocking on doors could easily damage his knuckles, the *shammash* was presented with a special wooden mallet. This practical insignia of office was frequently shaped like a *Shofar*—the traditional Jewish instrument for sounding an alarm—with ornamental carving at its wider end. Different communities had varying codes, based on the number of knocks, to indicate the nature of the summons. Where one knock was used for morning services throughout the year, two knocks might be used during the *Selichot* period, from the week before Rosh Hashanah until Yom Kippur, to underline the importance of not being late at these important services. Yet a further variation was used to denote some other occasions where the *shulklapper's* services were employed, for example to announce the approach of *Shabbat* and *Yom Tov*, and to summon people to attend funerals and important public meetings.

It was also the task of the *shammash* to ensure that decorum was maintained during the services. In an age before children's and youth services were thought of, and when a large family was the norm, the natural boisterousness of the young was often given free rein in synagogue. Sitting in bunches with their peers, strategically placing themselves just out of view of their fathers, they would constitute a regular irritant to those wishing to concentrate on their prayers.

This was the acid test of the authority of the *shammash*. In some instances, one disapproving glance was sufficient to strike fear into the young, and to restore silence.

The nature of the post thus necessitated a fairly thick-skinned personality. Where other, more sensitive, individuals feared to tread, the *shammash* was not averse to rushing in. This explains why the custom arose of allocating the *aliyah* for the reading of the biblical sections of the *Tokheichah* ("rebuke")[3] to the *shammash*. Because of the fearful curses and punishments enumerated there, people were unwilling to have such a portion read for them. In the hope that some brave person would come forward, the warden simply called out: *yaamod miy she-yirtzeh*, "let anyone who wishes come forward."[4] In the absence of volunteers, the broad-shouldered *shammash* was generally expected to save the day. And this subsequently became the *shammash's* "prerogative."

Gabbais (wardens) would come into office for a few years and then leave, but the *shammash* went on forever. He was an indispensable adviser to the wardens, filling them in on the background to members, their families, their *simchahs*, their domestic situation, and, of course, reminding them of who required to be called up to the Torah. He was frequently the first person to discover that a family had fallen on bad times, and he would pass a discreet word to that effect to the organizer of the *Gemilut Chasadim* (welfare) society.

Custodian of Local Customs

As the turnover of rabbis and *chazanim* was far greater than that of *shammashim*, and as different communities had many varying local customs, a new rabbi or *chazan* would regularly turn to the *shammash* for guidance as to the *minhag ha-makom*, the local tradition. In some communities his influence in this area was so generally recognized that, on taking up his appointment, the *shammash* had to take a formal oath to the effect that he would be a faithful custodian of the local customs, and would also ensure that any community decisions taken by the *kahal* were strictly enforced.

Because of the influence he inevitably acquired over the years, combined with his intimate knowledge of individual families and their affairs, the *shammash* was appointed to discharge a variety of functions and offices. Apart from doing the routine chores in the synagogue, which encompassed the role of caretaker and handyman, he was also called upon to discharge certain less pleasant tasks, such as tax collector and bailiff, calling for tact and background knowledge of family circumstances. He would also have to attend on the rabbi as a kind of bodyguard and secretary, as well as going around the community, and beyond, as his representative or messenger. He was also ideally placed to serve as community *shadchan*, marriage broker.

The *shammash* made all the public announcements in synagogue. Since the synagogue was, for all intents and purposes, the community meeting place, all events and functions, public and private, took place within its precincts. Publicity, when required, was therefore entrusted to the *shammash*.

Since there are many occasions during the year when additions or other changes are made in various prayers, it is the *shammash* who is charged with announcing these. He reminds the congregation of the changes by calling out, for example, *Yaaleh ve-yavo*, prior to the silent *Amidah* on Rosh Chodesh, or *Ve-tein tal u-matar* when the plea for winter rain is introduced during December. At the formal entry of mourners into the synagogue on the first Friday evening of their *shivah*, it is the *shammash* who calls out *"Nichum aveilim"* ("comforting of the mourners"), which is the signal to the congregation to recite the special formula of comfort.

The salary of the *shammash* was never generous; and it was understood that on certain occasions during the year, particularly at times of members' family celebrations, appropriate "appreciation" would be shown to him. Before a *Yom Tov* or on one's *Yahrzeit* it was traditional to "remember the *shammash*." It was frequently his exclusive prerogative to import and distribute the *Arba Minim* (*Lulav* and *Etrog*, etc.) for Sukkot, and to cut down and bind into bunches the *Hoshanot*. This was probably his major opportunity in the year for augmenting his earnings.

Demise of the Profession

The profession of *shammash* is now in its final death throe, and even large synagogues cannot afford to pay a living wage to such an official. More and more of the tasks originally performed by the *shammash* are now placed on the shoulders of the synagogue secretariat. Whereas, in less affluent days, the *shammash* also served as collector, making a weekly round of houses to collect synagogue membership dues and subscriptions to the Burial Society, in the modern era of checkbooks and computerized bills it is obviously far more cost-effective to leave all this to the synagogue office.

It is becoming more and more common to appoint an honorary *shammash*, from among willing members, to attend to the routine responsibilities that occur during the course of services. These include offering visitors a *tallit, Siddur,* and *Chumash,* and acting as representative of the *gabbais* to ask people their Hebrew names prior to their being "called up," or inviting them to open the Ark.

The demise of the professional *shammash* is to be regretted. In addition to the fact that the day-to-day routine of a synagogue with a *shammash* at its helm always proceeded more smoothly, that official was also invariably a colorful personality with a fund of experiences and anecdotes culled from the fascinating human-life situations of which he was such a close and perceptive observer.

20

Outward Signs

The *Tallit* and *Tzitzit*

Biblical law obliges us to tie "fringes" *(tzitzit)* upon the edges of our garment: "And they shall make for themselves, throughout their generations, fringes" (Numbers 15:38).

The basic meaning of the word *tzitzit* is "thread" or "fiber," and is used by the prophet Ezekiel to denote the thin locks of the hair: "And he took me by the locks of *(be-tzitzit)* my head" (Ezekiel 8:3).

Popular etymology explains the word in the sense of "looking," "gazing at," connecting it with the phrase in the Song of Songs (2:9), *meitzitz min ha-charakim,* "looking through the lattice." This interpretation takes account of the purpose of the *tzitzit,* as defined in the Torah: "And you shall *look at* them and remember all the commandments of the Lord, and fulfill them" (Numbers 15:39).

The stages by which this is achieved are expressed in the Talmud:[1] "Looking makes one remember, remembering makes one fulfill." The Torah long ago presupposed modern educational methods by appreciating the efficacy of visual aids.

Some pious Jews, particularly of the chasidic sect, take the biblical injunction "And you shall look at them" in its most literal application, and insist that their *tzitzit* be visible over their outer garments.

263

Since the purpose of the *tzitzit* is "to remember *all* the commands of the Lord," rabbinic fancy sees the entire corpus of Jewish law indicated in the numerical value of the word *tzitzit*, which is *six hundred*. Add to this the *eight* threads and the *five* knots, on each corner of the garment, and we have 613 – the sum total of the biblical laws.

According to biblical law the wearing of *tzitzit* is only obligatory upon a person wearing a garment with four corners. This is clearly stated in Deuteronomy 22:12, "Thou shalt make twisted cords *upon the four corners of thy covering.*" Since very few garments came to be made with four corners, the wearing of *tzitzit* would hardly have been incumbent upon most people. The rabbis of the Talmud, in their love for, and anxiety to fulfill, every *mitzvah* of the Torah, accordingly instituted a special four-cornered garment, the *tallit*, to be worn particularly during prayer, in order that the institution of *tzitzit* should not become neglected.

The *tallit* soon became accepted as an essential prerequisite for prayer; and one who refrained from wearing it was castigated as an *am ha-aretz* – an unobservant Jew.[2]

Before or after Marriage?

In some Ashkenazi communities unmarried men refrain from wearing the *tallit* before marriage. It must not be thought that any regulation exists limiting the wearing of it exclusively to married men, neither is there any merit in not wearing the *tallit*. The origin of that practice is most certainly due to difficult economic conditions, when most people could not afford to purchase such a luxury for their children. As a result, the acquisition of a *tallit* usually had to be postponed until the time of marriage, when it was customary for the bride (or her father) to present the groom with the gift of a *tallit*, which he wore for the first time during the marriage service.

As often happens, when the origin of a custom or practice has been forgotten, attempts are made to justify the practice, even though it began as an emergency measure or a concession to the times. Thus, some writers defend the practice of not wearing it before marriage, and even appeal to the words of the Torah to support their views! They point out the juxtaposition of the two verses in the Torah, "Make for thyself twisted cords upon the four corners of thy garments" (Deuteronomy 22:12) and, "If a man take a wife" (Deuteronomy 22:13). The doubtful conclusion they arrive at is that the law of the twisted cords, or the *tallit*, is only applicable when one has "taken a wife."

The Talmud states quite clearly, however, that "a minor (under thirteen years) who knows how to enwrap himself is obliged to wear *tzitzit*."[3] Since we know that minors do not actually have *obligations* to fulfill *mitzvot* of this kind, the *Tur*, in codifying this law, rephrases it to read, "a minor, who knows how to enwrap himself, his father should buy him *tzitzit* in order to train him religiously (for the future)."[4]

We have already drawn attention to the fact that, even for an adult, the obligation to wear *tzitzit* was originally only if he was wearing a four-cornered garment (*arba kanfot*). Hence the *Bach*, commenting on the above statement of the *Tur*, reminds us that this *obligation* of the father to provide his son with *tzitzit* arises since "nowaday, everyone has *the custom* of paying serious attention to the *mitzvah* of *tzitzit*." It is, therefore, an obligation rooted in custom (*minhag*), on the part of the father, to buy his son *tzitzit* in order to train him in the *mitzvah*.

Sephardi communities seem to have taken this principle of "training the young" more seriously than their Ashkenazi counterparts, and they are particular to provide a child, old enough to understand the purpose of the *mitzvah*, with a *tallit* to wear in synagogue, in addition to the *tzitzit* he wears all day long.

The Ashkenazi practice of waiting until marriage before donning a *tallit* continued even when economic conditions improved and people could afford to purchase one for their teenage children. The practice was justified by appeal to no less an authority than the distinguished R. Yaakov b. Mosheh of Moellin (*Maharil*) who refers to this custom with approbation in the section of his book dealing with the Laws of Marriage.

Maharil relates a case that prior to marriage a young man obtained a *tallit* for the first time, but he wore it in honor of the festival of Shavuot preceding his marriage. *Maharil* states that this was not a correct action, "since the day of one's wedding is more significant to a young man than any festival. Hence any new object should be saved for the wedding day."

The *Mishnah Berurah* is most unhappy with *Maharil's* implicit discouragement of the wearing of a *tallit* by people before marriage. After quoting his words, he observes, "But this is quite astonishing that, until the day one gets married, one must sit idly and forgo a positive commandment."[5]

The modern authority, Rabbi Chayyim David Ha-Levi, adds another argument to support the case for boys over *Bar Mitzvah* wearing the *tallit*. He points out that, since the *tallit katan* or *tzitzit* that we wear under our clothing is generally not large enough to conform to the halakhically required size, most of us are not really fulfilling that biblical *mitzvah* of *tzitzit*. Hence the basis on which it was assumed that thirteen-year-olds could delay wearing the *tallit* until marriage, namely because they were, in any case, fulfilling the biblical *mitzvah* by wearing their *tzitzit*, is now seen to be without foundation. Rabbi HaLevi consequently appeals to Ashkenazi young men to wear a *tallit* during prayer in order to ensure that the *mitzvah* of *tzitzit* is practiced effectively.[6]

Tzitzit (and *tallit*) is a *mitzvah* that is incumbent only upon men, not women. This is because it is placed in the category of "positive commands which are restricted to a specific time for their performance," from which women are exempt. This categorization is on account of the fact that *tzitzit* are restricted to daytime wear only, since it states (Numbers 15:39), "And you shall *see* them" (i.e., easily, by natural sunlight). Restricted usage means that women are absolved from performing such a *mitzvah*.

Wool or Silk *Tallit?*

The silk *tallit* is considered by Orthodox Jews to be inferior to the woolen one. The blessing that is made over the *tallit* is, "Blessed art thou . . . who has commanded us to enwrap ourselves with fringes." The silk *tallit* is normally made too small to adequately "enwrap oneself."

The preference for wool, according to some authorities, is inferred from the words "on the corners of their garments" (*bigdeihem*, Numbers 15:38). The word *beged* (garment) in the Torah, although not qualified in our passage, refers exclusively to either wool or linen. This qualification is explicitly mentioned in Leviticus 13:47, "A garment *(beged)* of wool or linen." For this reason only a wool or linen garment, or *tallit*, is definitely subject to the requirements of *tzitzit*, and a *tallit* of such material is therefore obviously to be preferred.

In the Middle Ages the Ashkenazi and Sephardi communities were distinguished by the materials from which they made their *tallit*. The Ashkenazim made theirs of wool, whereas the Sephardim preferred linen.

The Thread of Blue *(Tekheilet)*

A law no longer practiced, but one that is nonetheless an integral part of the biblical laws regarding the *tzitzit*, is the inclusion of a thread of blue:

"And they shall put with the fringe of each corner a thread of blue" (Numbers 15:38).

The color blue was, in Jewish tradition, always associated with the deity. In Ezekiel 1:26 the divine throne is described as "a work of sapphire." The biblical sapphire was the *lapis lazuli*, a blue stone. The Midrash[7] informs us that the Ark of the Tabernacle was covered in blue — the Ark being an earthy representation of the divine throne. According to another tradition the tablets of the Ten Commandments were of blue sapphire, as was the staff of Moses with which he performed the divine miracles.

The robe of the Ephod worn by the high priest was also a pure blue garment. The spiritual significance of the color blue is realized in modern-day Israel which proudly displays the blue *Magen David* on its national flag.

The Talmud explains why the color blue particularly calls to mind the deity: "Blue recalls the sea, the sea resembles the skies, and the skies denote the throne of glory."[8]

Although it was the single blue thread — *petil tekheilet* — that alone served as the trigger of recollection of the divine throne, yet, at an early period, the practice of including the *tekheilet* fell into disuse. The reason for this was undoubtedly an economic one. The dye used in order to produce the blue of the *tekheilet* was obtained from the blood of the *chalazon*, a shellfish found off the Mediterranean coast. This fish was very rare, and the process of extracting the dye was a difficult and costly operation. The *Mishnah*[9] found it necessary, therefore, to grant a dispensation in the matter, and maintained that the blue and white fringes are not interdependent, and a fringe of either color was permissible. Most people relied on this and contented themselves with the white fringes. The talmudic sages in the main could not afford the blue wool, and they characteristically attributed its rarity to the fact that the Almighty was hiding it away for the righteous in the world to come![10]

Some faithfuls could not witness the demise of a biblical law, and they concocted a vegetable compound that yielded an identical color. The Talmud, however, strongly objected to the use of this substitute, called *kela iylan (callainum)*, and the practice was curtailed.

Toward the end of the 19th century an attempt was made in some chasidic circles to revive the wearing and manufacture of the *tekheilet*. Rabbi Gershon Henikh of Rodzin claimed to have discovered a method of extracting the blue dye from a shellfish found off the coast of Italy. His followers joyfully reintroduced the wearing of the thread of blue. But the centuries had hallowed its neglect, and the innovation was resolutely and firmly opposed by most rabbinic authorities.

A Garment for Eternity

Apart from the other special ritual robes in which the dead are dressed prior to being buried, the *tallit* most clearly testifies to the cardinal Jewish principle that "a Jew, even if he sins, remains a Jew." However much he might have distanced himself in life from his kith and kin, and however insensitive he might have been to the message of the *tzitzit* symbol—"And you shall see it and *remember all the commandments* of the Lord"—the Jew lies for eternity enwrapped in a *tallit*.

But even then, a distinction is apparent; for the Jew who possesses his own *tallit*, the Jew who has retained some religious identity and affiliation, is enwrapped in his own *tallit*. Symbolically he enters before the judgment seat displaying his own evidence of merit. The other type of Jew, however, relies on the community to provide him with a *tallit*. Others have to testify for him that he was born a Jew and was interred as a Jew. Others have to petition on his behalf, that he might share in the collective spiritual rewards of the World to Come—"for thy people shall be *all* righteous" (Isaiah 60:21).

The association of the *tallit* with immortality and the reward for righteousness is clearly enunciated in the special meditation we recite before making the *berakhah* over the *tallit*:

> I am here enwrapping myself in this fringed robe, in fulfillment of the command of my Creator, as it is written in the Law, "And they shall make them fringes upon the corners of their garments throughout their generations."

> And even as I cover myself with the *tallit* in this world, so may my soul deserve to be clothed with a splendid spiritual *tallit* in the world to come, in the Garden of Eden. Amen.

Tefillin and Their Contents

Having enwrapped oneself in the *tallit*, we proceed to the *tefillin*. The fact that the *tallit* is put on first does not signify its superior importance. Quite the contrary. The *tallit* is put on first because of the well-established principle of *tadir u-she-eino tadir, tadir kodem*, "the mitzvah which is performed most frequently—irrespective of importance—is performed first." The *tallit* is worn more frequently, since it is used on Sabbaths and festivals when the *tefillin* are not.

Another reason for putting on the *tefillin* after the *tallit* is in order to satisfy another principle, that of *maalin ba-kodesh ve-ein moridin*, "we ascend in order of importance, but do not descend." Thus, since the *tefillin* are of greater sanctity than the *tallit*, they are placed in the climactic position.

In four separate passages in the Torah we are commanded to bind upon our body certain words of holy writ as a constant reminder of the unique relationship existing between God and Israel.

The first passage, *Kaddesh liy kol bekhor* (Exodus 13:1–10), refers to the Exodus from Egypt and the celebration of Passover. The relevance of the opening words—"Sanctify unto me every firstborn"—to the theme of the Exodus is clearly to contrast God's abandonment of the Egyptian firstborn to a tragic fate, on the one hand, with His close spiritual relationship with Israel's firstborn, on the other, a relationship that is emphasized in the ceremony of *Pidyon Ha-Ben*, the redemption of the firstborn. This exclusive consecration of Israel's firstborn foreshadows and symbolizes His selection of Israel who are in that same unique relationship: "Israel is my son, my firstborn" (Exodus 4:21).

The second passage, *Vehayah kiy yevi'akha* (Exodus 13:11–16), is a mere amplification of the first, detailing how the consecration of the firstborn is to be effected. Consecration does not mean child sacrifice, a feature of certain perverted cults in antiquity; and this is made abundantly clear by the directive to Israel, "And all the firstborn of man among thy sons shalt thou redeem" (Exodus 4:13).

The last two passages comprise the *Shema* (Deuteronomy 6:4–9), proclaiming the Unity of God and calling upon Israel to love Him and give Him undivided loyalty, and *Vehayah im shamo'a* (Deuteronomy 11:13–21), which is attached to the *Shema* in the liturgy and enunciates the doctrine of reward and punishment.

In each of these four passages the Torah prescribes, "And it shall be ('And thou shalt bind them,' Deuteronomy 6:8) for a sign upon thy hand and for frontlets ('As a memorial,' Exodus 13:9) between thine eyes." Hence the insertion of these four particular sections into the *tefillin*.

The Name *Tefillin*

The name *tefillin* is not mentioned anywhere in the Torah, which refers to either *totafot* (frontlets), *ot* (sign), or *zikaron* (memorial). The name *tefillin* occurs for the first time in the mishnaic period (1st–3rd centuries). The word is a plural form of the word *tefillah*, "prayer," which testifies to their, by then, restricted use as symbols to be worn only during prayer. The Torah does not confine their wearing, however, to any particular time or ritual of the day, but seems to demand constant wear. In mishnaic times however, probably in the aftermath of the Bar Kochba revolt and the attendant outlawing of religious practices by the Romans, it was only possible to wear them for a short while, and the period of prayer was the obvious choice. They were consequently given the name *tefillin*—"Prayer Accompaniments."

By the time the edict was lifted people had become accustomed to such a restricted usage, even though many pious people reverted to wearing them all day long. The great sage, Yochanan bar Napacha, compromised, wearing them all day long only in winter, while in summer, when the heat was unbearable, he only wore the arm *tefillin*.[11] This spirit of compromise gave the seal of approval to the ordinary people, working in the fields and the markets, to continue wearing *tefillin* only during prayer, a practice that subsequently became standard.

A modern-day authority, Rabbi Chayyim David Ha-Levi,[12] was asked why past and present rabbis and students of Torah have not embraced the original practice of wearing the *tefillin* all day long. In answer, he draws attention to the *Shulchan Arukh*, which lists as one of several fundamental preconditions of wearing *tefillin* that "one's mind must not wander *(heisech ha-daat)* from concentrating upon that mitzvah."[13] That source goes on to state that "since no one can these days be scrupulous in this respect, they abandoned the practice of wearing them all day." Furthermore, Isaac Luria is quoted as a support for the view that "the essential time for the wearing of *tefillin* is, in fact, in the morning during prayer. The rest of the day it is not such a *mitzvah* or obligation."[14]

Phylacteries

The popular translation of *tefillin* by the word "phylactery" is a misnomer. *Phylactery* is a Greek word derived from *phulakterion*, meaning "a guard," "protector," and reflects the superstitious notion that the *tefillin* were prophylactics, objects to guard against disease and neutralize the effect of evil demons. Some may well have viewed them in this light, but the majority of Jews have always regarded them as a unique stimulus to holiness and a symbol of our total immersion in both the theory and practice of our God-given mission.

Tefillin Shel Yad and *Shel Rosh*

The *tefillin* are black leather boxes containing the above-mentioned four biblical passages. Slotted through the base of the boxes (called *battim*) are thin leather straps *(retzuot)*, by means of which the boxes are held in position on the head and arm.

The arm *tefillin* is called the *tefillah shel yad*. It is placed high up on the muscle of the left arm, and, after the recitation of the blessing, it is wound seven times around the arm.

The choice of the left arm for the *tefillah shel yad* was determined by an unusual spelling of the word *yadkhah* ("your hand") in Exodus 13:16. Instead of employing the final letter *khaf*, as expected, the second person singular termination is written as *khah* (with the letters *khaf* and *hey*).

Although this orthographic variant is not unknown from ancient Hebrew and Moabite inscriptions, the rabbis[15] believed that it was employed here in this form—*yadkhah*—in order that the word should be immediately suggestive of two words: *yad keihah*, "the weak hand." In other words, the Torah employed variant orthography in order to teach the law that the arm *tefillin* should be placed on the *left* hand, which, for most people is, indeed, "the weaker." If someone is left-handed, then his right hand is the weaker, and the *tefillin* are, accordingly, placed on that hand.

The head *tefillin*, called *tefillah shel rosh*, is then lightly placed upon the head, with its horizontal base meeting the hair line at the top of the forehead. After reciting the appropriate blessing, it is tightened securely into position. The straps of the arm *tefillin* are then wound around the middle finger three times, and over the top of the hand so as to depict the letter *shin*, denoting *Shaddai*, one of the divine names. (There are easily available many books and booklets dealing with all aspects of the *tefillin*, many incorporating illustrations showing the proper method of putting them on. We accordingly confine ourselves in this particular chapter to mere basic principles.)

The same four biblical paragraphs are placed into both the head and arm *tefillin*. The difference is that within the head *tefillin* they are written on four separate pieces of parchment, each folded and placed into a separate compartment, whereas for the hand *tefillin* they are written on just one long strip which is rolled before being inserted.

Very ancient traditions govern these and the many other regulations associated with the *tefillin*. The precise reason for the difference in the way the portions are separated in the head *tefillin* may not be ascertained with certainty; though it is apposite that a singular word ("sign") is always employed in reference to the arm *tefillin*, whereas *totafot*, a plural noun, is used in three out of the four passages to denote the head *tefillin*. This may have inspired the separation of the four paragraphs within the head *tefillin*.

This, in turn, suggested a homiletical explanation that in "matters of the head"—interpretations and philosophies of the various *mitzvot* and concepts of Judaism—there is room for "separate compartments" and differing emphases. Indeed, the Torah itself has, over the ages, been treated to a variety of approaches: textual, allegorical, mystical, philosophical, etc. However, when it comes to the fulfillment of practical ritual—as symbolized by the arm *tefillin*—then we must have but the one compartment, denoting a unified, halakhically predetermined method of observance.

The *Tefillin* of Rashi and *Rabbeinu Tam*

There was a difference of opinion among our religious authorities of the Middle Ages as to the order in which the four biblical passages should be inserted in the *tefillin*. This arose out of an apparent ambiguity in the words of the Talmud:

> What is the correct order?—It is *Kaddesh* (Exodus 13:1–10) and *Ve-hayah kiy yevi'akha* (Exodus 13:11–16) on the right-hand side; *Shema* (Deuteronomy 6:4–9) and *Ve-hayah im shamo'a* (Deuteronomy 11:13–21) on the left-hand side.[16]

The great commentator Rashi (Solomon b. Isaac) interpreted the talmudic statement to mean that the order of the passages, from right to left, should be, *Kaddesh, Ve-hayah kiy yevi'akha, Shema, Ve-hayah im shamo'a*. Not only did the wording of the talmudic comment imply this, in his view, but this arrangement also had the merit of following the order of the passages as they occur in the Bible.

His grandson Jacob *(Rabbeinu)* Tam, a renowned authority in his day, understood the talmudic extract to require *Kaddesh* on the extreme right and *Shema* on the extreme left. Thus, *Rabbeinu Tam's tefillin* have the biblical passages in the following order (right to left): *Kaddesh, Ve-hayeh kiy yevi'akha, Ve-hayah im shamo'a, Shema.*

The opinion of Rashi was always followed by the vast majority of Jews, and our *tefillin* contain his order of the passages. However, the view of *Rabbeinu Tam* could not be rejected out of hand, and some pious Jews, eager to allay any possible doubt, lay both the *tefillin* of Rashi and (for the latter part of the morning service) the *tefillin* according to *Rabbeinu Tam.*

In the 16th century, the kabbalists of Safed wore both at the same time. Rashi's were worn higher up at the top of the arm, but in the case of the head *tefillin, Rabbeinu Tam's* were placed above Rashi's.

Though this dispute between Rashi and his grandson took place in the 11th century, it reflected a divergence of practice over many centuries. It is noteworthy that among the *tefillin* discovered at Murabbaat, and used by the ancient Essene sect of the Dead Sea Scroll fame before the destruction of the Temple, were those arranged according to the order later demanded by *Rabbeinu Tam!*

A Sectarian Explanation

The Karaites, who repudiated the rabbinic interpretation of the Torah, similarly denied the biblical foundation for the ritual of the wearing of *tefillin.* In the words of the famous Karaite spokesman, Moses Ha-dasi, in his *Eshkol Ha-Kofer,* "The biblical injunction to 'bind them as a sign upon your hands and as frontlets between your eyes' is mere metaphor and not to be taken literally. This biblical law merely calls upon us to have the divine will constantly before our eyes, and to fulfill it zealously."

The Karaites denied that the Bible referred to any physical act of binding. They supported their metaphorical interpretation of the words "and you shall bind them *(u-keshartam)*" by drawing a parallel with the verse from Proverbs 6:21, "Bind the divine commands *(koshreim)* upon the tablets of your heart," which is obviously metaphoric phraseology.

By "explaining away" the ritual *mitzvot* – the cement of Judaism – in this way, the Karaites were sowing the seeds of their own dissolution.

Tefillin on Sabbath and Festivals

Tefillin are only worn on weekdays, not on Sabbath or festivals. The reason usually given to account for this is that, since *tefillin* are "signs," denoting Israel's special relationship to God, they are only necessary on weekdays. On Sabbaths and festivals, however, the very day itself constitutes a "sign," so that the *tefillin* add nothing.

Some have suggested, however, that the prohibition against wearing them on Sabbath is, in fact, in the nature of a fence to ensure that people do not carry them from the home to the synagogue. For the sake of uniformity they were similarly not worn at festival services, according to this view.

The intermediate days of a festival are also termed *mo'ed* (festival), and for this reason Sephardim refrain from putting on the *tefillin* on those days.[17] The Ashkenazi authorities, on the other hand, recommended that they should be worn, since these days had acquired the character of ordinary working days. The *chasidim* of Poland adopted the Sephardi custom of *not* wearing the *tefillin* on *Chol Ha-Mo'ed*, and adherents of this sect—even those living today in other countries—have retained this practice.

Objectives of the *Tefillin*

We conclude our brief survey of the institution of *tefillin* with two quotations that draw attention to the basic objectives of this ritual:

> The sanctity of the *tefillin* is very great. As long as they are on a man's body he feels humble and is God-fearing. He will not be drawn into laughter and idle talk, neither will evil thoughts enter his mind, but he will turn his heart to words of truth and righteousness.
>
> (Maimonides, *Laws of Prayer* 4:25)

> He has commanded us to lay the *tefillin* upon the hand as a memorial of His outstretched arm, and opposite the heart to indicate the duty of subjecting the longings and designs of our heart to His service, blessed be He; and upon our head, opposite the brain, thereby teaching that the mind, whose seat is in the brain, together with all the senses and faculties, is to be subjected to His service.

May the effect of the precept thus observed be to extend to me long life, with sacred influences and holy thoughts, free from every association, even in imagination, to sin and iniquity. May the evil inclination not mislead or entice us, but may we be led to serve the Lord as it is in our hearts to do. Amen.

> (*Meditation of the Mystics*—recited before donning the *tefillin*)

The Head Covering:
Yarmulkah, Kippah

The sanctity of the synagogue is recognized even by those who do not regard themselves as observant. Thus, men who might not otherwise cover their head do so immediately upon stepping inside the synagogue building. The same people who, at other times, express skepticism of the historical and halakhic justification for insisting upon the wearing of a hat or *yarmulkah (kippah)* throughout the day, somehow *sense* the justification as they enter the house of God.

The wearing of a special garment or uniform has deep psychological significance. When the lady puts on her ball gown and the gent his tuxedo, they immediately experience the anticipation and spirit of the celebration to come. Upon donning his uniform the conscript becomes sensitive to his role and responsibility, and the graduate in his robes becomes more acutely conscious of his background, training, and achievements, and at the same time recollects the mission and objective to which he is expected to direct the knowledge and experience he has accumulated.

Symbolic Value

It is the same with the head covering. It may only be a small, insignificant item of clothing, but it is invested with tangible symbolic value. By covering one's head inside the synagogue, and when praying or making blessings, we make a gesture of separation between the sacred and the profane. Whether it has *intrinsic* meaning or not is quite irrelevant. *It is the meaning with which we invest it that is of importance.*

And its meaning for Jews lies in the area of our awareness of God's presence which the head covering serves to symbolize. This association may well have arisen out of the context of the priestly robes, conspicuous among which were the hats of the high priests and the officiating priests. Some rabbis of the talmudic period who aspired to a particularly high degree of piety adopted that priestly symbol, and were never seen without a head covering.[18] They felt "different"; the hat focused their attention upon the ever-present divine presence "above their head."[19]

In the course of time the custom ceased to be regarded as mere _middat chasidut_ ("token of piety"), and it was embraced first by all rabbis of the Babylonian community, after which it became fairly widespread among laymen as the distinctive badge of the Chosen People, reflective of their wish to maintain a constant association with the One who chose them.

Hence, the famous Codes of the 11th and 12th centuries (Alfasi and Maimonides) already embody a law not to pray with the head uncovered;[20] and Karo, following the decision of _Rabbeinu Yerucham_, puts the final seal of authority on that prohibition.[21]

A broader dimension to the symbolism of the head-covering was introduced by the 17th-century halakhic authority, Rabbi David Ha-Levi _(Taz)_:

> In my view there is a definite prohibition (not to go about bareheaded) for quite another reason: since it is now an established practice of the non-Jews that, as soon as they enter a house and sit down, they take off their hats. Bareheadedness must now be classified, therefore, under the prohibition of "Do not walk in their ways" (Leviticus 20:23). How much more important is it then, since, in addition, it is also a symbolic demonstration of fear of heaven.[22]

In recent centuries, as Jews became more and more isolated and discriminated against in Christian lands, the wearing of a hat, or _yarmulkah_, became a proud identification mark, particularly in East European countries. This is to be viewed as a response and reaction to a centuries-old method of insulting Jews by making them wear special hats. Even when the edict lapsed, Jews continued to wear their hat, for, in addition to its religious significance, it now became a symbol and gesture of defiance (like the wearing of striped pajamas at demonstrations by survivors of the concentration camps). It was a way of telling the Christian persecutors that the Jewish wish to remain isolated from their circles and way of life was even greater than the Christian wish to keep the Jew at bay. A distinctive garb ensured that the gap remained unbridged. Conversely, the first act of the Jew who wished to assimilate was to shed the practice of covering his head. It was for this reason that the wearing of a hat, which began as a token of special piety, and which was subsequently extended to become a prerequisite for prayer or mentioning the name of God, ultimately became a uniform to be worn at all times.

Badge of Affiliation

By the type of head covering worn by different religious factions in Israel today it is possible to identify their affiliation. The *chasidim* will wear nothing but a plain, large, black satin or velvet *yarmulkah*, covering most of their head. In the street, during prayer, and when reciting Grace After Meals, they will wear a dark hat over their *yarmulkah*. The Agudat Yisrael and yeshivah fraternity will wear a black velvet or satin *yarmulkah* of slightly smaller dimensions, whereas the *Mizrachi*, or religious modernists, will wear what has been designated as the *kippah serugah*, "the knitted kippah." This comes in any color or mixture of colors, and in a host of different designs, often incorporating the Hebrew name of the wearer. It is generally much smaller than that worn by the more "right wing" circles, and is consequently disparaged by the latter. It must be admitted that the *kippah serugah* does frequently attain minuscule proportions that cannot possibly conform to the halakhic requirement, as laid down by modern authorities, that it must cover at least "the majority of the head." There is a halakhic principle that *rubbo ke-kullo*, "the majority is equivalent to the whole," so that, providing it covers most (or at least more than half) of the head, it is considered as if the entire head was covered.

Unlike the uniform of an élite corps, anyone is free to don a *kippah*, and a recent development in the State of Israel is the adoption of this custom by unlikely groups, such as Reform, non-Jews, and even Arab traders, who regard it as "good for business." It is consequently in danger of losing its status and significance as an "outward sign," and becoming a mere item of national costume.

The *Mezuzah*—An Unnecessary Synagogue Symbol

Throughout this book we have adduced numerous examples of the democratic principles that served as the prime motivation of the institutions of the synagogue and Jewish prayer, and in which they continue to be rooted. This democratic ideal is highlighted, in a simple though compelling manner, even before one has stepped inside the synagogue prayer chamber, namely through the notable absence of a *mezuzah* on the doorpost of that holy chamber.

The Talmud tells us that no *mezuzot* were affixed to any of the doorposts of the Temple chambers, with but one exception. This was the *Lishkat Parhedrin*, where the high priest took up residence for seven days each year, to prepare himself for the Yom Kippur rituals.[23] Because it was used as a human habitation it required a *mezuzah*, whereas the rest of the Temple was considered God's house, and a holy residence does not require a *mezuzah*. This is inferred from the verse, "And you shall write them upon the doorposts of *your* house." Only on *your* house is the *mezuzah* required, not on *God's* house.

There is a salutary message here for all who attend the synagogue, and particularly for those involved in synagogue organization and leadership.

In our own homes we wield authority, we determine policies and make plans based upon our personal and circumscribed ambitions for ourselves and our families. We cocoon ourselves within our homes and close the doors upon the outside world. The *mezuzah's* message is definitely required in such a situation, to remind us that there are higher spiritual goals and perspectives which should transcend our narrow domestic priorities.

In the synagogue, in God's house, this message of the *mezuzah* should not be required. For the collective concept of a *kehillah kedoshah*, a holy community, automatically focuses our attention upon broader and loftier national and spiritual collective enterprises.

It follows from this that there should be no room in the synagogue for selfish, personal ambitions. The synagogue must, of necessity, expand our hearts and our desires to encompass the entire *minyan*, the needs and views of all its members. The synagogue is not our house; it is God's. We are all guests there, with no special title, no individual rights and privileges, with no claim to recognition on account of social or material status.

Democratic Ideal of the Synagogue

Our synagogues must lay greater emphasis on this doctrine of equality and democracy if we wish to stem the accelerating rate of defection from this nerve center of Jewish life and inspiration. Nothing is more calculated to deter the lukewarm from returning to synagogue affiliation than an atmosphere of authoritarianism, of an autocratic individual or clique imposing its views and policies upon a docile membership. Nothing will deter young, enthusiastic, and idealistic potential leaders more than the spectacle of exaggerated deference to the wealthy and the automatic investment of spiritual and communal influence into the hands of the materially influential.

The synagogue is rooted in the principle of democracy. Within its walls deference to God alone is appropriate. The prophet called upon us to "walk humbly with thy God" (Micah 6:8). If we cannot do so in the synagogue, of all places, then where shall we?

The synagogue is God's home. It belongs to no one man to call his own. It is mine; it is yours. It is ours; it is our children's. It belongs to every Jew, and it waits patiently to welcome them all.

It grieves when their seats go unoccupied, and it feels that abiding sense of loss when they depart this life, never again to occupy and grace their place, never again to contribute of their personality and fervor to the house of God and to the fund of collective spiritual vitality.

The synagogue shares all our joys and sorrows. It keeps our confidences as we dream, and wish, and pray. It yearns with us for better times, and it smiles with us when they come our way.

The synagogue is the *Bet Ha-Kneset*, the house of meeting. It is where a man meets his fellow to experience fellowship, and to express mutual spiritual kinship. It is where man meets God, to proclaim His fatherhood and to receive His blessing: "In every place where I cause My name to be mentioned, there shall I come to you and bless you."

Notes

Chapter 1

1. *Berakhot* 26b.
2. See *Targum Onkelos* and *Jonathan,* also *Rashi* on Genesis 4:26.
3. See *Rashi* on Genesis 6:9.
4. Genesis 24:12–15.
5. Genesis 24:26–27.
6. Genesis 24:52.
7. Genesis 25:21.
8. Genesis 27:28–29.
9. Genesis 32:10–13.
10. Exodus 2:23–24.
11. Exodus 15:1–18.
12. Eliezer Levi, *Yesodot Ha-tefillah* (Tel Aviv: Tzioni, 1963).
13. *Kiddushin* 71a.
14. See *Rashi* ad loc.
15. *Yoma* 39b.
16. Ibid. See also Maimonides, *Yad, Hilkhot Nesiat Kappayim,* 14:10.

17. *Menachot* 109b; J.T. *Yoma* 6:3.
18. Josephus, *Antiquities* 13:73; *Wars* 7:431.
19. *Kiddushin* 71a.
20. J.T. *Yoma* 3:7.
21. *Mo'ed Katan* 28b.
22. Theodore Friedman, "Some Unexplained Features of Ancient Synagogues," *Conservative Judaism* 36:3 (Spring 1983): 35–42.
23. See pp. 25–26, 159.
24. *Berakhot* 8a.
25. *Mishnah Taanit* 2:2; *Tamid* 5:1. See commentaries on mishnaic reference to *Shalosh berakhot*.
26. Cf. *Avot* 5:4. See also J. M. Cohen, *Understanding the Synagogue Service* (Glasgow: Private publication, 1974), pp. 45–46.
27. *Mishnah Taanit*, chaps. 1–3.
28. See J. M. Cohen, *Understanding the High Holyday Services* (London: Routledge and Kegan Paul, 1983), pp. 47, 164–165.

Chapter 2

1. Louis Finkelstein, *The Pharisees*, vol. 2 (Philadelphia: Jewish Publication Society, 1962), pp. 563–565.
2. See G. F. Moore, *Judaism in the First Centuries of the Christian Era*, 3 vols. (Cambridge, MA: Harvard University Press, 1927); W. Bacher, "Synagogue," in *Jewish Encyclopedia*, vol. 9 (New York, and London: Funk and Wagnalls Co., 1906), p. 619; S. W. Baron, *A Social and Religious History of the Jews*, 8 vols. (New York: Columbia University Press, 1960); R. T. Herford, *Pharisaism, Its Aim and Its Method* (London: Williams & Norgate, 1912).
3. *Megillah* 29a.
4. Isaiah 40:18–21, 45:20, 46:5–7.
5. Ezra, chaps. 9–10.
6. Nehemiah 7:61, 13:1–3, 15–31.
7. Cf. Deuteronomy 32:1.
8. See *Rashi* on I Samuel 1:13.
9. This reconstruction of the limited extent of personal prayer in the biblical period is not in conflict with the rabbinic tradition that the blessings of the Grace After Meals, for example, were composed by Moses, Joshua, David, and Solomon (*Berakhot* 21a). That our biblical ancestors composed, and recited, prayers regularly, we may indeed presuppose. What is less certain is that these were accepted and recited by the masses.
10. *Megillah* 17b.

11. *Berakhot* 33a.

12. *Pesachim* 50b.

13. S. Mowinckel, *The Psalms in Israel's Worship* (Oxford: Basil Blackwell, 1962), 2:198–201.

14. Ibid., p. 201.

15. Ibid., p. 199.

16. S. Zeitlin, *Studies in the Early History of Judaism* (New York: Ktav, 1973), 1:75–81.

17. *Taanit* 27b.

18. *Taanit* 23a.

19. Lee I. Levine, "Bet Kneset Bi-tekufat Bayit Sheni Ofyo Ve-hitpatchuto," in *Synagogues in Antiquity*, ed. A. Oppenheimer, A. Kasher, and U. Rappaport (Jerusalem, 1987), p. 230.

20. Cf. Y. Yadin, *Masada* (London: Wiedenfeld & Nicolson, 1966), pp. 183 ff.

21. S. Hoenig, "The Synagogue," *Jewish Quarterly Review* 54 (1963): 115 ff.

Chapter 3

1. *Yalkut Shimoni, Va-Yakhel*, sec. 408.

2. J.T. *Shabbat* 15:3.

3. *Pesikta Rabbati, Aseret Ha-dibrot*, 3.

4. *Mishnah Berakhot* 4:3.

5. *Vayikra Rabbah* 23:4.

6. *Berakhot* 34a.

7. *Mishnah Tamid* 5:1.

8. *Mishnah Yoma* 7:1.

9. This exaggerated form of worship is condemned even by the New Testament in a number of passages.

10. *Berakhot* 31a.

11. See *Chagigah* 14b.

12. *Berakhot* 28b.

13. *Shabbat* 33b.

14. *Sanhedrin* 11a.

15. *Bava Metzia* 59b; *Mishnah Rosh Hashanah* 2:9; *Berakhot* 27b–28a.

16. *Tosefta Berakhot* 3:25.

17. Several *Genizah* versions and formulae of the *Amidah* are published and discussed in several essays collected in *The Scientific Study of Jewish Liturgy*, ed. J. J. Petuchowski (New York: Ktav, 1970), and in I. Elbogen's classic work *Ha-tefillah Be-Yisrael*, ed. J. Heineman (Tel Aviv: Dvir, 1988), translation of his *Der Judische Gottesdienst* (Leipzig, 1913).

18. *Berakhot* 27b.
19. Daniel 6:11.
20. Psalms 55:18.
21. *Megillah* 15a; *Taanit* 27b.
22. *Berakhot* 16b.
23. Pupil of Judah Ha-Nasi, compiler of the *Mishnah*. Rav founded a talmudic academy in Sura in Babylon and revitalized religious life there.
24. *Pesachim* 117b.
25. *Menachot* 43b.
26. *Mishnah Tamid* 5:1.
27. See N. Wieder, "Berakhah biltiy yaduah al kriat perek Bameh Madlikin," *Sinai* 82 (*Shevat-Adar* 5738–1978):218.

Chapter 4

1. See S. Assaf, *Teshuvot Ha-Geonim* (Jerusalem, 1942), pp. 47–50.
2. *Asur leshannot mi-matbe'a shetavu chakhamim.*
3. See *Kobetz Al Jad* (Jerusalem: Mekitzey Nirdamim, 1939), 3(13), p. 11.
4. See J. Heinemann, "Al defus piyyuti kadum," *Bar Ilan* 4/5 (1967).
5. *Tur, Orach Chayyim*, sec. 621.
6. J.T. *Berakhot* 3:4.
7. J. Schirmann, "Hebrew Liturgical Poetry and Christian Hymnology," *Jewish Quarterly Review* 44:123–161.

Chapter 5

1. See p. 44.
2. Cf. Shem-Tov Gaguine's *Keter Shem Tov* (London, 1934).
3. It has even been suggested that the different pronunciation of Hebrew on the part of Ashkenazi and Sephardi Jewry is to be attributed to the original distinction between Hebrew as pronounced in Palestine and Babylon, respectively.
4. Gershom G. Scholem, *Major Trends in Jewish Mysticism* (London: Thames & Hudson, 1955), p. 101.
5. Solomon Schechter, *Studies in Judaism* (New York: Meridian & Jewish Publication Society of America, 1958), p. 252.
6. *Mishnah Shekalim* 6:1,3.
7. J.T. *Berakhot* 4:5.
8. Solomon of Lutzk, *Maggid Devarav Le-Yaakov* (Lublin, 1927), pp. 94–95.

Chapter 6

1. Jakob J. Petuchowski, *Prayer Reform in Europe* (New York: World Union for Progressive Judaism, 1968); Noah H. Rosenbloom, *Tradition in an Age of Reform* (Philadelphia: Jewish Publication Society of America, 1976), chap. 14.
2. J. Heinmann, "Toledot Ha-riformah shel Siddur Ha-tefillah," *Tarbiz* 39 (1970): 219.
3. See J. J. Petuchowski, "New Directions in Reform Liturgy," *Central Conference of American Rabbis Journal* (April 1969): 26 ff.
4. *Authorized Daily Prayer Book*, ed. S. Singer (London: Singer's Prayer Book, 1962), preface to first edition, July 1890.

Chapter 7

1. *Bava Batra* 15b.
2. On Numinous Hymns, see Jeffrey M. Cohen, *Understanding the High Holyday Services* (London: Routledge and Kegan Paul, 1983), pp. 17–18, 147, 160.
3. Rudolph Otto, *The Idea of the Holy* (trans. of *Das Heilige*) (Oxford: Oxford University Press, 1928), chap. 6.
4. Jeffrey M. Cohen, op. cit., p. 160.
5. See "Falashas" in *Encyclopaedia Judaica* 6:1147.
6. See n. 2 in this chapter.
7. The parallel is striking between this genre of hymn and some of our own *Selichot* and, in particular, *Hoshanot*, which represent the earliest form of postbiblical poetry known to us. J. Heinemann believes that they belong to a category of litanies originally chanted during processions or circuits round the altar (for references, see Jeffrey M. Cohen, op. cit., pp. 125–126). Heinmann's theory may well be corroborated from this Ethiopian source, for the sacrificial cult is an essential element in Ethiopian Jewry's worship, and we may assume that this particular hymn belongs to the section of their liturgy recited at the sacrifice, headed, *Tefillot Ha-Korban*.
8. See A. E. Cowley, *The Samaritan Liturgy* (Oxford: Clarendon Press, 1909).

Chapter 8

1. *Rosh Hashanah* 16a.
2. Maimonides *Yad, Hilkhot Yesodei Ha-Torah*, chap. 2.

3. *Berakhot* 54a.
4. See *Midrash Song of Songs Rabbah* 2(32); *Bereishit Rabbah* 45(5).
5. See "Prayer and Heart," in *Prayer,* ed. David Derovan, vol. 3 (New York: Yavne Studies, 1970), p. 78.
6. *Berakhot* 35a.
7. *Berakhot* 17a.
8. *Berakhot* 35b.

Chapter 9

1. *Berakhot* 23a.
2. *Shulchan Arukh, Orach Chayyim,* sec. 88.
3. This sect was known as the "Hemerobaptists."
4. *Berakhot* 22a.
5. Maimonides, *Yad, Hilkhot Tefillah* 4:9.
6. *Shabbat* 11a.
7. Maimonides, *Yad, Hilkhot Tefillah* 4:5.
8. *Berakhot* 34b.
9. See Maimonides, *Yad, Hilkhot Tefillah* 10:1.
10. *Mishnah Berakhot* 5:1.
11. *Shabbat* 118b.
12. *Shulchan Arukh, Orach Chayyim* 98:1.
13. Maimonides, *Yad, Hilkhot Tefillah* 4:15.
14. *Shulchan Arukh, Orach Chayyim* 98:2.
15. See *Tosafot* on *Berakhot* 12b.
16. This was probably emphasized in order to justify the removal of the Ten Commandments from the daily prayers, see pp. 13, 47.
17. See *Be'er Heiteiv* on *Shulchan Arukh, Orach Chayyim* 61:1.
18. A. J. Heschel, *Man's Quest for God* (New York: Charles Scribner's Sons, 1954), p. 17.
19. Joseph B. Soloveitchik, "The Lonely Man of Faith," *Tradition* 7:2 (Summer 1965): 43.
20. *Pirkei Avot* 1:15.
21. Psalms 100:2.
22. S. Schechter, *Seminary Addresses and Other Papers* (Westmead, England: Gregg International Publishers, 1969), pp. 84–85.

Chapter 10

1. See pp. 22–23.
2. Opening prayer of morning service.

3. *Tosefta Megillah*, chap. 4.
4. *Shulchan Arukh, Orach Chayyim* 150–155.
5. See *Perishah* on *Tur*, sec. 150.
6. I Kings 8:27–30.
7. Daniel 6:10.
8. *Bava Batra* 25a.
9. For a full discussion of this subject, see Epraim E. Urbach, *The Sages* (Jerusalem: Magnes Press, 1969), pp. 44–49; F. Landsberger, "The Sacred Direction in Synagogue and Church," H.U.C.A. 28 (1957): 181–203.
10. *Mishnah Sukkah* 5:4.
11. Nehemiah 13:24.
12. Maimonides, *Yad, Hilkhot Tefillah* 1:4.
13. A. J. Heschel, *Man's Quest for God*, p. 55.
14. *Megillah* 23b.
15. Numbers, chap. 14.
16. Numbers 14:27.
17. Genesis 18:33.
18. *Berakhot* 47b–48a.
19. See *Tosafot* ad loc.
20. *Bet Yoseph, Orach Chayyim*, sec. 55.
21. Mosheh Feinstein, *Iggrot Mosheh, Orach Chayyim*, vol. 4 (New York: Moriah, 1959), p. 188.
22. See Ovadiah Yoseph, *Sefer Yechavveh Da'at*, vol. 3 (Jerusalem: Yeshivat Porat Yoseph et al., 1977), pp. 23–27.
23. For a graphic description of that joyous Temple ceremony and festivity, see *Mishnah Sukkah* 5:1–4.
24. *Sukkah* 51b.
25. Mosheh Feinstein, *Iggrot Mosheh, Orach Chayyim*, 1:102–104.

Chapter 11

1. *Mishnah Berakhot* 9:2.
2. See Numbers 34:7.
3. *Sefer Ha-terumot*, quoted in *Magen Avraham, Orach Chayyim* 228:1.
4. *Shulchan Arukh, Orach Chayyim* 223:4–5.
5. *Rema* on *Shulchan Arukh, Yoreh De'ah* 28:2.
6. *Rema* on *Shulchan Arukh, Orach Chayyim* 223:6.
7. Loc. cit.
8. Maimonides, *Hilkhot Berakhot* 1:6. On the extent of the use of vernacular translations of prayers in synagogue worship, see I. Abrahams, *Jewish Life in the Middle Ages* (Cleveland and New York: Meridian and Jewish Publication Society of America, 1958), pp. 345–347.

9. See Alan Henkin, " 'The Two of Them Went Together,' (Genesis 22:6): Visions of Interdependence," *Judaism* 32:4 (Fall 1983): 460.
10. *Shulchan Arukh, Orach Chayyim* 46:8.
11. See *Rema*, ad loc.
12. *Mishnah Berakhot* 9:5.
13. *Berakhot* 14b.
14. Zevi Karl, *Mechkarim Be-toldot Ha-tefillah* (Tel Aviv: N. Twersky, 1950), p. 185.
15. S. Zeitlin, *Studies in the Early History of Judaism*, vol. 1 (New York: Ktav, 1963), p. 92.
16. Ibid., p. 95.
17. See O. Eissfeldt, *The Old Testament* (Oxford: Basil Blackwell, 1965), p. 405.
18. S. R. Hirsch, *The Pentateuch*, ed. I. Levy (London: Isaac Levy, 1959), pp. 212–213, 347–348.
19. See Exodus 29:40; Leviticus 2:4, etc.
20. See Deuteronomy 32:31; I Samuel 2:25, etc.
21. S. R. Hirsch, op. cit., p. 348.
22. Genesis 27:4,7,19.
23. Genesis 33:22; Joshua 15:19; Judges 1:15; I Samuel 25:27, 30:26.
24. See "Prayer before retiring to sleeping"—"May Michael be at my right hand, Gabriel at my left. . . ."
25. *The Authorized Selichot for the Whole Year*, ed. A. Rosenfeld (New York: Judaica Press, 1979), pp. 21, 39, 57, etc.
26. See Genesis 28:12–17.
27. *Sotah* 34b.
28. *Taanit* 23b.

Chapter 12

1. *Megillah* 29a.
2. *Berakhot* 8a.
3. *Kli Yakar* on Deuteronomy 11:21.
4. *Zohar, Raya Meheimna, Beshalach* 59:2.
5. *Tosefta, Bava Metzia* (Zuckermandel ed.), 11(23).
6. *Magen Avraham, Shulchan Arukh* 144 (end), in name of *Rivash*.
7. See *Shaar Ha-tziyyun, Mishnah Berurah* 2:140 (3).
8. *Mishnah Ketubot* 12:3.
9. This decision is based on the fact that the wording of the talmudic *ketubah* was: "You shall dwell *in my house* and be fed from my sustenance." Thus, the deceased's home, now occupied by the heirs, is the only place where she can rightfully claim sustenance under the terms of her *ketubah*.

10. This responsum of the *Ridbaz* was published for the first time in *Zikhron Shelomo* (Jerusalem, 1972), pp. 1–3.

11. *Megillah* 29a.

12. *Mishnah Berakhot* 9:5.

13. This is how Maimonides understands the term *afundato* (see his *Peirush Ha-mishnayot, Berakhot* 9:5). *Rashi*, on the other hand, understands the term as denoting "a money belt."

14. *Megillah* 28a; *Rambam, Hilkhot Tefillah* 11:6.

15. *Mishnah Megillah* 3:1.

16. For a full treatment of this subject, see *Encyclopaedia Talmudit*, vol. 3 (Jerusalem: Talmudic Encyclopedia Publications, Ltd., 1954), pp. 200–205.

17. See *Shulchan Arukh, Yoreh De'ah* 270:1.

18. *Shulchan Arukh, Orach Chayyim* 151:6.

19. See Shaul Yisraeli, "Al Shimush be-Ramkol," *Berkai* 5 (1989): 152–158.

20. *Shabbat* 18a.

21. *Shulchan Arukh, Orach Chayyim* 252:5.

Chapter 13

1. Exodus 25:10.

2. Genesis 50:26.

3. II Kings 12:10,11.

4. See F. Brown, S. R. Driver, and L. A. Briggs, *Hebrew and English Lexicon of the Old Testament* (Oxford: Clarendon Press, 1906), p. 75.

5. See Song of Songs 5:1; Psalms 80:13.

6. *Shabbat* 32a.

7. *Mishnah Taanit* 2:1; *Megillah* 3:1.

8. J.T. *Megillah* 4:5.

9. J.T. *Megillah* 3:1.

10. *Shabbat* 133b.

11. *Megillah* 9b.

12. Ibid.

13. See J. M. Baumgarten, "Art in the Synagogue: Some Talmudic Views," *Judaism* 19 (1970): 196–206.

14. *Rosh Hashanah* 24b.

15. See R. Ovadia Yoseph, *Yechavveh Daat*, vol. 3 (Jerusalem: Yeshivat Porat Yoseph et al., 1977), p. 199.

16. See *Bi'ur Ha-gra* ad loc., n. 21.

17. *Shulchan Arukh, Yoreh De'ah* 142:6.

18. *Shakh*, ad loc.

19. *Taz,* ad loc., n. 14.

20. R. Chaim David Halevi, *Asei Lekha Rav,* vol. 4 (Tel Aviv: Committee for the Publications of HaGaon Rabbi Chaim David Halevi, 1981), pp. 240–255.

21. R. Ovadia Yoseph, op. cit., p. 201.

22. *Sanhedrin* 92a.

23. See *Be'er Heitev* on *Shulchan Arukh, Orach Chayyim* 1:1(3).

24. See Psalms 4:7, 44:4; Proverbs 6:23, 20:27, et al.

25. *Mishnah Tamid* 6:1.

26. See *Rashi* on *Shabbat* 22b. *Rambam, Hilkhot Bet Ha-bechirah* 3:8, actually designates the *central* lamp as the *ner maaraviy. Rashi* (ad loc.) explains the background to this difference of opinion.

27. *Sukkah* 51b.

28. *Midrash Pesikta Derav Kahana* (ed. Buber), p. 12.

29. See I. Renov, "The Seat of Moses," *Israel Exploration Journal* 5 (1955): 262–267.

30. See C. H. Kraeling, *The Excavations at Dura-Europos, Final Report* VIII, part I: *The Synagogue* (New Haven: Yale University Press, 1956), pp. 17, 260.

31. Jeffrey M. Cohen, *A Samaritan Chronicle* (Leiden: Brill, 1981), p. 71.

32. Ibid., pp. 178, 182, 224, et al.

33. L. Landman, *The Cantor* (New York: Yeshiva University, 1972), p. 18.

34. *Rambam, Hilkhot Tefillah* 11:3.

35. *Sukkah* 51b.

36. See *Kesef Mishneh* ad loc.

37. Rachel Wischnitzer, "Mutual Influences between Eastern and Western Europe in Synagogue Architecture from the 12th to the 18th Century," *YIVO* (Annual of YIVO Institute for Jewish Research) 2–3 (1947–1948): 26.

38. See *Sedei Chemed, Asefat Dinim,* Laws of the Synagogue, no. 13. For full discussion on this subject, see I. Jakobovits, *Jewish Law Faces Modern Problems* (New York: Yeshiva University, 1965), pp. 43–46.

39. *Magen Avraham, Orach Chayyim* 90:3.

40. *Berakhot* 10b.

41. See *Ketav Sofer,* II, nos. 1 and 2.

42. J. David Bleich, *Contemporary Halakhic Problems* (New York: Ktav, 1977), p. 66.

Chapter 14

1. See pp. 174–175.

2. *Ketubot* 19b.

3. *Menachot* 29b.

4. *Bet Yoseph* on *Tur, Orach Chayyim, sub Vekatav Ha-Mordechai.*

5. *Avodah Zarah* 24b.

6. *Shabbat* 133b.

7. See *Midrash Song of Songs Rabbah* on Song of Songs 4:2.

8. Exodus 28:17–20.

9. *Pirkei Avot* 4:13.

10. *Berakhot* 22a.

11. *Rambam, Hilkhot Sefer Torah* 10:8.

12. *Rema* on *Orach Chayyim* 88:1.

13. A. Weiss, "Women and Sifrei Torah," *Tradition* 20:2 (Summer 1982): 106–118.

14. Ibid., p. 113. See his most recent study, *Women at Prayer* (Hoboken, NJ: Ktav, 1990), chap. 7.

15. *Shulchan Arukh, Orach Chayyim* 135:14.

16. See *Arukh Ha-shulchan* ad loc.

17. *Megillah* 29b.

18. *Rosh Hashanah* 11a.

19. *The Itinerary of Benjamin of Tudela*, ed. A. Asher (London: A. Asher & Co., 1840–1841), p. 98.

20. Ibid., p. 70.

Chapter 15

1. *Tur, Orach Chayyim* 139.

2. Ibid.

3. *Megillah* 23a.

4. *Tashbatz*, cited by *Magen Avraham* on *Shulchan Arukh, Orach Chayyim* 282:1.

5. *Shulchan Arukh, Orach Chayyim* 282:2.

6. See *Arukh Ha-shulchan* ad loc.; *Siddur Ha-gra*, vol. 2 (Jerusalem, 1971), p. 103.

7. *Mishnah Gittin* 5:8.

8. *Gittin* 60a.

9. *Roshei Knesiyyot*. The precise function performed by this official is not known with certainty, nor is the origin of his title.

10. See *Magen Avraham* on *Orach Chayyim* 136:1.

11. See Jeffrey M. Cohen, *Understanding the Synagogue Service*, p. 46 n. 4.

12. *Megillah* 32a; *Bava Kamma* 82b; J.T. *Megillah* 4:1 (75a).

13. *Bava Kamma* 82b.

14. See p. 20.

15. *Midrash Shemot Rabbah* 40:1.

16. See *Bach* on *Tur, Orach Chayyim* 139, *sub Ha-korei*.
17. *Mishnah Berurah*, vol. 2, 139:1 (3).
18. *Sefer Ha-Eshkol*, Laws of the Synagogue.
19. *Yoma* 70a; *Rambam, Hilkhot Tefillah* 12:23; *Tur, Shulchan Arukh, Orach Chayyim* 144:3.
20. *Rashi* on *Yoma* 70a.
21. *Pirkei Avot* 5:25.
22. Genesis 3:11.
23. *Hullin* 139a.
24. *Shabbat* is regarded as more stringent than Yom Kippur since the penalty for disregarding Yom Kippur is *karet* (divine punishment), whereas for deliberately profaning *Shabbat* it is but a human punishment: *sekilah*, death by stoning.
25. See introduction to *Mishnah Berurah*, vol. 3.
26. Ibid. The converse is also true, and the rabbis state that "whoever observes the Sabbath is regarded as if he had observed all the other laws of the Torah."
27. This subject is dealt with in a responsum by Rabbi Mosheh Feinstein. See *Iggrot Mosheh, Orach Chayyim*, vol. 1, no. 23.
28. *Shabbat* 67b–68a.
29. *Rambam, Hilkhot Mamrim* 3:3.
30. *Rambam, Iggeret Kiddush Ha-shem* (end).
31. For further halakhic treatment of this issue, see article by Rabbi M. D. Schiff in *Machanayim* (July 10th and 17th, 1959), summarized in "Review of Halakhic Periodical Literature," *Tradition* (1960): 305–307.
32. *Megillah* 32a.
33. *Rema* on *Orach Chayyim* 147:1—"But *now* that the practice has been introduced that one person lifts it up and another rolls it. . . ."
34. See *Sefer Ha-Eshkol*, part 2, p. 69.
35. Ibid.
36. *Megillah* 52a.
37. Ibid.
38. *Shulchan Arukh, Orach Chayyim* 147:1.
39. This is the reason for the *mitzvah* of *Gelilah* as offered by *Shitah Mekubbetzet* on *Berakhot* 13b in the name of *Rashba*.
40. See n. 33.
41. *Mishnah Berurah*, vol. 2, sec. 147 (19).
42. Quoted in *Dover Shalom* commentary, as printed in *Otzar Ha-tefillot*, vol. 1 (New York, 1966), p. 416.
43. *The Pentateuch and Haftorahs*, ed. J. H. Hertz, commentary on Numbers 10:35.
44. See *Masekhet Soferim* 14:4; *Shulchan Arukh, Orach Chayyim* 134:2.
45. *Shulchan Arukh, Orach Chayyim* 14:13.

46. *Shulchan Arukh, Orach Chayyim* 149:2.

47. A commonly quoted, though unconvincing, reason for *hagbahah* is that it is in order to show the congregation that the blessings about to be recited are not actually written down inside the scroll.

48. See Jacob Chagiz, *Halakhot Ketanot* (Cracow: Josef Fischer, 1897), part 2, sec. 225.

Chapter 16

1. See *Sanhedrin* 52b; *Avodah Zarah* 11a; *Rashi* on Deuteronomy 16:22.

2. See Exodus 9:33; I Kings 8:54; Ezra 9:5, etc. See *Encyclopaedia Talmudit* 17:318 n. 168.

3. *Masekhet Semachot* 2:10; *Tur, Yoreh De'ah* 345:5.

4. *Gittin* 68a–b.

5. *Zohar, Vayyikra* 73.

6. Jeremiah 52:19.

7. Ezra, chap. 41.

8. See L. Ginzberg, *Legends of the Jews*, vol. 4 (Philadelphia: Jewish Publication Society of America, 1913), p. 321.

9. I Maccabees 1:21–24.

10. *Rosh Hashanah* 24b.

11. *Menachot* 28b, which refers to its "legs" *(raglayyim);* also *Rambam, Hilkhot Bet Habechirah* 3:2; *Rashi* on Exodus 25:31.

12. *Menachot* 28b.

13. See P. Bloch, "Seven-Branched Candelabra in Christian Churches," *Journal of Jewish Art*, vol. 1 (Chicago: Spertus College of Judaica Press), pp. 44–47.

14. See Gad Ben-Ami Zorfati, "The Tables of the Covenant as a Symbol of Judaism," *Tarbiz* 29 (1960): 370–393.

15. British Museum Cotton MS. Claudius B.iv.

16. J.T. *Shekalim* 6:1 (25a).

17. *Tosafot* to *Menachot* 99a *(melammed).*

18. R. Mellinkoff, "The Round-Topped Tablets of the Law: Sacred Symbol and Emblem of Evil," *Journal of Jewish Art* I, p. 38.

19. Ibid., p. 42.

20. P. Kidson, "Arch and Vault," in *Encyclopaedia Britannica* (1970 ed.), p. 287.

Chapter 17

1. A sketchy chronology of the Chain of Tradition, and the scholars who were its bearers down the ages, is given in *Pirkei Avot*, chaps. 1–2; for Rabban Gamliel, see pp. 211–212 *(Avot* 1:16).

2. I. H. Weiss, *Dor Dor Vedorshav*, vol. 1 (Jerusalem/Tel Aviv: Ziv Publishers, n.d.), chap. 20, p. 179.

3. Sherirah Gaon was of the opinion, however, that the title "Rabbi" only became universally employed in the succeeding period of R. Yochanan ben Zakkai.

4. *Mishnah Sotah* 9:15. The traditional explanation of this statement is that, until his day, students studied Torah standing up, whereas subsequent generations were not hardy enough to accord it honor in that way.

5. *Bava Metzia* 84b; *Gittin* 88b.

6. See J. Newman, *Semikhah* (Manchester, England: Manchester University Press, 1950), pp. 95–97.

7. *Rosh Hashanah* 20b.

8. J. Newman, op. cit., p. 41.

9. *Pirkei Avot* 6:4.

10. *Pirkei Avot* 6:6.

11. *Arakhin* 17a.

12. *Sanhedrin* 14a.

13. Rabbi Shelomo Dichowsky, "Al ha-derekh ha-ne'otah li-bechirat rabbanim," *Barkai* 1 (1983): 33–36.

14. Ibid., p. 34.

15. *Berakhot* 55a.

16. Dichowsky, op. cit., pp. 35–36.

17. *Nedarim* 35b; *Kiddushin* 23b.

18. Shaul Yisraeli, "Ha-rav ve-ha-rabanut be-aspaklariat ha-dorot," *Barkai* (1983): 27–28.

19. See *Ran* on *Nedarim* 36a.

20. *Midrash Shemot Rabbah* 2:2.

21. *Shulchan Arukh, Yoreh De'ah* 244:1.

22. Ibid., 244:7.

23. Ibid., 243:10.

24. Ibid., 243:1–2.

25. *Bava Batra* 8a.

26. *Litra*, the Roman *Libra*, "a pound."

27. *Shulchan Arukh, Yoreh De'ah* 243:2.

28. Ibid., 243:4.

29. *Pirkei Avot* 4:5.

30. M. Davis, *The Emergence of Conservative Judaism* (Philadelphia: Jewish Publication Society of America, 1963), p. 155.

31. Ibid., p. 133.

32. Abraham J. Karp, "Rabbi, Congregation, and the World They Live In," *Conservative Judaism* 26:1 (Fall 1971): 38.

Chapter 18

1. *Rosh Hashanah* 34b.
2. See L. Ginzberg, *Commentary on the Palestinian Talmud*, vol. 1 (New York: Jewish Theological Seminary of America, 1941), p. lxx.
3. *Shabbat* 115b.
4. *Sukkah* 51b.
5. *Pirkei Derabbi Eliezer*, chap. 12 (end); chap. 16.
6. *Ketubot* 5b.
7. *Masekhet Soferim* 19:12.
8. Ibid., 11:14.
9. *Shabbat* 11a.
10. Ibid., 56a. See *Rashi ad loc., sub lachazaneihem*.
11. *Yoma* 24b.
12. *Bava Metzia* 93b, and *Rashi*'s explanation of *chazanei mata* as referring to members of the police force!
13. Exodus 24:11.
14. *Mishnah Taanit* 2:1.
15. *Taanit* 16a.
16. Ibid.
17. J.T. *Sukkah* 3:15; *Shulchan Arukh, Orach Chayyim* 53:8.
18. *Mishnah Bikkurim* 3:7.
19. This responsum is quoted in full in *Tur, Orach Chayyim* 53.
20. See *Taz* on *Orach Chayyim* 53:6.
21. *Shulchan Arukh, Orach Chayyim* 53:11.
22. See *Mafteach Li-Teshuvot Ha-Geonim*, ed. J. Miller (Berlin, 1891), p. 208.
23. Isaac Alfasi, *Teshuvot*, ed. S. Leiter (Leghorn, 1781), no. 281; *Kol Bo* (Venice, 1547), p. 155b.
24. For fuller treatment of this subject, see L. Landman, *The Cantor* (New York: Yeshiva University, 1972), chap. 2.
25. See *Magen Avraham* on *Orach Chayyim* 53:19 (20).
26. Loc. cit., sec. (22).
27. *Shulchan Arukh, Orach Chayyim* 53:21.
28. Ibid.
29. Loc. cit., sec. (23).
30. See *Rema* and *Taz* ad loc.
31. *Shulchan Arukh, Orach Chayyim* 53:24.
32. I am grateful to my dear colleague, Rev. Geoffrey L. Shisler, for allowing me to quote these three paragraphs from his report, "The Role of the Chazan in Anglo-Jewry," submitted as an internal memorandum to the United Synagogue in 1983.

33. M. S. Geshuri, "Le-toldot Ha-chazanut Be-eretz Yisrael," in *Bet Ha-kneset*, ed. Mordechai Ha-Cohen (Jerusalem: Ha-madpis Ha-memshalti, 1955), pp. 143–144.

Chapter 19

1. The pronunciation of the last letter, *shin*, as *sin*, is a relic of the way northeastern, Lithuanian, Ashkenazi Jews pronounced that Hebrew letter. This was also a dialectal feature of their pronunciation of Yiddish. It was probably attributable to topographical influences. However, the confusion of the phonemes *sh* and *s* was already a dialectal feature of spoken Hebrew in early biblical times (see Judges 12:6). The Samaritans, as well as some communities in Greece and Italy, also pronounce the *shin* as *sin*.

2. Israel Abrahams, *Jewish Life in the Middle Ages* (Cleveland and New York: Meridian and Jewish Publication Society of America, 1958), p. 55.

3. Leviticus 26:14–45; Deuteronomy 28:15–68.

4. *Rema* on *Shulchan Arukh, Orach Chayyim* 428:6.

Chapter 20

1. *Menachot* 43b.
2. *Berakhot* 47b.
3. *Sukkah* 42a.
4. *Tur, Orach Chayyim*, chap. 17.
5. *Mishnah Berurah, Laws of Tzitzit*, 17:3 (10).
6. Chayyim David Halevi, op. cit., vol. 3, pp. 9–13.
7. *Midrash Bamidbar Rabbah* on Numbers 4:13,14.
8. *Sotah* 17a.
9. *Mishnah Menachot* 4:1.
10. *Bamidbar Rabbah* on Numbers 15:37–41.
11. J.T. *Berakhot* 1:11 (4c).
12. Chayyim David Halevi, op. cit., vol. 5, p. 327.
13. See, for example, *Shulchan Arukh, Orach Chayyim* 28:1; 37:2.
14. Quoted from *Shaar Ha-kavvanot*, no. 5.
15. *Menachot* 37a.
16. *Menachot* 34b.
17. *Shulchan Arukh, Orach Chayyim*, chap. 31.
18. *Shabbat* 118b; *Kiddushin* 31a.
19. *Hagigah* 14b; *Rosh Hashanah* 17b; *Taanit* 20a.

20. *Rambam, Hilkhot Tefillah* 5:5.
21. *Bet Yoseph, Hilkhot Tefillah* 9:1.
22. *Taz* on *Shulchan Arukh, Orach Chayyim* 8:2 (3).
23. *Yoma* 10a.

References

This reference list is restricted to major works actually referred to, or sources quoted, in the body of the text or notes to the text. Where no publisher is listed, a private publication—usually the author's himself—may be assumed.

Abrahams, I. *Jewish Life in the Middle Ages.* Cleveland and New York, Meridian and Jewish Publication Society of America, 1958.

Asher, A. (ed.). *The Itinerary of Benjamin of Tudela.* London: A. Asher & Co., 1840–1841.

Assaf, S. (ed.). *Teshuvot Ha-Geonim.* Jerusalem, 1942.

Bacher, W. "Synagogue," in *Jewish Encyclopedia*, vol. II, p. 619. New York and London: Funk and Wagnalls Co., 1906.

Baer, S. (ed.). *Seder Avodat Yisrael.* Roedelheim, Israel: Lehrberger, 1868.

Baron, S. W. *A Social and Religious History of the Jews.* 8 vols. New York: Columbia University Press, 1960.

Baumgarten, J. M. "Art in the Synagogue: Some Talmudic Views." *Judaism* 19 (1970): 192–206.

Birnbaum, P. *Tefillot Yisrael Umusar Ha-yahadut.* New York: Shulsinger, 1971.

Bleich, J. David. *Contemporary Halakhic Problems*. 2 vols. New York: Ktav, 1977.

Bloch, P. "Seven-Branched Candelabra in Christian Churches." *Journal of Jewish Art* 1:44–47. Chicago: Spertus College of Judaica Press.

Brown, F., Driver, S. R., and Briggs, L. A. *Hebrew and English Lexicon of the Old Testament*. Oxford: Clarendon Press, 1906.

Chagiz, J. *Halakhot Ketanot*. Cracow: Josef Fischer, 1897.

Cohen, J. M. *The History of Jewish Prayer*. London: United Synagogue, 1973.

_____. *Outward Signs*. London: United Synagogue, 1967.

_____. *A Samaritan Chronicle*. Leiden: Brill, 1981.

_____. *Understanding the High Holyday Services*. London: Routledge and Kegan Paul, 1983.

_____. *Understanding the Synagogue Service*. Glasgow: Private publication, 1974.

Cowley, A. E. *The Samaritan Liturgy*. Oxford: Clarendon Press, 1909.

Davis, M. *The Emergence of Conservative Judaism*. Philadelphia: Jewish Publication Society, 1963.

Derovan, D. (ed.). *Prayer*. Vol. 3. New York: Yavne Studies, 1970.

Dichowsky, S. "Al ha-derekh ha-ne'otah li-bechirat rabbanim." *Barkai* 1 (1983): 33–36.

Dov Baer (The Maggid) of Mezhirech. *Maggid Devarav Le-Yaakov*. Lublin: Herszenbhorn-Strazberger, 1927.

Eissfeldt, O. *The Old Testament*. Oxford: Basil Blackwell, 1965.

Elbogen, I. *Ha-tefillah Be-yisrael* (revision of original German edition, Leipzig, 1913). Tel Aviv: Dvir, 1972.

Encyclopaedia Judaica. Jerusalem: Keter Publishing House, 1972.

Encyclopaedia Talmudit. Jerusalem: Talmudic Encyclopedia Publications, Ltd., 1955.

Feinstein, M. *Iggrot Mosheh* (responsa on four sections of *Shulchan Arukh*). New York: Moriah, 1959.

Finkelstein, L. *The Pharisees*. Philadelphia: Jewish Publication Society of America, 1962.

Gaguine, S. *Keter Shem Tob*. London, 1934.

Geshuri, M. S. "Le-toldot ha-chazanut be-eretz yisrael," in *Bet Ha-Kneset*, ed. Mordechai Ha-Cohen, pp. 143–144. Jerusalem: Ha-madpis Ha-memshalti, 1955.

Ginzberg, L. *Legends of the Jews*. 7 vols. Philadelphia: Jewish Publication Society of America, 1908–1938.

_____. *Peirushim Ve-chiddushim Bi-yerushalmi* (Commentary on the Palestinian Talmud). 3 vols. New York: Jewish Theological Seminary, 1941.

Goldman, S. (ed.). *Otzar Ha-tefillot*. New York: Hebraica Press, 1966.

Halevi, Ch. D. *Asei Lekha Rav*. 5 vols. Tel Aviv: Committee for the Publications of Ha-Gaon Rabbi Chaim David Halevi, 1981.

Heinemann, J. "Al defus piyyuti kadum." *Bar Ilan* 4/5 (1967): 132–137.

_____. *Ha-tefillah Bi-tekufat Ha-tanna'im Ve-ha-amora'im*. Jerusalem: Magnes Press, 1964.

_____. "Toledot ha-riformah shel siddur ha-tefillah." *Tarbiz* 39 (1970): 219.

Herford, R. T. *Pharisaism, Its Aim and Its Method*. London: Williams & Norgate, 1912.

Hertz, J. H. (ed.). *The Authorised Daily Prayer Book with Commentary*. London: Shapiro Vallentine, 1947.

_____. (ed.). *The Pentateuch and Haftorahs*. London: Soncino, 1978.

Heschel, A. J. *Man's Quest for God*. New York: Charles Scribner's Sons, 1954.

Hirsch, S. R. *The Pentateuch*. Ed. I. Levy. London: Isaac Levy, 1959.

Hoening, S. "The Supposititious Temple-Synagogue." *Jewish Quarterly Review* 54 (1963): 115.

Hyamson, A. M. *Jews' College, London: 1855–1955*. London: Jews' College Publications, 1955.

Idelsohn, A. Z. *Jewish Liturgy and Its Development*. New York: Schocken Books, 1932.

Jacobson, B. S. *Meditations on the Siddur*. Tel Aviv: Sinai, 1966.

_____. *Netiv Binah*. 5 vols. Tel Aviv: Sinai, 1976–1978.

Jakobovits, I. *Jewish Law Faces Modern Problems*. New York: Yeshiva University Press, 1965.

Josephus, Flavius. *Jewish War (Bellum Judaicum)*. London: The Loeb Classical Library, 1926–1963.

Karl, Z. *Mechkarim Be-toldot Ha-tefillah*. Tel Aviv: N. Twersky, 1950.

Karp, A. J. "Rabbi, Congregation and the World They live in," *Conservative Judaism* 26:1 (Fall 1971): 38.

Kidson, J. "Arch and Vault," in *Encyclopaedia Britannica*, p. 287. Chicago: William Benton, 1970 ed.

Kohn, A. *Prayer*. London: Soncino, 1971.

Kraeling, C. H. *The Excavations at Dura-Europos; Final Report, VIII pt. I: The Synagogue*. New Haven: Yale University Press, 1956.

Landau, I. E. *Dover Shalom* (commentary on the liturgy). Published in *Otzar Ha-tefillot*. New York: Hebraica Press, 1966.

Landman, L. *The Cantor*. New York: Yeshiva University, 1972.

Landsberger, F. "The Sacred Direction in Synagogue and Church." *Hebrew Union College Annual* 28 (1957): 181–203.

Levi, E. *Yesodot Ha-tefillah*. Tel Aviv: Tzioni, 1963.

Medini, Ch. *Sedei Chemed*. 18 vols. Warsaw, 1891–1912.

Mellinkoff, R. "The round-topped tablets of the Law: Sacred symbol and emblem of evil," *Journal of Jewish Art* 1:38.

Menachem Ha-Cohen (ed.). *Machanayim*, Journal of the Israel Defence Forces (First appearance, 1948).

Miller, J. (ed.). *Mafteach Li-Teshuvot Ha-Geonim*. Berlin, 1891.

Moore, G. F. *Judaism in the First Century of the Christian Era*. 3 vols. Cambridge, MA: Harvard University Press, 1927.

Mowinckel, S. *The Psalms in Israel's Worship*. 2 vols. Oxford: Basil Blackwell, 1962.

Munk, E. *The World of Prayer*. 2 vols. New York: Feldheim, 1951.

Newman, J. *Semikhah*, Manchester, England: Manchester University Press, 1950.

Oppenheimer, A., Kasher, A., and Rappaport, U. *Synagogues in Antiquity*. Jerusalem, 1987.

Otto, R. *The Idea of the Holy*. Translation of *Das Heilige*. Oxford: Oxford University Press, 1928.

Petuchowski, J. J. "New Directions in Reform Liturgy." *Central Conference of American Rabbis Journal* (April 1969): 26 ff.

———. *Prayer Reform in Europe*. New York: World Union for Progressive Judaism, 1968.

Reif, S. C. (ed.). *Published Material from the Cambridge Genizah Collections—A Bibliography 1896–1980*. Cambridge: Cambridge University Press, 1988.

Renov, I. "The Seat of Moses." *Israel Exploration Journal* 5 (1955):262–267.

Rosenbloom, N. H. *Tradition in an Age of Reform*. Philadelphia: Jewish Publication Society of America, 1976.

Rosenfeld, A. (ed.). *The Authorized Selichot for the Whole Year*. New York: Judaica Press, 1979.

Rosenthal, E. K. J. (ed.). *Saadya Studies*. London: Oxford University Press, 1943.

Sarfatti, G. B. "The tables of the Covenant as a symbol of Judaism." *Tarbiz* 29 (1960): 370–393.

Schechter, S. *Seminary Addresses and Other Papers*. New York: Gregg International Publishers, 1969.

———. *Studies in Judaism*. New York: Meridian and Jewish Publication Society of America, 1958.

Schirmann, J. "Hebrew liturgical poetry and Christian hymnology." *Jewish Quarterly Review* 44 (1953–1954): 123–161.

Scholem, G. *Major Trends in Jewish Mysticism*. London: Thames & Hudson, 1955.

Shisler, G. L. "The Role of the Chazan in Anglo-Jewry." Report submitted as internal memorandum to the United Synagogue, London, 1983.

Singer, S. (ed.). *The Authorised Daily Prayer Book*. London: Singer's Prayer Book, 1962.

Solomon of Lutzk. *Maggid Devarav Le-yaakov* (Lublin, 1927; repr. Jerusalem, 1962).

Soloveitchick, J. B. "The lonely man of faith." *Tradition* 7:2 (Summer 1965): 43.

United Synagogue. "Beginning Anew: Report and recommendations of the Honorary Officers of the United Synagogue on the Role, Career Structure, Remuneration and Communal Involvement of Rabbis/Ministers and Readers of the United Synagogue," London, June 14, 1984.

Urbach, E. E. *The Sages*. Translation of *Chazal: Pirkei Emunot Vede'ot*. Jerusalem: Magnes Press, 1969.

Weiss, A. "Women and Sifrei Torah." *Tradition* 20:2 (Summer 1982): 106–118.

———. *Women at Prayer*. Hoboken, NJ: Ktav, 1990.

Weiss, I. H. *Dor Dor Vedorshav*. 5 vols. Jerusalem/Tel Aviv: Ziv, undated (reprint of original edition, New York and Berlin, Platt & Minkus, 1924).

Werner, S. *Zikhron Shelomo*. Jerusalem: A. Werner, 1972.

Wieder, N. "Berakhah biltiy yadua al kriat perek Ba-meh Madlikin." *Sinai* 82 (*Shevat-Adar* 5738/1978): 218.

Willowski, J. D. *(Ridbaz)*. Unpublished responsum published in *Zikhron Shelomo*, ed. A. Werner (Jerusalem, 1972), pp. 1–3.

Wischnitzer, R. "Mutual influences between Eastern and Western Europe in Synagogue architecture from the 12th to the 18th century." *YIVO Annual*

2-3 (1947-1948): 2.

Wurmbrand, M. "Falashas" in *Encyclopaedia Judaica*, vol. 6, p. 1143. Jerusalem: Keter Publishing House, 1972.

Yadin, Y. *Masada*. London: Wiedenfeld & Nicolson, 1966.

Yisraeli, Sh. "Al Shimush be-ramkol le-tzorekh mitzvah be-shabbat ve-mo'ed." *Barkai* 5 (1989): 152-158.

_____. "Ha-rav ve-ha-rabanut be-aspaklariat ha-dorot." *Barkai* 1 (1983): 27-28.

Yoseph, O. *Sefer Yechavveh Daat*. 3 vols. Jerusalem: Yeshivat Porat Yoseph et al., 1977.

Zeitlin, S. *Studies in the Early History of Judaism*. Vols. 1 and 2. New York: Ktav, 1963.

Zorfati, Gad Ben-Ami. "The Tables of the Covenant as a Symbol of Judaism." *Tarbiz* 29 (1960): 370-393.

Zulay, M. *Piyyutey Yannai*. Berlin: M. Zulay, 1938.

Zunz, L. *Die Ritus des Synagogalen Gottesdienstes*. Berlin: Julius Springer, 1859.

_____. *Die Synagogale Poesie des Mittelalters*. Berlin: Julius Springer, 1855.

Primary Rabbinic Sources

Alfasi, Isaac, *see Teshuvot Ha-Rif.*

Arukh Ha-Shulchan, Commentary on the *Shulchan Arukh* by R. Yechiel Michal Ha-Levi Epstein. Compiled 1884-1906, 8 vols. Modern ed., Tel Aviv, undated.

Bayit Chadash, Commentary (referred to by acronym *Bach*) of R. Yoel Sirkes on the *Tur Shulchan Arukh.*

Be'er Heiteiv, Commentary on the *Shulchan Arukh* by R. Zechariah Mendel of Belz and R. Yehudah Ashkenazi (on *Orach Chayyim* and *Even Ha-Ezer*, respectively).

Bet Yoseph, Commentary on the *Tur* by Joseph Karo. First published 1555. Appended to most editions.

Bi'ur Ha-Gra, Commentary on the *Shulchan Arukh* by R. Eliyahu b. Shelomo Zalman of Vilna (Vilna Gaon). Appended to most editions.

Derishah, Commentary on the *Tur* by R. Yehoshua Falk. Appended to many editions. See also *Perishah.*

Halakhot Pesukot Min Ha-Geonim, Geonic responsa, ed. J. Miller, Cracow, 1897.

Kesef Mishneh, Commentary on Rambam's *Mishneh Torah* by Joseph Karo. First published Venice, 1574-1575. Appended to most editions.

Ketav Sofer, Responsa (and commentary on Pentateuch) by R. Avraham Shmuel Binyamin Sofer of Pressburg. Publ. 1873-1938.

Kol Bo, Anonymous halakhic work, Venice, Marco Giustiniani, 1547.

Magen Avraham, Commentary on the *Shulchan Arukh* by R. Avraham Abeli Gombiner. Appended to most editions.

Maimonides, see *Rambam.*

Masechet Semachot, Minor tractate of the Talmud. Generally appended to editions of Babylonian Talmud. Critical edition by M. Higger, *Mekitzei Nirdamim*, 1931. English edition by D. Zlotnick, 1966.

Masechet Soferim, Late minor tractate of the Talmud. Printed at end of *Seder Nezikin.* Critical edition by M. Higger, Mekitzei Nirdamim, 1937.

Midrash Pesikta DeRav Kahana, ed. S. Buber, Lyck, *Mekitzei Nirdamim,* 1868; D. Mandelbaum, Jewish Theological Seminary of America, 2 vols., 1962.

Midrash Pesikta Rabbati, ed. M. Friedman, Vienna, 1880; W. S. Braude, New Haven and London, Yale University Press, 1968.

Midrash Rabbah, Various editions: Jerusalem, Rome, Vilna, etc.

Midrash Yalkut Shimoni, Salonika, 1521–1526.

Mishnah, Various editions. Translation: H. Danby, Oxford, 1933; Commentaries: P. Blackman, Oxford, 1951–1956 (7 vols.); P. Kehati, Jerusalem, 1963 (12 vols.). See *Rambam.*

Mishnah Berurah, Halakhic Code and commentary on *Shulchan Arukh Orach Chayyim* by R. Yisrael Meir Ha-Cohen *(Chafetz Chayyim).*

Perishah, Commentary on the *Tur* by R. Yehoshua Falk. Appended to many editions. See also *Derishah.*

Rambam, Commentary to the *Mishnah (Peirush Ha-mishnayot Le-Ha-Rambam),* var. editions.

Rambam, Maamar Kiddush Ha-Shem (or *Iggeret Ha-Shemad*). Epistle contained in *Iggrot Ha-Rambam,* Jerusalem, Mosad Ha-Rav Kuk, 1944, pp. 15–65.

Rambam, Mishneh Torah (or *Yad Ha-Chazakah*). Major Code of Jewish Law. Var. editions.

Ran, Commentary to Talmud *Nedarim* and to *Halakhot* of Isaac Alfasi (see *Rif*) by R. Nissim b. Reuven of Gerondi.

Rashba, Talmudic novellae *(Chiddushei Ha-Rashba)* by R. Shelomo b. Avraham Adret. Var. editions.

Rashi, Major commentator on Bible and Talmud. Numerous editions.

Rema, Glosses to *Shulchan Arukh* by R. Moses Isserles. Incorporated into text of all editions.

Rif, See *Teshuvot Ha-Rif.*

Sedei Chemed, Halakhic encyclopedia by R. Chayyim Chizkiyahu Medini, 18 vols., Warsaw, 1891–1912.

Sefer Ha-Eshkol, Halakhic commentary, reflecting traditions of southern France, by R. Avraham b. Isaac of Narbonne. Var. editions (First published, Halberstadt, H. Meyer, 1867).

Shaar Ha-tziyyun, Notes on sources of *Mishnah Berurah,* compiled by Israel Meir Ha-Cohen *(Chafetz Chayyim).*

Sherirah Gaon, Author of talmudical commentaries. Best known for his *Iggeret Rav Sherirah Gaon,* Jewish historiographical source, written in 987 and now published in standard editions of Babylonian Talmud.

Shitah Mekubbetzet, Novellae on various talmudic tractates, and supplement to *Tosafot* and other *Rishonim,* by R. Bezalel ben Avraham Ashkenazi. Commentary on *Bava Batra* (quoted in notes) published Livorno, 1774.

Siddur Ha-Gra, Edition of the Prayer Book by R. Eliyahu b. Shelomo Zalman of Vilna (Vilna Gaon), with commentary on text, laws and customs of prayer, Jerusalem, 1971.

Talmud Bavli, Babylonian Talmud, var. editions, Jerusalem, Rome, Vienna, Vilna. English translated edition, ed. I. Epstein, London, Soncino,

1948–1957. Hebrew annotated edition, A. Steinsaltz; several tractates issued to date, Jerusalem, Israel, Institute for Talmudic Publications, 1967– .

Talmud Yerushalmi, Palestinian Talmud, ed. Krotoschin, 1886; *Talmud Yerushalmi Ha-Gadol*, 6 vols., Vilna, 1922.

Targum, Aramaic versions of Bible; *Onkelos*, Pseudo-Jonathan *(Targum Yonatan)*, fragmentary Targum *(Yerushalmi*, etc.), as printed in var. editions of rabbinic Bible.

Tashbatz, Responsa of R. Shimon b. Tzemach, Duran, Amsterdam, 1738–1741.

Taz, Halakhic commentary *(Turei Zahav)* to *Shulchan Arukh*, by R. David b. Shemuel Ha-Levi (first edition, on *Yoreh De'ah*, Lublin, 1646), now published in most editions.

Teshuvot Ha-Rif, Responsa of I. Alfasi (Leghorn, 1781), ed. Z. Leiter, Jerusalem, 1954.

Tosafot, Collection of comments on Talmud and earlier authorities (especially *Rashi*). Printed, together with *Rashi*, in all standard editions of Talmud.

Tosefta, Ed. M. S. Zuckermandel, Jerusalem, 1963.

Tur, Major halakhic Code of Jacob b. Asher (full title, *Arbaah Turim*), First complete edition, Piove di Sacco, 1455, Warsaw, 1882, Jerusalem, 1969.

Zohar, Central work of mystical literature, in form of commentary on Pentateuch, as well as independent kabbalistic studies. First editions, Mantua (1558–1560) and Cremona (1559–1560). English ed., ed. M. Simon, 5 vols., London, Soncino, 1932.

Index

307

About the Author

Rabbi Jeffrey M. Cohen has distinguished himself in the field of religious affairs as a broadcaster, lecturer, writer, and reviewer. A graduate of the Yeshivot of Manchester and Gateshead, Rabbi Cohen received a master's degree in philosophy from London University and a Ph.D. from Glasgow University. He is the author of several books, including *Understanding the Synagogue Service, Understanding the High Holyday Services, A Samaritan Chronicle, Horizons of Jewish Prayer, Moments of Insight, Prayer and Penitence: A Commentary on the Holy Day Machzor,* and *1,001 Questions and Answers on Pesach,* as well as over 200 articles. He is a member of the cabinet of the chief rabbi of Great Britain. He currently serves as the rabbi of Stanmore and Canons Park Synagogue, the largest Orthodox congregation in Great Britain. He and his wife, Gloria, reside in London. They have four children and five grandchildren.